the Making of Michigan

BY LYNNE DEUR & SARA MICHEL

River Road Publications, Inc.

Contributors

Marion H. Smith
Manuscript Editor

Patricia Wilson
Copy Editor

Jean Shafer, Ph.D.
Educational Consultant

Donna J. Knoth, M.A.
Educational Consultant

Lee S. Brown
Cover & Illustrations

Colleen A. Rockey
Book Design

Sheila B. Warners
Maps

Delbert Michel
Illustrations

Kip Wiersma
Illustrations

Published by River Road Publications, Inc.
Spring Lake, Michigan 49456

ISBN: 0-938682-17-2

Contents

Photo Credits

The illustrations are reproduced through the courtesy of: pp. 6, 129, 143, 210, Lee S. Brown; pp. 17, 24, 54, 65, 75, 84, 105, 106, 121, 125, 132, 134, 139, 146-152, 155-159, 162-167, 171-176, 178-185, 188, 196, 197, 201, 203, 206-209, 214-217, 220-224, 233, 239, 241, 243, 244, 248-253, 258-260, 269, 272-275, 281, Michigan State Archives; 23, 56, The American Museum of Natural History; 26, Field Museum of Natural History; 39, 131, 144, Delbert Michel; 44, 46, 53, 116, State Historical Society of Wisconsin; 51, 60, Public Archives Canada; 61, Library of Michigan; 62, 63, 122, 204, 205, Kip Wiersma; 77, 82, 102, Michigan Bell; 80, 161, 194, 226, Burton Historical Collection, Detroit Public Library; 89, George Rogers Clark National Historical Park; 92, 108, 127, Mackinac Island State Park Commission; 95, Ohio Historical Society; 110, Chicago Historical Society; 124, 186, 187, Marquette County Historical Society; 154, 192, 195, 199, 218, 231, 255, Grand Rapids Public Library; 177, 200, Hackley Public Library; 191, Tri-Cities Historical Museum; 230, Michigan State University; 232, 234, 268, 270, 271, Detroit News; 238, Ottawa County Road Commission; 262, Michigan Department of Transportation; Gerald R. Ford Library, 276.
p. 282, Harold Bretschneider

Introduction

Four thousand years ago, even before pyramids were built in ancient Egypt, Indian people were mining copper in what is today the Upper Peninsula of Michigan. They traded the metal with Indians in other parts of North America. Copper from the Lake Superior region has been found in all parts of the United States, Mexico, and Central America.

Before the Pilgrims landed at Plymouth Rock, French traders and explorers had found their way to the Michigan region in search of furs, the resource on which America's first industry was built. While the thirteen colonies were being formed on the Atlantic coast, settlements along the Straits of Mackinac were lively, busy places. Fur traders, French soldiers, and thousands of Indian people gathered in the spring and summer to trade for furs and enjoy each other's company after a long winter season in the wilderness.

It was not until the 1830s, more than two hundred years after the first Europeans arrived in Michigan, that white settlers began to come to the state in large numbers. When they finally came, they set records. Michigan's population increased at a faster rate in the 1830s than that of any other state or territory.

Later in the same century, there were other rushes to the state. Businessmen wanted to be a part of the copper "boom" in the Upper Peninsula. Lumbermen recognized the wealth lying in the state's white pine forests that seemed to have no end.

As the twentieth century dawned, Michigan was the center of another booming industry. Henry Ford and Ransom E. Olds experimented with their early cars on the bumpy, muddy streets used by horses and buggies. Then they began the auto industry, which helped change the life of the entire nation.

And so Michigan's history stretches back much further than its 150 years of statehood. Its stories of the past are among the oldest in our country. They are also stories that contain much more than local color and information. Nestled in the heart of the Great Lakes, Michigan has been an important theater for the pageant of the nation's history. Its people, its natural resources, and its industries have shaped more than a state. They have played a vital role in the American story.

One Hundred and Fifty Years— and More

SI QUAERIS
PENINSULAM
AMOENAM
CIRCUMSPICE

·

IF YOU SEEK
A PLEASANT
PENINSULA,
LOOK AROUND
YOU

Chapter 1

The Place Called Michigan

When the jet reached ten thousand feet,
it was clear why the country
had cities where rivers ran
and why the valleys were populated.
The logic of geography—
that land and water attracted man—
    from "Geography Lesson" by Zulfikar Ghose © 1900 by
Zulfikar Ghose. Used with permission of Dufour Editions, Inc.

There is something about Michigan that celebrates the past. Not that it isn't a modern industrial state. Signs of that are everywhere. Breathtaking buildings form the landscapes of its cities. Interstate highways run in every direction. Jet service to any part of the world is available from a number of its cities.

Yet four Great Lakes still wash the shores of the two peninsulas that form Michigan just as they did thousands of years ago. Rivers once traveled by Indian people in their birchbark canoes still wind through thickly forested areas. And it's possible to imagine a farmer with his plow and six oxen trying to break through the sod of the rich prairie lands—or perhaps the sound of an axe ringing in a grove of giant white pines.

Many of Michigan's present links to the past have been created by its people. In Dearborn, Greenfield Village offers visitors a look at homes and shops from a century ago. In the southwestern part of the state, villages sit quietly along the St. Joseph River much the way they did when Michigan was a young state. Farther north, in Holland, a giant windmill turns slowly in the breeze, reminding the inhabitants and their visitors of the Dutch immigrants who carved the town out of the wilderness there.

In the Mackinac Straits area, the link to the past is perhaps most dramatic. In both Mackinaw City and Mackinac Island forts have been restored. On Mackinac Island visitors crowd the streets searching for good times as they did during the fur trading years or in the late 1800s when tourism on the island became fashionable. But it is not possible to stay lost in history. Crossing the straits is the mighty Mackinac Bridge, a great feat of modern times. It seems to serve as a reminder of the many years that have passed and the many changes that have taken place since the days of the fur trade.

Some of the links to Michigan's past are, perhaps, less obvious. In the Upper Peninsula there are the crumbled remains of old iron forges. Weeds and brush disguise the land that was mined for copper during the boom years of the late 1800s. In some areas the land is still scarred from the lumbering that took place there nearly a century ago. The cutover land looks barren and wasted with no promise of a new crop of fine, strong trees.

Michigan's story is as closely linked to its land and to its resources as any history can be. It is, in fact, difficult at times to decide where geography ends and history begins. And so to appreciate the story fully, it is necessary to know something about the two peninsulas, the endless waters, and the rich resources that make up the place called Michigan.

Michigan's beginnings

Understanding Michigan from its very beginning includes something more than just learning about its historical past. The state's history is made up of a continuing collection of stories written down by people who lived or heard about important events in the past. But Michigan also has a geological past. Geology, or the history of the earth, is recorded by scientists who study the earth's surface as well as the layers that lie beneath its crust. Unlike Michigan's history, which takes us back only a few hundred years, geology forces us to measure time in millions of years!

Understanding Michigan's geological past demands imagination. Millions of years ago the two peninsulas that now form the state did not exist. Neither were there any Great Lakes. Much of North America had a very hard rocky surface often called the Canadian, or Laurentian, Shield. This surface covered what is now eastern and central Canada, and dipped down into what is now part of Michigan's Upper Peninsula. South of the Canadian Shield the earth's surface was a mixture of softer rocks that were more easily worn away by erosion. Salty, shallow seas often covered much of the area that is now Michigan.

Throughout the huge spans of geological time, there were many changes. At times the earth's surface actually rose, making drastic changes in the rock and its formations. In the present area of Lake Superior, volcanoes erupted, and deposits of minerals such as iron ore were formed. At other times the seas dried up, leaving behind salt deposits in the earth.

Throughout these long periods of change, there were forms of plant and animal life unlike those of today. During some stages the weather was very warm, and there were ferns and various

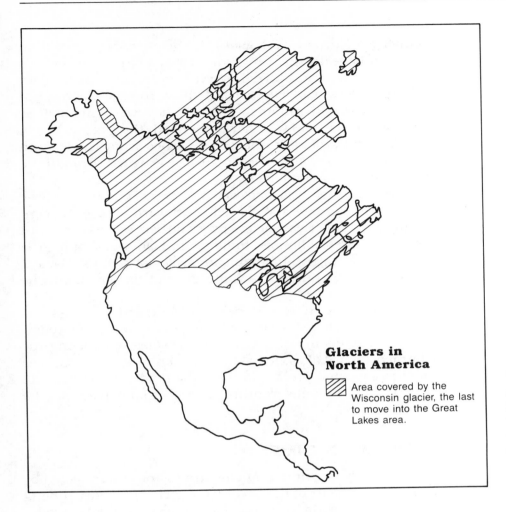

Glaciers in North America

Area covered by the Wisconsin glacier, the last to move into the Great Lakes area.

While glaciers shaped Michigan's land, their melting waters created the many lakes, rivers, and waterfalls that make the state a water wonderland.

types of tropical plants and trees. There were insects resembling dragonflies and large reptiles such as dinosaurs. In the seas were countless shellfish. When these died, their shells became mixed with mud and in time formed limestone. In some areas the tropical plants and trees died and decayed in the mud, forming coal deposits.

The power of the ice

To geologists, a million years is a rather short period of time. And so it was only a recent one million years ago that the earth's northern climate became very cold. Snow that fell in the winter did not completely melt during the summer. Each new winter added another layer of snow. Over a period of many years, the piles of snow grew into huge and heavy sheets of ice called glaciers.

The glaciers began to move by the force of their own tremendous weight. Slowly they pushed southward from the Arctic into

North America, Europe, and Asia. The glaciers did more than bury the land beneath them in snow. These giant earth movers gouged and ripped and scarred everything in their path. They scooped out valleys, carried soil and rocks to new places, and wore down jagged mountains. Finally, they were stopped by warmer weather. As slowly as they had grown, the glaciers began to melt. Huge piles of rock and soil loosened from the ice and formed hills. Water from the melting masses rushed through the valleys, creating rivers and lakes.

The great Ice Age was not over, however. Four times these giant ice masses formed and moved southward across the continents. In North America glaciers pushed their way as far south as the present states of Illinois, Indiana, and Ohio, reshaping the face of half the continent. In Michigan, geologists tell us, glaciers two miles in height buried the state on and off for about one million years!

As the last glacier retreated over four thousand years ago, the Great Lakes region at last resembled the area as we know it today. What is now Michigan, with its two peninsulas, lay among the newly formed Great Lakes. It was a land rich in water resources and mineral deposits. Trees and plant life gradually returned to stay, and wildlife became plentiful. It was a land ready for its people.

Front row, center

From the very beginning, Michigan's history was affected by its location in the heart of the Great Lakes. The five lakes, among the largest in the world, are connected by rivers, a lake, and a strait, making a natural transportation network. (See the map on page 11.) Much of the early activity in the region took place on the Great Lakes and along their shores. It was as if what is now Michigan, with 3,121 miles of coast along this magnificent waterway, occupied the front row, center seat in a Great Lakes theater. Across the stage moved Indian people, French explorers and missionaries, fur traders, French and British soldiers, and early white settlers.

As history progressed, it was natural for ports to develop along Michigan's many miles of coastline. Ships that first brought immigrants looking for new homes later carried tourists looking for relaxation and enjoyment along the beaches and in the resort towns. Other ships carried copper, iron ore, and limestone from Michigan's mineral deposits and lumber from the forests. Manufactured goods were brought in to meet the needs of its growing population. Decade after decade, the Great Lakes helped shape the history of the place called Michigan.

The Great Lakes have also had an important effect on Michigan's climate. As other large bodies of water do, the lakes gain and lose their heat much more slowly than land. Therefore, they remain cold long into the spring and warm far into the fall. This has helped make some of Michigan's shoreline areas ideal for growing fruit. In the spring, cool breezes from Lake Michigan keep fruit crops from blooming while there is still the danger of frost. At the same time, the warm winds off the lake in the fall protect the fruit from being destroyed by early frost.

The cool breezes from the Great Lakes help make the shoreline areas popular on hot summer days. The lake effect also increases the amount of snowfall in the winter. This fact is appreciated by those who love winter sports and causes others to vacation in southern states during the winter months. Overall, however, the Great Lakes make it possible for Michigan to enjoy a more moderate climate than other areas located as far north.

Nestled in the heart of the Great Lakes, Michigan's name is an appropriate one. It comes from an Indian word generally meaning "great water."

The rugged Upper Peninsula

Stretching between Lake Superior, Lake Michigan, and Lake Huron is Michigan's Upper Peninsula. From east to west, it is about three hundred miles long. Forests, lakes, rivers, rocky cliffs, and waterfalls make up its rugged beauty. Only a few towns and cities interrupt its seemingly endless wilderness landscape.

What is most striking of all, however, is this peninsula's link to the geological past. In the western part of the peninsula are the Huron and Porcupine mountains. Once high and jagged, these ancient peaks were worn down by glaciers into low, rolling mountains. Still, they are higher and more rugged than the highlands in other parts of Michigan. Mount Curwood, located in the Hurons, is the highest point in the state, with an elevation of 1,980 feet.

Along with the Porcupine and Huron mountains, the Upper Peninsula has other reminders of Michigan's geological past. In the western half of the peninsula are copper and iron ore deposits that had their beginnings millions of years ago. Some of the old-

Pictured Rocks National Lakeshore lies along the cold, deep waters of Lake Superior. It has both huge sand dunes and colorful sandstone cliffs that have been carved by wind and water.

Michigan's Land
a closer look

Land versus water

Michigan makes up an area of 96,675 square miles. Its land area, 56,817 square miles, ranks it 23rd among the states. But much of Michigan, about 41%, is made up of water! Since its boundaries extend out into four Great Lakes, Michigan has 38,459 square miles of Great Lakes waters. The state also has 1,399 square miles of inland waters.

Sand, a precious resource

Sand dunes along some of the shores of the Great Lakes are one of Michigan's most unique landforms. Michigan's sand, which is made up mostly of quartz, is moved from the lakes to the beach by wave action. When the sand dries, the wind carries it inland. Eventually mounds of sand, or dunes, are created. The dunes continue to change with time and wind. Spectacular dunes line 270 miles of Michigan's Great Lakes shoreline.

A variety of soils

To a large extent Michigan's soils are made up of materials dumped by the glaciers. They include the natural soils from Canada, along with a wide assortment of rocks, boulders, sand, and clay. Through thousands of years they have been changed by the breaking down of rocks, the decomposing of plants and animals, and other factors.

Famous stones

Michigan is famous for its Petoskey stones found in the northern counties of the Lower Peninsula. These stones come from a coral reef that once existed in a sea that covered the area. Greenstone, or chlorastrolite, is a deep green gemstone with traces of pebbles within. It is found on Lake Superior shores, particularly on Isle Royale. The Greenstone is the official gem of Michigan, and the Petoskey stone is the official state stone.

Sand mining along Lake Michigan

est rocks in North America appear at the earth's surface in this region. Rock hounds are attracted to this part of the state to hunt for agates, greenstones, and other gems—souvenirs of the strange events in Michigan's geological past.

Not all the Upper Peninsula is high and hilly. Most of the eastern half of the peninsula is made up of low plains. There are also large swampy areas, or bogs, in this part of the state. Dolomite and limestone quarries border the shoreline of Lake Michigan and Lake Huron, and fossils can readily be found in the area.

Forests cover much of the land in the Upper Peninsula. Before the 1800s the eastern half of the peninsula had many pines, with cedar and spruce growing in the bog areas. In the western half there were fewer pines, but a variety of hardwoods that included sugar maples and basswood grew. Today the large pine forests are gone in both parts of the peninsula. In their place are white birch, aspen, and open fields.

The population of the Upper Peninsula is much smaller than that of the Lower Peninsula. This is partly due to the long, cold winters. In the area around Houghton and Hancock, for example, more than 160 inches of snow falls in the winter, while the area around Lansing in the Lower Peninsula usually receives less than sixty inches! Also, much of the Upper Peninsula has soil that is poorly suited to farming. In areas where the soil is fertile, the short growing season limits the kinds of crops that can be raised.

A variety of landscapes

Michigan's Lower Peninsula, which stretches for 277 miles from north to south, has a greater variety of landscapes than the Upper Peninsula. There are rolling, forested hills, miles of level farmland, and large urban areas. Scenic sand dunes make up the Lake Michigan coastline. The land area in the Lower Peninsula makes up about two-thirds of the state.

The northern part of Michigan's Lower Peninsula resembles the Upper Peninsula. There are many forests, but these forests differ from those that once covered the high, hilly land here. The huge white pine forests have been replaced by white birch, aspen, and jack pines. Limestone quarries are also familiar sights in this part of the state. Industrial plants in the area combine the limestone with clay, another available resource of the area, to make cement. Oil and natural gas deposits are also found here.

The southern half of the Lower Peninsula is made up largely of lowlands and plains and is the state's most populated area. All of the large cities and most of the farms are located here. Even in prehistoric times this seems to have been an area of activity for wildlife, for there are numerous sites where bones of such ancient

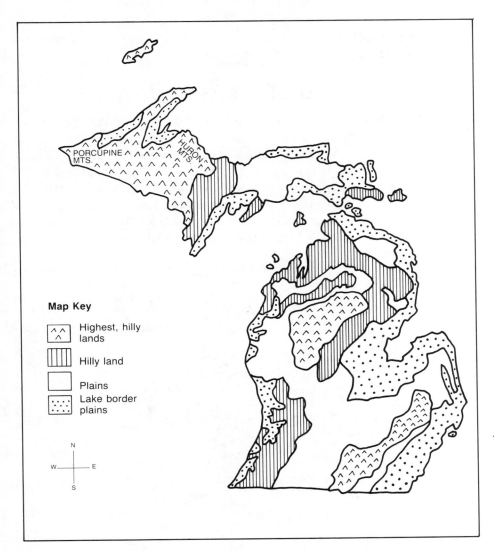

Map Key

^ ^
  ^ Highest, hilly
     lands

||||| Hilly land

[   ] Plains

[...] Lake border
      plains

N
W — E
S

PORCUPINE MTS.

HURON MTS.

Michigan has many landscapes that vary from swamplands to rolling, forested hills. It also has a greater variety of soils than most states. For this reason, many types of farming are carried on in the state.

animals as mammoths, mastodons, giant beaver, and musk-oxen have been found. Beneath the earth are other reminders of the past. Here there are such minerals as salt and peat, the latter formed by decayed plants and used largely to enrich soil. There are also oil and natural gas deposits.

There are few forests in the southern half of the Lower Peninsula, although this was not always so. Except for some small prairies and open areas between the trees, the land was once covered by hardwoods such as oak, hickory, and maple. The first farmers settled in the prairie and open areas, but those that followed had to cut the trees and clear the land for farms. They found the soil beneath these forests fertile. That, along with flatness of the land and the long growing season, made this part of Michigan most popular for farming. Today farming is still important, although most of Michigan's people live in urban areas and work in the state's many industries.

A wonderland of lakes and rivers

Michigan's natural resources have had a tremendous impact on the state's history.

It is impossible to describe the land of Michigan without mentioning its many inland lakes and rivers. Over eleven thousand lakes dot the state, with four counties (Marquette, Luce, Gogebic, and Oakland) claiming more than four hundred each! Naming this vast number of lakes has been a problem, and it is not surprising that the state has several Round Lakes, Silver Lakes, Mud Lakes, as well as others bearing the same names. Rivers are also plentiful within the state. Although none of these

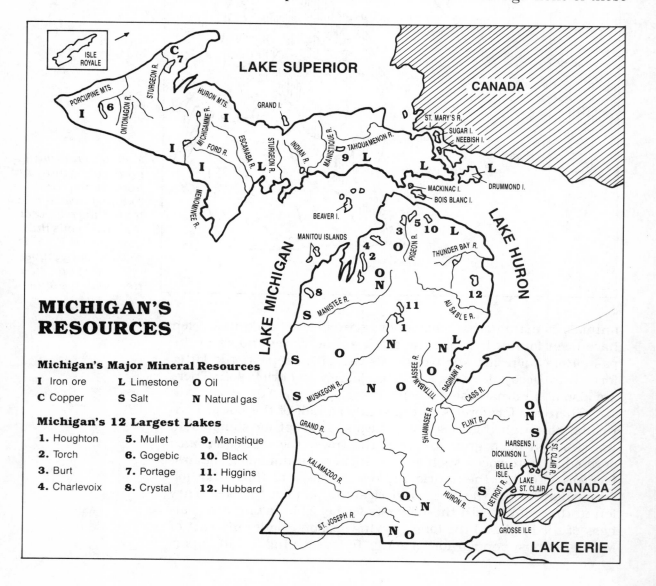

MICHIGAN'S RESOURCES

Michigan's Major Mineral Resources

I Iron ore   **L** Limestone   **O** Oil

C Copper   **S** Salt   **N** Natural gas

Michigan's 12 Largest Lakes

1. Houghton   **5.** Mullet   **9.** Manistique

2. Torch   **6.** Gogebic   **10.** Black

3. Burt   **7.** Portage   **11.** Higgins

4. Charlevoix   **8.** Crystal   **12.** Hubbard

rivers is considered among principal rivers of the United States, some of them are important waterways. All together, their winding paths add up to over 36,000 miles!

Just as the Great Lakes have played an important part in Michigan's past, so have its inland lakes and rivers. It is easier to appreciate the importance of these water resources by imagining Michigan as a land of thick forests and tangled underbrush. Lakes and rivers were of great benefit to early travelers, since it was far easier to journey by canoe or boat than to walk or use a horse and wagon. Long after the land was cleared for farms and towns, it was cheaper to move farm products and manufactured goods by boat than by other types of transportation.

Rivers and lakes were especially important during Michigan's lumber boom of the late 1800s. Logs were cut from forests and hauled to the rivers, where they were floated to sawmills. The finished lumber from the sawmills was then shipped to other areas in the Midwest. The Muskegon River, stretching two hundred miles inland, and the Saginaw, which connected with a number of smaller rivers, led the rest in their importance to the logging industry.

Rivers and lakes were important to Michigan's development. Here schooners are being loaded with lumber at a sawmill on Manistee Lake near Lake Michigan. The photo was taken about 1900.

48

Transportation was not the only use for the state's many lakes and rivers. They provided water for drinking and fish as a basic food source. Ice was cut from the lakes each winter and stored to preserve food during warm weather. From the late 1800s to the middle of the 1900s, a large share of the state's electric power was generated by the force of rushing river waters.

Today, recreation is the most important use of Michigan's lakes and rivers. Residents and tourists alike enjoy a wide variety of water sports. It is as if these water resources have retired from their more active and functional past, devoting themselves now to leisure.

The islands

Michigan has about 150 waterfalls, most of which are in the Upper Peninsula. These tumbling waters are located on the Presque Isle River in the western Upper Peninsula.

An added attraction to Michigan's geography is its islands, many of which are quite large. Some of the islands have residents who live there throughout the year. Others attract tourists and visitors from the spring through the fall. All in all, Michigan's islands have their own special beauty and make up an interesting chapter in the state's past.

A number of Michigan's islands are located in northern Lake Michigan. The largest of these is Beaver Island, where a Mormon leader named James Strang once declared himself king. Among the smaller islands in that area are North Manitou and South Manitou. Both these islands are largely wilderness and are part of the Sleeping Bear Dunes National Lakeshore.

Michigan's famous Mackinac Island is located in Lake Huron. Part of Mackinac is a state park which preserves the island's colorful past as the home of a fur trading post and a British fort. During the summer, thousands of visitors tour the island by bicycle or horse and buggy, since automobiles are not allowed there.

Several other large islands lie in northern Lake Huron and the nearby St. Marys River. Bois Blanc Island is located near Mackinac Island, and except for one small village, is largely forested. Drummond Island is a large island lying near the Canadian border. The island has inland lakes and a large dolomite quarry. Farther north, in the St. Marys River, are Sugar and Neebish islands, which are largely forested and have a few summer residents.

Isle Royale is a Michigan island in western Lake Superior. Indians once mined copper on the island, perhaps as long as 4,500 years ago. Today the island is a national park that is dedicated to preserving the wilderness, and attracts only the most enthusiastic lovers of the outdoor life.

A number of small islands are located in southeastern Michigan in Lake St. Clair and the Detroit River. Among these are Harsens Island, Dickinson Island, Belle Isle, and Grosse Isle. These islands are all inhabited except for Belle Isle, which is used for recreation.

A document of the past

In many ways, then, the land is a valuable document of Michigan's past. It is as if glaciers, the natural changes of erosion, and people have all made their imprints in its surface. Discovering these imprints that link a place with its history can do more than reveal an interesting story. In the search we may find both lessons and promises for the future.

M I C H I G A N

I·N T·I·M·E

Date	In Michigan	Outside Michigan
10,000 B.C.	First people come to the Michigan area hunting mastodons, mammoths, and other large animals	
9,000 B.C.		
8,000 B.C.	Deer, bear, and other smaller animals replace mastodons and mammoths	Southwest Indians gather wild plants for food and make baskets
7,000 B.C.		Northwest coast Indians fish and hunt sea mammals
6,000 B.C.	People begin to fish and gather some wild foods	Indians in Mexico begin to grow their own foods and develop corn
5,000 B.C.	Copper Culture Indians begin using copper in Upper Peninsula area	
4,000 B.C.		
3,000 B.C.	Indians live in bands and villages more than early hunters	Northeast Indians begin making pottery / Egyptians build pyramids
2,000 B.C.	Indians bury their dead with some of their belongings in cemeteries	Moses leads people out of Egypt
1,000 B.C.	Hopewell Indians live in the Michigan area and build mounds	Indians in Mexico build Pyramid of the Sun / Golden Age of Greece
A.D. 1	Indian people making pottery and growing some food	Roman Empire at its peak / Vikings sail to North America
A.D. 1,000	Arrival of Europeans (1600s)	Iroquois Indians form league Arrival of Europeans (1600s)

Chapter 2

"Under every rock in this land there is a trace of us."
from *Anpao* by Jamake Highwater.

**The First
People**

Prehistory from traces on the land

With the slow retreat of the glaciers, life began to unfold in the area we now know as Michigan. Trees and other plant life returned, as well as animal life. After the animals, which included mammoths and mastodons, came Michigan's first people. Experts believe that these people did not settle in any particular area. Instead they camped and moved, hunting the beasts that furnished them with food and clothing.

The huge block of time from the early hunters to the arrival of the Europeans in the early 1600s is referred to as Michigan's prehistory. There is no written account of life during this time. Scientists called archeologists have long been studying traces on the land to determine how people lived during the many years of prehistory. By carefully digging in an area where Indians once lived, they have recovered bones, broken tools, spearpoints, and bits and pieces of items used by Indian people. From these clues the archeologists are able to give at least some account of how these early people lived.

Even with very sophisticated methods of studying prehistory, some of the information can only be educated guesses. It cannot be said with certainty, for instance, how people first came to North America. It is generally believed that a land bridge once connected Asia and North America near the present Bering Strait (a narrow body of water that separates Alaska and the U.S.S.R.). This would have made it possible for people to walk from Asia to North America and then gradually travel southward.

When did these people first come to North America? The dates keep changing as experts discover more and more about prehistory. Although scientists once said that people came to the North American continent about 25,000 years ago, some now believe it may have been over 100,000 years ago! It was probably

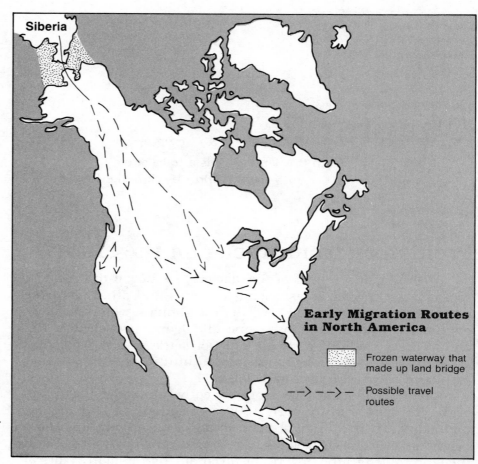

Siberia

Early Migration Routes in North America

Frozen waterway that made up land bridge

Possible travel routes

Knowledge about prehistory changes as experts uncover clues about the past. Clues become more difficult to find, however, as cities, highways, and other changes reshape the land.

much later, however, that their descendants made their way to Michigan—perhaps about 10,000 B.C.

The first copper miners

As the climate grew warmer and the glaciers retreated, activity in the area of the Great Lakes continued to increase. Both plant life and animal life became more abundant. The large animals such as mastodons, with their limited numbers, became extinct as they were killed by hunters or became mired in swamps and bogs. In their place were deer and the smaller animals that are familiar to us today. More people moved into the area to live, people whom Columbus, thousands of years later, mistakenly named Indians.

Among the early Indians in the Great Lakes area were the Copper Culture people. These people began to mine the copper in the Lake Superior region about four thousand years ago, even

Jefferson mammoths once lived in the Michigan area. They had long hair, long curved tusks, and ate grass and shrubs.

before Egyptians began building pyramids. By heating chunks of copper ore in a fire and quickly cooling them with water, the miners were able to crack these rocks and dig into the pure, soft copper within. They then hammered the copper into items such as spearpoints, fishhooks, knives, and axes. The Copper Culture Indians were among the first people in the world to use metal in place of stone for their tools. They also traded their copper objects with Indian people in distant areas, such as the present states of New York and Kentucky.

Although the Copper Culture Indians secured most of their food by hunting, they clearly had a more settled way of life than the first hunters. Along with hunting, they fished and gathered some wild foods, such as berries. They used boats for travel, perhaps even an early type of birchbark canoe. They also tamed dogs, which they probably used for hunting.

The Copper Culture Indians lived in the Lake Superior area for several thousand years. Experts say they then moved northwestward into Canada. A few other Indian groups continued to mine the copper, but never as much as the Copper Culture Indians. When the French arrived in the 1600s, Indian tribes had not been mining copper for hundreds of years. And it was not until the mid-1800s that Michigan's copper deposits were mined again.

A changing way of life

The Copper Culture Indians lived in the Michigan area during a period archeologists and other experts in Indian study call the Archaic period. Copper Culture people, along with other Indian groups of the period, made their living mainly by hunting and fishing. Instead of spending most of their time in family

Early Indian copper miners found ways to reach large beds of copper which lay under the earth. They built fires to heat the rocks that covered the copper and then poured cold water over the hot rock to crack it. Gradually they made deep mining pits.

groups as the early hunters did, people of the Archaic period lived in communities or bands, and their dead were buried in cemeteries. During this period the tool called the atlatl was developed. This was a wooden spearholder that allowed the hunter to throw his weapon with greater power.

Gradually the Archaic way of life changed, marking the beginning of another huge block of time that experts call the Woodland period. Slowly people began to gather more wild foods and also to grow some of their food. They learned to make pottery and hunt with bows and arrows. The Woodland period began sometime between 1,000 and 500 B.C. and continued until the arrival of the Europeans. It is a period often divided into early, middle, and late stages.

The Hopewell Indians

During the middle Woodland period a distinctive group of Indians moved into the Michigan area. These people, now called the Hopewells, built mounds, usually to bury their dead. One of their mounds, when it was found hundreds of years later, was located on an Ohio farm owned by a man named Hopewell. Thus, "Hopewell" became the unlikely name for these mound-building people.

The Hopewell Indians lived throughout the Midwest for about seven or eight hundred years. In Michigan their settlements were located largely in the southwest up to the lower Muskegon River. Although other groups of Indian people lived in the same areas and sometimes even built mounds, their ways of life did not match the Hopewells'. For the Hopewells established something of a golden age of Indian culture.

The Hopewell mounds show the planning skills, energy, and way of life of these early Indian people. Without the help of oxen, horses, or machinery they created their mounds, some of them as high as thirty feet. Although most of these huge piles of earth were dome-shaped, some Hopewell mounds outside the Michigan area were built in the shape of animals, such as a snake. Within the mounds were rectangular or oval areas enclosed by walls. The dead were usually buried here. Items such as pottery, jewelry, and pipes were placed with the bodies in these tombs. Not everyone who died was buried in a mound, however. A mound burial seems to have been reserved for important leaders, rich people, or perhaps a beloved family member. It is likely, experts say, that great ceremonies went along with the construction of a mound.

The Hopewell mounds that have been studied by archeologists have supplied a wealth of information about the Indian past. Not only did the Hopewells hunt, fish, and gather wild foods, they also farmed. They grew beans, squash, tobacco, and a type of corn and worked with tools made of stone, bone, and copper. Like the Copper Culture Indians, the Hopewells were traders. Their burial items included grizzly bear teeth from lands far to the west, large shells from the Gulf of Mexico, and sheets of a mineral called mica that came from the eastern United States.

Unlike any Indian people before them, the Hopewells were interested not only in adding artistic touches to the things they used, but also in making things purely for decoration. In addition to attractive pottery, pipes, and tools, they made stone sculptures, probably for their religious ceremonies. The Hopewells revived the metal-working skills of the Copper Culture Indians. Unlike these earlier people, however, they made a great deal of jewelry and other ornaments from copper. They also learned to weave, twisting the stringy material that grows inside the bark of certain trees to make thread for cloth. They did not build looms, but used a finger method of weaving cloth. Musical instruments have also been found in the mounds, the most common being rattles and panpipes, a type of wind instrument.

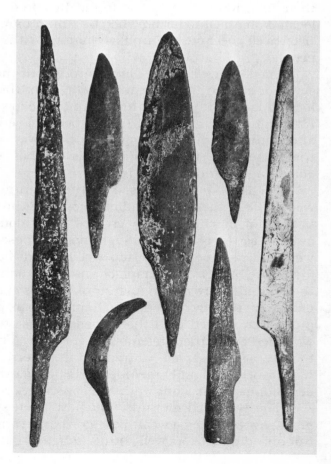

The copper mined by early Indians was used largely for tools, such as knives, awls, and spearpoints. The Hopewells also made some copper jewelry.

Unusual traces of the Hopewell culture are the garden beds that were discovered by pioneers in the southwestern part of the state. These beds covered many acres of land and were made of low mounds or ridges of earth in various rectangular shapes. Although they resembled formal gardens, experts are not sure why the beds were built or how they were used. The beds were destroyed when settlers came to Michigan in the 1800s and began farming.

Strangely, neighboring Indian groups of the Hopewells did not adopt Hopewell customs, but lived much simpler lives. Some still made their living by hunting, fishing, and gathering. Although a few built burial mounds, they were small and their burial ornaments less elaborate. Even the Hopewells themselves were unable to sustain their way of life, which placed importance on ceremony and art. Around 700 B.C. the golden age of their culture was beginning to fade. The traces of their lives remained, however, buried deep within their mounds.

The Woodland Indians

By the late Woodland period, the Hopewell way of life had come to an end. The different groups of Indian people that lived here shared a culture that can probably be best described as practical. There were many more people gathered in larger villages.

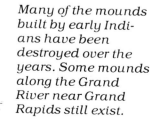

Many of the mounds built by early Indians have been destroyed over the years. Some mounds along the Grand River near Grand Rapids still exist.

They were kept busy raising food, making clothes and tools, and learning better ways to hunt. They made pottery, but did not take time to decorate it. Although at a much slower pace than we are accustomed to today, times were changing.

The Indians in the Michigan area during the late Woodland period lived in ways that were similar to those of Indian people throughout the area that is now the northeastern United States. The people in this large area are called the Eastern Woodland Indians. Although their languages differed in some ways, many of them were related to a broader language called Algonquian. Their daily activities, such as farming, hunting, and making pottery, were also much the same. They built dome or rectangular-shaped houses and sometimes constructed palisades, or fences of stakes, around their villages.

In the southern part of what is now Michigan, the Woodland Indians lived by hunting, fishing, and farming. Their three main crops were squash, beans, and corn, which they often called the "three sisters." In the northern areas farming was more difficult since the growing season was shorter and the soil generally poorer. Here people depended largely on hunting and fishing for their food supply.

The people of the late Woodland period were the ancestors of the Indians who greeted the French explorers. They lived together in bands, or small groups, but were part of larger groups called tribes which shared the same language and way of life. At the time of the French arrival, three main tribes were living in the Michigan area. They were the Ottawa, the Potawatomi, and the Ojibwa, or Chippewa. Each tribe was loosely knit. Although the word "nation" is often used in place of tribe, there were no strong political ties between bands, but rather a sense of community and cooperation. The Ottawa, Ojibwa, and Potawatomi, all friends, often referred to themselves as the Three Fires.

The arrival of Europeans

With the arrival and eventual takeover by Europeans, the differences between the tribes grew smaller. They were the people who had lived here for hundreds of years, almost a part of the land that was officially to become Michigan. Yet the government saw them as one people. Many of America's leaders and people believed all tribes needed to be moved west or south to a common Indian territory. Gradually laws were passed that forced Indians from their land, and even from Michigan itself. Through conflicts, disease, and poverty the tribes were reduced until, in time, Indian villages were made up not of an Ojibwa or Ottawa band, but of Potawatomi, Ojibwa, and Ottawa survivors.

Indians in Michigan did not live in one area throughout prehistoric and historic times. After the arrival of Europeans, however, they generally occupied the areas shown on the map.

The arrival of Europeans in the Great Lakes area marked more than the beginning of the end of the Indian way of life. It also marked the end of Michigan's prehistory. And Michigan's history began to be written, not by the Indian people who lived here, but by Europeans, people who had stumbled upon a continent they had not known existed. The Europeans found that the Indians were vastly different from themselves and decided that the natives were an inferior race. Even as the Indians fed, guided, and welcomed them, few Europeans were able to appreciate the Indian culture. Unfortunately, this negative viewpoint toward the Indian people dominated the history that was written. It was many years before the Indian culture was recognized as a rich part of both our Michigan and our American heritage.

The Ojibwa

The largest tribe of Indians to live in the Michigan area at the time of contact with the Europeans was the Ojibwa tribe. The Ojibwa had several different names. They called themselves Anishnabeg, meaning Indian or person. Other tribes referred to them as Ojibwa. The first French explorers met a group of Ojibwa fishing in the rapids at Sault Ste. Marie in the early 1600s. They called them Saulteurs, or people of the rapids. About one hundred years later the English traders and soldiers gave them the name of Chippewa. This name is commonly used today.

The Ojibwas lived and traveled throughout the northern Great Lakes region from Lake Huron westward to the present North Dakota. The tribe was made up of so many bands of different people it could barely be called a single tribe. Each band lived, hunted, and traveled in an area that extended for hundreds of miles.

As in other Indian tribes, the size of each Ojibwa band varied. For example, one band might be made up of five hundred people. Within the band there might be twenty to twenty-five family groups, or extended families. Within the extended family were a man and wife and children, along with the man's parents, his younger brothers and sisters, and so forth. The extended families belonged to a broader family group called a clan, which was named for an animal such as a beaver, loon, or turtle. Each child was part of his or her father's clan and was expected to marry a member of another clan. Thus, clan relationships extended from band to band and kept a certain bond between people.

The Ojibwa people depended largely on hunting or fishing for their food, a way of life that kept them moving. During the warm seasons, the bands of Ojibwa lived in villages that were often built along the Great Lakes and near the mouths of rivers where fishing was good. During the winter months bands would break apart into families and move inland where hunting was better. At special times of the year they might also move and set up temporary camps to gather wild rice or collect sap from maple trees to make maple sugar.

In a few places, such as the area around Sault Ste. Marie, there was enough food to sustain a band throughout the year. When two French priests named Dollier and Galinee visited that area, they commented on the Saulteurs and the supply of fish in the St. Marys River. They wrote the following in their journal: "This river forms at this place a rapid so teeming with fish, called white fish, that the Indians could easily catch enough to feed ten thousand men. It is true the fishing is so difficult that only Indians can carry it on. No Frenchman has hitherto been able to succeed in it, nor any other Indian than those of this tribe, who are used to this kind of fishing from an early age."

For the most part, however, the Ojibwa moved around, and their way of life reflected this pattern. Their homes were wigwams, dome-shaped structures that were quick and easy to build. A wigwam was made by arching saplings to form a framework and then covering it with birchbark, animal skins, or woven mats. When a family moved, they rolled up the outside covering and carried it to another location. In less than a day, a frame could be built and covered, making a new wigwam ready for occupancy.

Using Birchbark

The birch tree, with its handsome and useful bark, was an important raw material for Indian people in the northern Great Lakes area, a region where many of these trees grow. In the spring, when the bark was especially strong, it was cut from the trees in large strips. The Indians were careful not to cut so deeply into the trunk that the tree would die, even though the bark that would grow back would never be suitable for their needs.

One of the common uses of birchbark was in the manufacture of mocucks, or containers that could be made watertight. A single piece of bark was steamed until it was easy to bend, molded into shape, and cooled. Spruce roots were used to sew the seams of the container and also to hold splints of wood around the top edge. A gummy solution made from pitch of spruce trees was used to seal the seams or repair any cracks in the bark. The finished containers were then used to store wild rice, maple sugar, dried berries, and other foods. The Ojibwa were proud of their mocucks and often decorated them with paints and dyes made from various roots, berries, and barks. Sometimes small birchbark containers were highly decorated with porcupine quills dyed in various colors.

The birchbark canoe is probably the most famous item made by Indian people in the area that is now the northeastern United States and southern Canada. In late spring pieces of bark were cut from large silver birch trees, and then rolled and stored in cool places. When a new canoe was needed, the Indians cut down cedar trees and made strips for the boat's framework. Just as in the manufacture of mocucks, the Indians used spruce roots for thread and pitch to seal the seams. They kept the birchbark wet to keep it soft and pliable. Stones and stakes helped hold the bark in shape as the Indian craftsmen and craftswomen sewed and sealed seams and lined the interior with cedar strips. Often designs were painted on the finished canoes.

Although they seemed light and fragile, Indian canoes were remarkably durable. A well-made canoe might last as long as ten years with normal use. Pitch and sometimes extra spruce roots were carried, however, to make repairs that were often necessary.

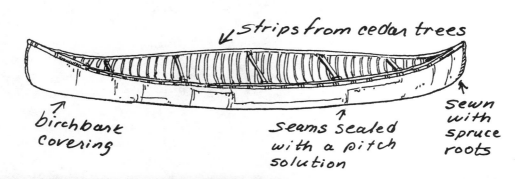

strips from cedar trees

birchbark covering

seams sealed with a pitch solution

sewn with spruce roots

The Ojibwa also found practical ways to travel through a land thick with forests and dotted with lakes and rivers. Their handsome birchbark canoes were lightweight, allowing them to travel on even the shallow, rapid rivers and streams. Canoes could also easily be carried, or portaged, around waterfalls or other impassable parts of a river. Although other tribes of the Eastern Woodland area also made canoes, the Ojibwa were especially skillful at this craft. Their canoes were admired by other tribes as well as by European traders and explorers. In the winter the Ojibwa traveled by snowshoes or toboggans, two more inventions that were quickly adopted by European fur traders and explorers.

The Ottawa

A French trader once called the Ottawa "a nation of raised hair." Another Frenchman said the Ottawas had "hair like a brush turned up." Still another commented that the Ottawa people were the ones that always traveled loaded with trade goods.

It was true that the Ottawa could be distinguished from other tribes in the Michigan area because of the brushed-up hairstyle of the men. The Ottawa tribe had not spent hundreds of years in the Michigan area. They came from an area east of Lake Huron where it was not uncommon for Indian men to wear their hair in this fashion. Because of threats by the powerful Iroquois tribes that dominated the eastern Great Lakes region, the Ottawa moved

Although wigwams were probably the most common type of Indian houses in the Michigan area, the Ottawa also built longhouses. Longhouses lodged more than one family.

westward in the mid-1600s. Ottawa bands lived in many places in Michigan, but especially near the Straits of Mackinac and southward along Lake Michigan.

It was also true that the Ottawa were more involved in trading than other Michigan tribes. Their name, in fact, means traders. While other tribes were teaching their boys to hunt and fish, the Ottawa were also teaching theirs essential business skills. Although they had been traders before the arrival of the French, they quickly found a place as middlemen between the Europeans and other Indian tribes. They bought furs and food from Indians and traded them to the French for items such as guns, beads, and kettles.

The Ottawa way of life was more settled than that of the Ojibwa. An Ottawa village was made up of longhouses, usually with roofs shaped like half a barrel. Just like small apartment buildings, the longhouses lodged several families. Fences or palisades were often built around the village. These helped protect the women and children who were left alone for long periods of time while the men hunted, fished, and traded.

Generally, the Ottawa people lived in their villages throughout the year. When food was scarce during the long winter months, the men often traveled inland to winter hunting camps. After they had killed enough animals, they dressed the meat and returned to the village. Occasionally, a band would move their entire village, perhaps to protect themselves from enemies.

It was important to the Ottawa that their villages be located near lakes or rivers, since fishing occupied more of the men's time than hunting. Generally the Ottawa fished with nets, although hook, line, and spears were also used. Fish that were not eaten fresh were dried over fires or in the sun.

Ottawa women kept busy preparing food, making clothes, and carrying on the farming. With the help of the old men who were no longer able to hunt and travel, they raised enough corn to supply their own needs and to trade to Ojibwa bands. The women were also skillful weavers. Using cornhusks, cattail leaves, and other reeds they made mats, bags, and baskets.

The Potawatomi

Among the tall hardwood forests that once covered southwestern Michigan were scattered open fields belonging to Indian farmers, mainly the Potawatomi. More than the Ojibwa or the Ottawa, the Potawatomi relied on their farming skills to supply their food. They grew beans, squash, melons, and corn, burying fish with their seeds to help produce better crops. As was com-

Living From Nature

Indian people throughout North America were extremely skillful at finding both food and medicine in the natural world around them. The Menominee Indians and certain bands of Ojibwa gathered the wild rice that grew in the quiet, shallow waters of lakes, rivers, and streams of northern Michigan. In the late summer an Indian family would slowly push their canoe through a rice bed, bending the rice stalks over the canoe and beating them until the heads of rice fell into the canoe. The Indians returned with their loaded canoes to dry the rice in the sun and store it in birchbark containers. They also replanted some of the rice so that there would be enough for the following year's harvest.

Indians also discovered that certain maple trees yielded a sap in late winter that could be made into delicious syrup and sugar. Nearly all the tribes that lived in the Michigan area gathered sap from sugar-maple trees each year, usually in the month of March. The sap was boiled by placing steaming rocks in birchbark or skin containers filled with sap. The process was continued until the sap became a sweet, rich syrup, or boiled down to sugar. Both the syrup and the sugar could be easily stored and used throughout the year to make foods more flavorful.

While Michigan's Indian people ate nuts and berries, as we might expect, they also used plants that surprise us today. The cattail, for instance, had many uses for the Indians. In the spring, the pure white shoots of the root were cooked and eaten. Fresh root was used to treat burns or wounds. Dried, ground root was used to cure stomachaches. Indians also ate the pointed tips or spikes of the cattail in the spring. Later, the yellow pollen on some of the spikes was used as flour. Indians also dried the long, flat leaves of the cattails and wove them into mats or baskets.

Milkweed was another valuable plant to the Indians. When regular or swamp milkweed blossomed, it was picked and eaten much like asparagus. It was also used in soup or mixed with cornmeal. Tea was made from milkweed roots and used for medicine.

Acorns from white or red oak trees were also gathered by Michigan's native people. The Indians put them through a long process, which included roasting and then boiling them in wood ashes, so that the nuts could be eaten safely. When the process was complete, the acorns were usually ground into flour for thickening soup or making pancakes.

Cattail

mon among Indian tribes, the women planted and tended the gardens while the men hunted and fished.

Although the Potawatomi seem to have lived only in southwestern Michigan in the early 1600s, they moved farther south and west as time went on. By the 1800s bands of Potawatomi lived in the areas that are now eastern Wisconsin, northern Illinois, and northern Indiana. Often they would take over territories of smaller, weaker tribes. Still, the Potawatomi were not known for making war. A French trader named Nicolas Perrot said that the tribe's leaders made careful decisions and were unwilling to undertake activities that were unreasonable. "The old men," he wrote, "are prudent, sensible, and deliberate."

As with other tribes in the Great Lakes area, the extended family was extremely important to the Potawatomi way of life. Children called their own father and their father's brothers all by the name of "father." "Mother" was the word used for a child's real mother and also the mother's sisters. If a child's parent died, there was another parent to love and care for the child. The extended family assured that everyone had a place and would not be left to struggle alone.

For many years Potawatomi men usually had more than one wife, a practice that was not uncommon among Indian tribes. This made an extended family larger and more powerful within the band. French missionaries who came to the Great Lakes region were greatly upset by this practice and worked to convince the Indians to abandon it. Thus, by the 1800s the Potawatomi men had only one wife in each household.

Missionaries were also upset by the complex and involved religious practices of the Potawatomi and other Michigan tribes. There were feasts and ceremonies involving dancing and other rituals. The Feast of the Dead, for example, was held about every three years and was a huge ceremony for all those who had died during that period. As part of the ceremony, the dead were dug up and then reburied.

The Potawatomi, as well as the Ojibwa and Ottawa, had a religious organization called the Midewiwin, or Grand Medicine Society. People in this society healed the sick and were believed to have special spiritual powers. Although missionaries convinced some Indians to adopt the Christian religion, the importance of the Midewiwin was not drastically reduced. Most native people kept their own beliefs or combined ideas from both religions.

Michigan's other Indian tribes

A number of other, smaller Indian groups lived in the Michigan area after contact with the Europeans. Among them were the Hurons, a tribe that had once numbered about thirty thousand people and lived east of Lake Huron, in Canada. While living in Canada, however, about half of the Huron people had died of smallpox and other diseases brought by Europeans. They also fought with the powerful Iroquois who lived in the area that is presently New York State. These violent battles reduced their numbers even more. Finally, the Hurons who remained were adopted by the Iroquois or moved westward. Some that escaped went to live near the Straits of Mackinac. Later they moved to the Detroit area and became known as the Wyandottes.

The Huron people were actually closely related to their Iroquois enemies. They spoke similar languages, lived in longhouses, and usually surrounded their villages with palisades. Many Huron men had hairstyles like Iroquois men, pulling out all of their hair except for a narrow strip that stretched across the top of their heads from the forehead to the neck.

The social organization of the Hurons also resembled that of the Iroquois people. Children of a family belonged to the clan of their mother, not of their father as in the Ojibwa, Ottawa, and Potawatomi tribes. Families who lived together in a longhouse were also related through the women instead of the men. This type of family organization is called matrilineal, or the tracing of one's descent through the women.

In some ways the Huron way of life was much like that of other Michigan tribes. Huron men fished, hunted, and traded while the women worked in the gardens raising corn, beans, squash, and sunflowers. They also gathered wild foods, such as acorns, cranberries, and grapes. Although the Hurons had permanent villages, they often left them and built temporary houses while they fished, hunted, and even farmed.

The Miami Indians also lived in the Detroit area, as well as in what is now the southwestern corner of Michigan. Their villages were permanent ones, although many families left for winter hunts. Farming was very important to the Miami, and they raised a variety of crops. Although women generally were in charge of the crops, men often returned from hunting to help with the harvest. What was not immediately eaten was stored in underground pits lined with bark.

In several ways the Miami differed from other tribes in the Michigan area. Although they lived in wigwams, they often wove mats from reeds and used them to cover the wigwam frame. They traveled westward to hunt the buffalo that lived on the prairies.

Gifts From Bosh-Kwa-Dosh, The Mastodon

According to an Ojibwa legend, there was once an Indian man, an Anissinape, who was alone in the world. A tiny animal appeared to him, saying that his name was Bosh-Kwa-Dosh and that he could help him find other people. "Take me up and bind me to your body," the animal commanded, "and never put me aside." The Anissinape did as the animal asked, sewing Bosh-Kwa-Dosh into his belt.

With the help of the tiny animal, the Anissinape at last came to a village where he was asked to take some tests. With two other young men the Anissinape was forced to lie on a frozen lake for as long as he could endure. The other men died, but the Anissinape was only a little cold, protected by Bosh-Kwa-Dosh who was sewn into his belt.

The Anissinape was then asked to race. But his opponent in the race was a large, fierce black bear which could run faster than the young man. But Bosh-Kwa-Dosh again came to the aid of the Anissinape and helped him to move as quickly as a bird and win the race.

The people of the village were still not satisfied. They asked the Anissinape to take the ice test again. But he asked to rest first and took off his belt to sleep. When he awoke to take the test, he forgot to put the belt back around his waist. Thus, he froze and died, and the villagers cut his body into pieces.

One of the villagers was deeply saddened by the Anissinape's death, because the two had become friends. He picked up the belt worn by the Assinape and heard noises coming from within it. The villager carefully opened the seams. Inside was a tiny animal that quickly grew to the size of a dog. The mysterious dog began running through the village, collecting the bones of the Anissinape. When he had them in place, he let forth a strange howl that brought life to the Anissinape.

"Now," Bosh-Kwa-Dosh declared, "I will show you who I am." Then he began to shake himself. As he shook he began to swell. He grew into a mastodon, with two great shining tusks. "The Great Spirit created me to show his power when there were only animals on the earth. But the earth was made for man, not for beasts. And if all were as large as I, there would not be enough grass for food. So now I will go, giving you some of those great gifts which I possess. All the animals shall be your food, and you are no longer to flee before them, and be their sport and food." He then walked away, leaving all the smaller animals trembling.

An Ojibwa tale told by an old hunter of the Saulteur band at Sault Ste. Marie and recorded by Henry Schoolcraft.

Unlike the Ojibwa and Ottawa, the Miami chose to walk rather than travel by water. Their only canoes were crude dugouts.

The family structure of the Miami was different and more complex than that of other tribes in the Michigan area. Children were members of the clan of their mother's brother, called an uncle. The uncle's male children were also called uncles, and his female children were called mothers. It was a system that totally confused the Europeans. They could not understand why the old men claimed that young girls were their mothers!

Still another tribe of Indian people lived in what is now the western part of Michigan's Upper Peninsula and northern Wisconsin. They were the Menominee, a group admired by the Europeans and called a handsome, peaceful people. Although the Menominee farmed and hunted, they depended largely on wild rice and a large fish called sturgeon for the bulk of their food supply. The women of the tribe were also excellent weavers, making baskets, bags, and large mats used to cover their houses.

A shared view of life

Although Michigan's Indian peoples were different in many ways, they shared certain ideas about life. One of these common ideas concerned leadership. Each tribe had a chief, but this was not a position of power. Instead chiefs were supposed to listen to the thoughts of others. They were also expected to act in a generous, dignified, and responsible way.

Another important aspect of life common to all the tribes was the sharing of food, work, and even some household goods. Life was difficult, often a matter of survival, but the harder the times, the more this idea triumphed! If only one hunter brought back food, everyone had food. Generosity was a great virtue, and it was far better to give away your goods than to pile them up for yourself. With this attitude there was little or no stealing. No old, sick, or poor people were left to struggle on their own.

Indians of different tribes also held a common belief that plants, animals, and people were all linked in a web of life. Each had a reason for its life and needed the other. A bee, for example, depended on a flower for its food, while a bear depended on the bee's honey. In turn, an Indian needed the meat of the bear for food and its fur for robes. As time went by, all returned to the earth where life began again. With this idea as their guide, Indian people believed that taking more than was needed from the world around them would disturb the balance of nature.

In addition to being linked with plants and animals, the Indians felt these things had a living spirit of their own. For ex-

ample, a bear had a special spirit and in some tribes, such as the Ojibwa, ceremonies were held when one of these animals was killed. Clans of every tribe also named themselves after animals and felt that they had a special tie with those animals and their spirits.

The arrival of the Europeans was upsetting to the Indian view of life. The Europeans tried to buy or claim land when the Indians believed it was impossible for any man or woman to own land. To them, the land belonged to everyone, just as the sun and moon and stars belonged to all.

The beginning of the fur trade also created a conflict with the Indians' values. Hunters had never killed more than was needed, and each part of the animal was put to use: the meat for food, the skin for clothes, the bones for tools. Supplying the traders meant the Indians had to kill far more animals than they could use themselves.

Finally, the settlers themselves were a danger to the Indian philosophy of life. They cut the trees and scarred the land with their plows. Most of all, they wanted the Indians to move and change, to learn to think and live as white people, and to worship their god. The settlers' demands, along with their lack of understanding of Indian values, entangled the Indian people in Michigan's history in sad, even tragic ways, and led to solutions that are still being patched and repaired.

The European fur traders and missionaries changed the Indian way of life. Indians struggled to hold on to their beliefs, their land, and their language for many years.

M I C H I G A N

I·N T·I·M·E

Date	In Michigan	Outside Michigan
1400		Columbus sails to America (1492) Cabot brings Europeans news of rich fishing waters near Newfoundland (1497)
1500		Cartier sails the St. Lawrence & claims land for France (1535) De Soto claims Florida for Spain (1539) Coronado explores the Southwest (1540) Sir Walter Raleigh comes to Virginia (1584)
1600	Brulé reaches Lake Superior (1622) Nicolet travels across Lake Michigan to Green Bay (1634) Raymbault & Jogues visit Sault Ste. Marie (1641) Radisson & Grosseillier travel along Lake Superior (1658) French make short peace with Iroquois (1667) Marquette founds a mission at St. Ignace (1668) Marquette & Jolliet explore the Mississippi (1671) La Salle comes to Michigan on the *Griffon* & builds Fort Miami (1679)	Jamestown, Virginia, is founded (1607) Champlain founds Quebec (1608) The Pilgrims land at Plymouth Rock (1620) The Dutch begin building fur trading posts along the Hudson River (1624) Hudson's Bay Company is formed (1670)

Chapter 3

Something in the hazy distance,
Something in the mists of morning . . .

. . . A birch canoe with paddles
Rising, sinking on the water,
Dripping, flashing in the sunshine;
And within it came a people
From the distant land of Wabun,
From the farthest realms of morning
Came the Black-Robe chief, the Prophet,
He the Priest of Prayer, the Pale-face,
With his guides and his companions.
    from "The Song of Hiawatha" by Henry Wadsworth Longfellow

Explorers, Traders, and Priests

By the time the Pilgrims landed in Plymouth in 1624, the land we now call Michigan had been visited by Europeans. They did not come on a ship like the *Mayflower*, but as Longfellow later wrote, in "a birch canoe with paddles." Canoes were supplied by Indians to these visitors who pushed westward from eastern Canada. They were French, and it was not their plan to settle here with their families. Instead, some were priests who wanted to bring the Christian religion to the Indians. Others were traders who were hoping to become wealthy in the search for furs. And still others were explorers who dreamed of discovering a water passage across the North American continent, the elusive Northwest Passage.

The search begins

It was this dream, this search for a Northwest Passage, that led the French to the Michigan area in the early 1600s. They, like other European explorers, were looking for a water route to the Indies, as they called China and other countries in Asia. There they could trade for spices, silks, diamonds, rubies, and other valuable goods from these lands. It was possible to sail south to the tip of Africa and then turn east, but that trip took far too long. Sailing westward seemed to be the answer, but North and

South America blocked the way. A number of explorers sailed along the coast of North America, but not because of their great interest in this continent. They simply wanted to find a waterway through this mass of land!

Among the European explorers who searched for a Northwest Passage through the North American continent were John Cabot and Jacques Cartier. Shortly after Columbus's voyage of 1492, Cabot, an Italian sailor exploring for England, sailed along the coast of present-day Newfoundland. More than forty years later, Cartier, sailing for France, went beyond Newfoundland into the Gulf of the St. Lawrence River. From the Gulf he followed the St. Lawrence River inland as far as the site of the present city of Montreal and claimed the land for France. He also named it Canada after the name of an Indian village.

Cartier had good things to say about the territory he explored. In his journal he wrote that it was as "goodly and pleasant a country as possibly can be wished for, full of all sorts of goodly trees, that is to say, oak, elms, walnut trees, cedars, firs, ash, box, willows, and great store of vines, all as full of grapes as could be, so that if any of our fellows went on shore, they came home laden with them." Still, it was nearly fifty years before other French people came to explore the lands further.

The fishing connection

The explorers were not the only ones to come to the Newfoundland area. Shortly after Cabot returned to Europe and told stories of the wonderful fishing waters off the Newfoundland coast, a few hardy fishermen set off to find out if this was true. By the early 1500s a number of fishermen from Portugal and other European countries began sailing to these waters in their tiny boats. They brought back huge catches of Atlantic codfish, a favorite fish in Europe.

The fishermen who made the long and risky sail to the fishing banks off Newfoundland began a chain of events that eventually led to the exploration of the Great Lakes area. Although many fishing boats packed their catches in barrels of salt to preserve them for the long voyage back to Europe, other fishermen took them to shore. There they cleaned and dried them in the sun on flakes, or platforms made of poles and branches. Once on shore, these fishermen discovered another valuable resource of the region. The Indian people had clothes and other items made of beautiful furs. These would be welcomed in Europe, where furs were in style.

It was apparent to the fishermen that they could make bigger profits from their trips by taking back furs to Europe along with their cargoes of codfish. They began to give Indians beads, knives, and other items in exchange for deer, beaver, bear, otter, and seal skins. It was the beginning of the fur trade, one of the most important industries in Michigan's, and America's, past.

Samuel de Champlain

The supply of furs in Europe had dwindled with the ever-growing demand for fur-trimmed clothing and hats. With this in mind, French businessmen began to see profit in sending men to North America to trade with the Indians for furs. One of the men they sent to carry out this job was Samuel de Champlain, a capable man who was eventually to become governor of Canada, or New France. After several attempts, Champlain and his group established a settlement at Quebec in 1608.

In order to survive as a stranger in this land, Champlain made friends with the Indians and urged them to bring their furs to the Quebec settlement to trade. Gradually the fur trade grew. Ships from France came to Quebec loaded with goods such as cloth, beads and iron cooking pots and returned to France with beautiful furs.

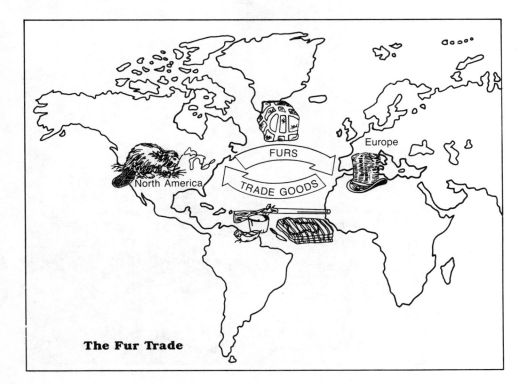

The Fur Trade

The fur trade, along with the search for the Northwest Passage, brought the French to the Michigan area. The trade was the main industry in the upper Great Lakes region for over two hundred years.

Champlain was more than a fur trader and leader. He was also a skilled geographer and explorer who traveled as far south as present-day New England. He also traveled westward, probably as far as Lake Huron, hoping to find a passage that would lead to the Pacific Ocean. Of course, he failed in that task, but the many lakes and rivers seemed promising. When injuries ended his explorations, he sent younger, stronger men to continue the search. Those Frenchmen were the first to reach the Michigan area.

Brulé and Nicolet

Indian guides accompanied the fur traders and explorers in the Great Lakes region. Often these Europeans did not want to leave the wilderness and lived and dressed like Indians.

If any explorer could have lived up to a movie or television image of a daring adventurer, it probably would have been Etienne Brulé. As a young boy Brulé had been a captive of an Indian tribe and proven his strength and courage at an early age. Now he was chosen by Champlain to live with the Huron Indians. He was to learn their language and find out as much as he could about the forests, lakes, and rivers of this vast land. The large Huron villages at this time were located near Georgian Bay on Lake Huron. "Push westward," Champlain instructed. Perhaps if the daring

Brulé reached the other side of the lake, he would discover some route to the Pacific Ocean.

Brulé set out westward with another Frenchman named Grenoble in 1622. Following the northern shore of Lake Huron, the pair paddled their canoe up the St. Marys River to Lake Superior. It's uncertain how far they traveled into Lake Superior. But Brulé was the first Frenchman to bring back the news to his people that "an enormous inland ocean" lay beyond the shores of Lake Huron. The explorer also brought back pieces of copper and told a French priest that he had learned of rich mines farther to the west. The French, however, were not interested in the possibility of copper resources. It was news of a water route that they wanted to hear.

Brulé never returned to live with his own people. His interest lay in the wilderness, and he remained with the Hurons. Unfortunately, he wrote nothing of his life or adventures. Not only would it have been an interesting story, but it is likely that he explored the region again after his trip for Champlain. He was later killed by a Huron as they argued over an Indian woman.

Another man sent by Champlain to live with Indians was Jean Nicolet. Like Brulé, Nicolet was to learn the Indian language and customs, and something about the geography of the region. After Nicolet became used to living in the wilderness, Champlain planned to have him search for the Northwest Passage. The Hurons had told Champlain about a strange tribe living in the west. It seemed to Champlain that these people might be inhabitants of the Indies!

Nicolet and his Indian guides set out in canoes in 1634. They paddled from Lake Huron, through the Mackinac Straits, and into Lake Michigan, making Nicolet the first European ever to see this lake. According to stories, the group went as far as present-day Green Bay, Wisconsin. There, Nicolet put on a fancy Chinese robe that had been sent with him by Champlain. But much to his disappointment, Nicolet was not in China or any part of the Indies. The strange tribe of people were the Winnebagos. These Indians spoke Siouan, a language unfamiliar to the Hurons.

Even with Nicolet's failure, the hope for the discovery of the Northwest Passage did not die. He took back the news of a great river that lay farther to the west. It was possible, he believed, that this river would flow westward to an ocean and beyond that, the Indies.

The story of Nicolet's robed landing and his geographical mistakes makes him seem a less romantic historical figure than Brulé. But in spite of his errors, his explorations gave the French new knowledge and encouraged other explorers to search for the "great river." Nicolet returned to live in Quebec, where he served as an Indian interpreter. Strangely, the man who had traveled by canoe across two great lakes died five years later when his small boat was swamped by waves. Nicolet, it seems, could not swim.

The Black-Robe chiefs

Among the first Frenchmen to come to America were Catholic priests. It was not the love of adventure or the hope of money from the fur trade that brought these men, but the knowledge that there were people here who did not know about Christianity. The Indians, the priests felt, must be taught to live and worship as Christians. These priests, most of whom were very well educated, were so dedicated to this cause that they left their comfortable homes in France to establish missions and risk their lives in the wilderness.

The task of changing the Indians' way of living and worshipping was a huge one. The priests from the Recollect order that had begun the work soon called for help from a larger order, the Jesuits. Still, most Indian people did not want these men telling them how to live their lives. At times French missions were burned

Nicolet hoped to reach the Indies as he crossed Lake Michigan. Instead he was greeted on the Wisconsin shores by a group of Winnebago Indians.

and the missionaries killed. Some priests lost their lives in the battles between tribes.

Even French traders did not always welcome the priests. The Indians' time, they felt, should be spent in the fur trade, not learning about Christianity. Men such as Brulé did not want the wilderness to be changed and refused to give help or aid to the missionaries. On the other hand, the priests were often angry at the traders for living like the Indians and supplying them with alcohol, a European trade item that was disrupting Indian life.

In spite of the problems, the priests were helpful to France. Their journeys helped establish French claims in America. They also provided new knowledge about the region, and some of their missions grew into important settlements. Perhaps even more important, the priests kept excellent records and journals that have been extremely valuable in our understanding of the past.

After Brulé and Nicolet, the priests were the first Europeans to come to the Michigan area. Isaac Jogues and Charles Raymbault journeyed northward on Lake Huron and the St. Marys River to preach to the Indians. A fellow priest at a mission in a Huron settlement on Georgian Bay wrote about the trip: ". . . After seventeen days of navigation on the great lake or fresh-water sea that bathes the land of the Hurons, they reached the Sault, where they found about two thousand souls, and obtained information about a great many other sedentary nations, who have never known Europeans and have never heard of God. . . ." The pair spent several weeks preaching to the Indians at the Sault, or the rapids on the St. Marys, and then returned to Georgian Bay. Before they left, they named the area Sault Ste. Marie.

In 1668, twenty-seven years after Jogues' and Raymbault's journey to the Sault, a Jesuit priest arrived to establish a mission there. He was Father Jacques Marquette. The young priest had studied Indian languages and was anxious to begin his first missionary assignment. For several years Marquette worked at the Sault, until he received a new assignment to establish a mission farther south along the Straits of Mackinac. He named the mission St. Ignace after the founder of the Jesuit order. Marquette's missions are remembered as the first two settlements in Michigan.

The fur trade

France's interest in its North American claims revolved almost entirely around the fur trade. While the English were building colonies along the Atlantic coast, the French settlements remained few and were located along the St. Lawrence River. Although there was some farming and necessary industries, the fur trade was the main business.

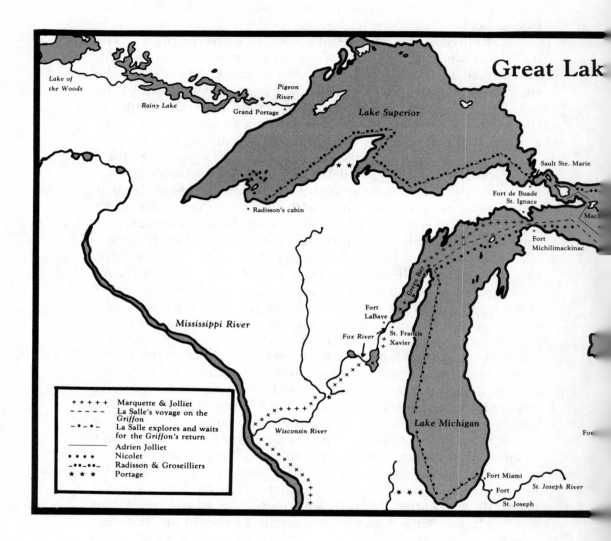

Great Lak

Lake of
the Woods

Rainy Lake

Pigeon
River

Grand Portage

Lake Superior

Sault Ste. Marie

Fort de Buade
St. Ignace

Macl

* Radisson's cabin

Fort
Michilimackinac

Mississippi River

Green Bay

Fort
LaBaye

St. Francis
Xavier

Fox River

Lake Michigan

Fo

+ + + + +	Marquette & Jolliet
– – – – –	La Salle's voyage on the *Griffon*
– • – • –	La Salle explores and waits for the *Griffon's* return
————	Adrien Jolliet
• • • •	Nicolet
–••–••–	Radisson & Groseilliers
★ ★ ★	Portage

Wisconsin River

Fort Miami

Fort

St. Joseph River

St. Joseph

Trade Routes

The early traders and explorers who came to the Michigan area did not come from the east through the Great Lakes. Instead they left the St. Lawrence River at Montreal, which was established in 1641, and traveled up the Ottawa River. At a small river called the Mattawa, they paddled and portaged their canoes to Lake Nipissing and then followed the French River to Georgian Bay on Lake Huron. From there they traveled westward to Lake Superior or Lake Michigan.

The late exploration and use of Lake Ontario and Lake Erie was due to the powerful Indian tribes called the Iroquois who lived in what is today New York State. The Iroquois tribes, who all spoke the same language and had created a

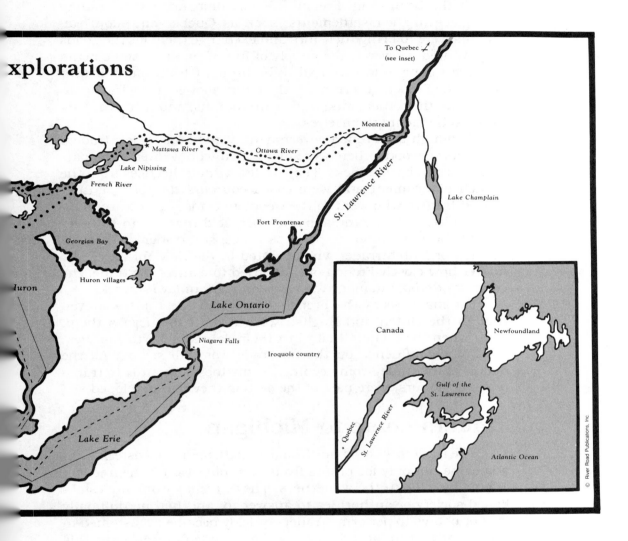

xplorations

To Quebec (see inset)

Montreal

Mattawa River · Ottawa River

Lake Nipissing

French River

St. Lawrence River

Lake Champlain

Fort Frontenac

Georgian Bay

Huron villages

Huron

Lake Ontario

Niagara Falls

Iroquois country

Lake Erie

Canada

Newfoundland

Gulf of the St. Lawrence

Quebec

St. Lawrence River

Atlantic Ocean

© River Road Publications, Inc

To Michigan

workable government, kept French traders from invading their lands. The goal of the Iroquois was to control the fur trade, and they often went to war to protect their interests. The French, as well as their Indian friends, often found themselves battling the well-trained forces of the Iroquois.

For many years the strength and fury of the Iroquois kept the French from exploring the upper St. Lawrence River, Lake Ontario, and Lake Erie. It was not until the late 1660s that a short peace was made with the Iroquois. The French then discovered the eastern Great Lakes and an improved route to the Michigan area.

In the beginning, French officials demanded that trading take place in their settlements, such as Quebec and Montreal. Indians were to bring their furs and exchange them for the goods they wanted. However, the supply of furs near these settlements was soon gone, and furs had to be brought from more distant areas. The French government, therefore, allowed a few traders to go beyond the settlements, trade with Indians, and bring the furs to the settlements themselves.

Although the French government wanted only a few traders to roam the woods, there were many men who wanted to be part of this profitable business. They traded without licenses from the French government and were called *coureurs de bois,* or unlicensed traders who went to the woods to trade. The *coureurs de bois* traded with the Indians and then sold the furs to whoever offered the most money—perhaps a licensed trader or even an English or Dutch trader who operated in the New York area. No matter how closely French officials tried to control the trade, the *coureurs de bois* managed to carry on their unlawful work.

For many years the French dominated the fur trade even though the Dutch and English worked hard to surpass them. Even when the French finally lost their claims in North America, the French influence on the fur trade was still strong. All the details of the trade, from keeping the business accounts to transporting the furs, were part of the system they had developed.

Traders come to Michigan

The traders who set out from the settlements of eastern Canada came not only for profits from furs, but also for the freedom offered by a life in the wilderness. They were far from any established society or authorities to answer to, and had no dull daily jobs or chores to perform. Traders quickly became accustomed to lives of adventure and danger as they traveled and lived in this unfamiliar land. They also came to enjoy life in those Indian villages where traders were welcome guests. Many of them dressed like Indians and married Indian women.

Among the first traders to explore the Michigan area were Medard Chouart, who carried the title Sieur de Groseilliers, and Pierre Radisson, both *coureurs de bois* from Quebec. On a journey that began in 1658, the pair paddled along the northern shores of Lake Huron and up the St. Marys River, carrying their canoe around the rapids at the Sault. When they reached Lake Superior, they paddled westward along the shore. Radisson kept a journal of this early French expedition on Lake Superior, and he frequently commented on its beauty. Its shores, he wrote, were "most delightfull and wounderous."

Radisson and Groseilliers continued along the southern shore of Lake Superior to what is now Wisconsin, and perhaps as far as Minnesota. After a two-year journey through lands north of the Great Lakes, they returned to Quebec loaded with beautiful furs. Their travels had given them new knowledge that a wealth of furs could be obtained north of Lake Superior up to the Hudson Bay region. The two, however, were not forgiven for trading without a license. French officials fined the pair and ignored their stories of Hudson Bay. The two angry traders later went to Europe and convinced businessmen from England to build trading posts along the bay. The Hudson's Bay Company, formed in 1670, became a leader in the business and gradually helped the British to surpass the French in the fur trade.

The fine furs brought back to Quebec by Radisson and Groseilliers encouraged other traders to come to the upper Great Lakes area. Many of them, like Radisson and Groseilliers, were *coureurs de bois.* Through their travels they gained valuable information about the region. Unfortunately, they did not keep written records of their journeys. They did name places, however, and often passed their knowledge along to mapmakers.

The voyageurs made up a colorful part of the history of the upper Great Lakes area. After long hard days of paddling, they had few comforts as they camped on the shores.

The voyageurs

Bringing furs to eastern Canada required a system of transportation that became almost legendary in the upper Great Lakes region and Canada. Large canoes were used to carry trade goods into the interior and furs back to Canadian settlements. They were manned by boatmen called voyageurs.

The life of a voyageur was a hard one. Journeys were long and difficult, and voyageurs paddled fifteen to eighteen hours each day, with only a few hours to sleep along the rocky shores. In many places they had to portage, or carry their cargoes and canoes around a waterfall or the rough stretch of a river. A voyageur had to be able to carry at least 180 pounds on his back, and some were said to be able to carry well over 300 pounds! To make it even more difficult, portages might lead them through underbrush and swamps or over rocky trails.

To help pass the long hours the voyageurs created their own entertainment. They often sang, usually songs that helped them keep time with the strokes of their paddles. They sometimes raced with each other or tried to outdo one another as they guided their canoes through the rapids. They did this knowing full well that the fun could quickly turn to tragedy.

Much like the traders, the voyageurs combined European and Indian dress, often wearing breechcloths, leggings, and moccasins. However, they were especially well known for their red wool caps, shirts with colorful ties or bandanas, and bright sashes worn around their waists. Their dress, along with the songs and sense of adventure, have made them an unforgettable part of history.

The priest and the trader

Even though the French were beginning to realize that the North American continent was much larger than they had ever imagined, they were unwilling to give up the idea that a water route could be found across it. The French governor in Quebec decided to send an exploring party westward and find the "great river" that was so often described by the Indians. It was hoped, of course, that this river would lead to the Pacific Ocean. The man selected to lead the expedition was a fur trader and mapmaker named Louis Jolliet. He was joined on the journey by Father Jacques Marquette and several other Frenchmen.

Marquette described the beginning of the journey in his journal: ". . . We embarked—Monsieur Jollyet and myself, with five men—in two bark canoes, fully resolved to do and suffer everything for so glorious an undertaking. Accordingly, on the 17th

day of May, 1673, we started from the mission of St. Ignace at Michilimackinac, where I then was. The joy that we felt at being selected for this expedition animated our courage, and rendered the labor of paddling morning to night agreeable to us."

The party paddled along the northern shores of Lake Michigan and into Green Bay and the mouth of the Fox River. Following the Fox, they were able to reach the Wisconsin River, which flows into the Mississippi, the Indians' "great river." "We safely entered Missisipi on the 17th of June, with a joy I cannot express," Marquette continued.

On their journey down the Mississippi, the explorers stopped and talked to Indian people who told them that the great river did not flow to a western sea but southward to the body of water now called the Gulf of Mexico. The Indians warned that tribes in the Gulf area had been given guns by Spanish explorers and would likely attack the French.

When they reached the mouth of the Arkansas River, Marquette and Jolliet decided it was dangerous to go on and so began their journey home. This time they followed the Illinois and smaller rivers to what is now Chicago. Marquette, who was ill, remained with Indian tribes, hoping to regain his health and do missionary work there. Jolliet returned to Quebec, but unfortunately lost his

Marquette and Jolliet were impressed by the great Mississippi River even though it did not lead to the Pacific Ocean. It is unlikely that their canoe was the same style as the one shown in this old painting.

Father Jacques Marquette

A city, county, and a river in Michigan bear the name of Marquette, an explorer-priest who is credited with establishing Michigan's first permanent settlements. Jacques Marquette was born in France in 1637, the son of a well-to-do family. Deeply religious, he began to prepare for priesthood in the Jesuit order, a process that then took fourteen years. When he finished he wanted to be a missionary, and he sailed to Canada to await his orders from the Jesuits.

After studying Indian languages at a college in Quebec, Marquette was sent to start a mission at Sault Ste. Marie, a place that had been visited only by missionaries. There, in 1668, he established the first European settlement in Michigan. Later, after a trip to a mission along Chequamegon Bay in present-day Wisconsin, Marquette established Michigan's second European settlement at St. Ignace along the Straits of Mackinac.

Marquette was a man interested in life beyond his priestly duties. Intelligent and curious, he wrote an account of his great explorations with Louis Jolliet. The priest described everything from the Indians' use of wild rice to the size of the fish in the Mississippi River. His warm personality, combined with his skill in speaking the Indian languages, made him a welcome visitor in Indian villages.

Marquette died as he made his way back to St. Ignace from the Illinois country. Several priests who accompanied him buried him along the shore of Lake Michigan near Ludington. Although the priests were shaken by the loss of this outstanding man, the Indians near the Straits of Mackinac were also overcome with grief when they learned of the death of their friend. Members of an Ottawa band journeyed to search for Marquette's grave. They then took his body to St. Ignace where they buried him again near the mission he had established.

journals and maps in a canoe accident. Although he was able to redraw some maps from memory, he was very discouraged and felt that the trip had failed.

Marquette remained in the Wisconsin and Illinois area for about a year and a half. His health was poor, however, and in the spring of 1675 he began the journey back to his mission at St. Ignace. He and his companions paddled northward along the eastern shore of Lake Michigan. But Marquette never reached the mission that he considered home. Somewhere along the lakeshore, perhaps near present-day Ludington, the priest became too ill to travel. Shortly after the party stopped to rest, Jacques Marquette died, only 37 years old.

The journeys of La Salle

It was the older brother of Louis Jolliet who helped inspire another journey to the Michigan area. Adrien Jolliet was an experienced trader who was returning to Quebec from Sault Ste. Marie. His Indian guide introduced the trader to a natural Great Lakes route still unknown to Europeans. From Lake Huron the pair canoed southward on Lake Huron to Lake Erie and then into Lake Ontario. There they came to Fort Frontenac, a trading post run by Robert Cavelier, who was called Sieur de la Salle.

It was La Salle's dream to build a great fur-trading empire for the French, and he had received permission from King Louis XIV of France to travel westward and build trading posts. Jolliet's discoveries gave La Salle new ideas about his trip westward. On the Niagara River, near Niagara Falls, he built a sturdy sailing ship named the *Griffon*. The ship, he hoped, would provide a new way to transport furs from the west.

In 1679 La Salle and his crew journeyed across Lake Erie in the *Griffon*, probably the first large sailing ship on the Great Lakes. Father Louis Hennepin, who was aboard the vessel, kept a journal and wrote about the trip:

> . . . We reached the entrance of the Detroit [strait] by which Lake Orleans [Huron] empties into Lake Conty [Erie] . . . This strait is thirty leagues long and almost everywhere a league wide, except in the middle where it expands and forms a lake of circular form, which we called Lake St. Clare, on account of our passing through it, on that Saint's day.
>
> The country on both sides of this beautiful strait is adorned with fine open plains, and you can see numbers of stags, does, deer, bears, by no means fierce and very good to eat. . . . The rest of the strait is covered with forests, fruit trees like walnuts, chestnuts, plum and apple trees, wild vines loaded with grapes, of which we made some little wine. There

The "Griffon" was the first European sailing vessel on the Great Lakes. Here it is welcomed at Michilimackinac.

is timber fit for building. It is a place in which deer most delight.

In spite of storms and other dangers, the ship and its crew continued northward into Lake Huron and westward into Lake Michigan. They then went on to the Green Bay, Wisconsin, area where they loaded the *Griffon* with furs and prepared it for the return to the Niagara River. Neither La Salle nor Hennepin sailed back with the *Griffon's* crew. Hennepin wrote: "Contrary to our opinion, the Sieur de la Salle, who never took any one's advice, resolved to send back his bark [ship] from this place, and continue his route by canoe. . . ."

La Salle's trip by canoe took him around the southern shore of Lake Michigan until he reached the St. Joseph River. There he built Fort Miami and waited for the *Griffon* to make a second voyage to Lake Michigan. The ship, however, did not arrive.

Meanwhile, La Salle journeyed westward and built a fort in Illinois country. Then he returned to Fort Miami, where there was still no sign of the *Griffon*. Deeply discouraged and desperate for supplies, La Salle and his companions headed back to Fort Frontenac on the eastern end of Lake Ontario. The most direct route, La Salle reasoned correctly, was to cross what is now Michigan's Lower Peninsula. And so in the early spring of 1680, he and his men walked from Fort Miami to the Detroit area, probably the first Europeans to venture into the interior of Michigan. From the Detroit River they made their way back through Lake Erie and Lake Ontario.

The fate of the *Griffon* still remains a question. According to Father Hennepin, who had been sent by La Salle to explore the northern part of the Mississippi River, the *Griffon* was lost in a storm. He wrote:

> It came to anchor at the mouth of Lake Illinois [Michigan], where it was seen by some savages, who told us that they advised our men to sail along the coast, and not toward the middle of the lake, because of the sands that make the lake dangerous when there are high winds. Our pilot, as I said before, was dissatisfied, and would steer as he pleased without hearing the advice of the savages, who, generally speaking, have more sense than the Europeans think at first. But the ship was hardly a league from the coast when it was tossed up by a violent storm in such a manner that our men were never heard from since; and it is supposed that the ship struck on the sand, and was there buried.

Historians and others are still searching for an answer, since no trace of the *Griffon's* wreck has ever been found. Hennepin's writings, which were bestsellers in Europe, are considered questionable since he was known to exaggerate for the sake of a good story.

La Salle continued his efforts to build a fur-trading empire for the French. He later returned to his Illinois fort and journeyed down the Mississippi to the Gulf of Mexico, an exploration for which he is famous. La Salle's plans for great fur-trading posts never became a reality, and even Fort Miami was abandoned by the French. However, he did help the French learn more about the Michigan area. And his lost *Griffon* was the first large ship to sail the Great Lakes waterway.

M·I·C·H·I·G·A·N
I·N T·I·M·E

Date	In Michigan	Outside Michigan
1670	Pageant of the Sault (1671) Marquette dies near Ludington (1675)	Indian power is broken in New England (1676)
1680	Duluth builds Fort St. Joseph near the present site of Port Huron (1686) A mission is built along the St. Joseph River (1686)	La Salle claims Louisiana territory for France (1682) French & British begin wars that last 100 years (1689)
1690	Fort De Buade is built at St. Ignace Fort St. Joseph is built near the present site of Niles (1691) Cadillac commands Fort De Buade (1694) Michigan forts are closed (1696)	King Louis XIV closes all French forts west of Montreal (1696)
1700	Cadillac established Fort Pontchartrain (1701) French make a new peace with the Iroquois (1701)	French make a new peace with the Iroquois (1701)
1710	Fort Michilimackinac is built at the present site of Mackinaw City (1715)	French construct a fort at the present site of Green Bay, Wisconsin (1717)
1720		
1730		American colonies have about 565,000 free people & 90,000 slaves
1740		Pennsylvania fur traders begin working their way into the Ohio valley
1750	Indians & French soldiers from Michigan fight in the French and Indian War (1754-1760)	French built Fort Duquesne & seize Ohio Valley (1754) Langlade leads raid against a Miami village (1752) French lose Quebec (1759)
1760	French soldiers leave Michigan forts (1760)	French surrender (1760) Peace of Paris gives most of France's American lands to Great Britain

Chapter 4

New France, New Spain, New England,
Which will it be?
Who will win the new land?
The land across the sea?

from "French Pioneers" by Rosemary and
Stephen Vincent Benét

**Claiming
the
Empire**

It was a day to remember. Indian people from seventeen different tribes assembled outside the mission at Sault Ste. Marie. And then the gates swung open. Out marched Jesuit priests in their long, black robes and voyageurs with their brightly colored sashes. They were followed by an officer of the French army, dressed in his colorful uniform and silver helmet.

The procession made its way to a hill outside the mission where a wooden cross lay upon the ground. There the group stopped and a ceremony began. The cross was raised, and along with it a post that displayed the royal seal of France. Prayers were offered, and the group sang a hymn. Then St. Lusson, the French officer commissioned by the King of France, scooped up a piece of earth and held it in the air. In the French language he proclaimed:

> In the name of the Most High, Most Mighty, and most Redoubtable Monarch Louis the Fourteenth, Most Christian King of France and Navarre, we take possession of the said place Sainte Marie du Sault, as also of Lake Huron and Superior, the island of Manitoulin and all other countries, rivers, lakes, and their tributaries contiguous and adjacent thereto, those discovered and to be discovered, bounded on one side by the Northern and Western seas, and on the other by the South Sea, this land in all its length and breadth.

After St. Lusson's proclamation was translated for the Indians by an important French trader named Nicolas Perrot, the celebration began. Muskets were fired and cheers went up from the hillside. When dusk fell, a huge bonfire was lit and the singing and celebrating continued. The Pageant of the Sault, as it was later called, would go down in history.

Although colorful and grand, this great Michigan ceremony of 1671 took place partly out of fear. Although France had claimed eastern Canada, no real boundaries had been set. With the establishment of the Hudson's Bay Company in the north, it was likely that English fur traders would drift into the Great Lakes region. Leaders of New France now had to worry not only about controlling their own fur traders, but also about competing with Great Britain for the trade and the territory.

Those who celebrated the great proclamation were also ignorant about a number of things. The French (as well as the British) did not yet have a true picture of the size or geography of the North American continent. Claims that were described vaguely in "lengths and breadths" were bound to come into dispute, especially as both nations began to view the land as a valuable addition to their empires. The Indians did not really understand St. Lusson's declaration. What could it mean that they were now subjects of a great and powerful king? They had no way of knowing that they would soon be caught in the struggle between the French and the British.

The French at Michili-mackinac lived and dressed much like the Indians. This man is holding passenger pigeons, which made good meals and were plentiful in Michigan at the time.

The French forts

For many years the French leaders in New France were undecided as to how to develop their claims in America. They believed it was best to concentrate on building strong settlements along the St. Lawrence River that would form the hub of the fur trade. However, the growing threat of the British traders invading the territory was mounting in the late 1600s. The Iroquois, too, presented a grave problem as they struck out at tribes that traded with the French and even attacked Montreal itself.

Out of necessity, then, the French began building forts in the west, the area that now includes Michigan, Illinois, and Wisconsin. They reasoned that the forts, as well as missions, would add to France's reputation as a strong power. They also hoped to keep the Indians in the area on their side in case of Iroquois attacks.

The governor of New France, the Marquis de Denonville, carefully chose people to help secure this western Great Lakes region. He made Nicolas Perrot commander of the west, charged with protecting the trading route from Green Bay to the Mississippi River. He gave Jesuit priests land for a mission along the St. Joseph River near the present city of Niles, in southern Michigan.

This French map of 1744 shows that the Europeans had much to learn about the geography of the area. One of the islands in Lake Superior never existed, but it was on maps for many years.

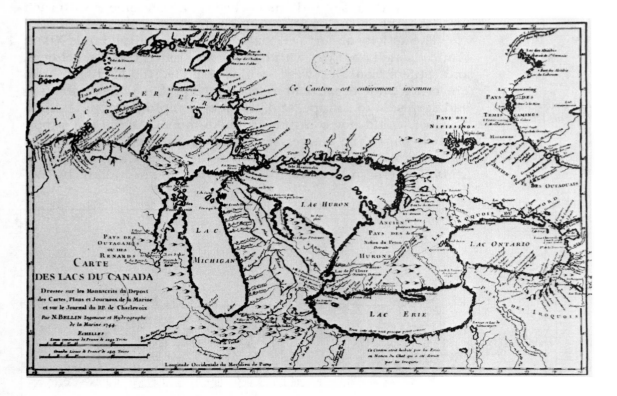

This, he felt, would help prevent the Potawatomi and Miami Indians from trading with the Iroquois and their allies, the British. Denonville sent another leading fur trader, Daniel Greysolon, Sieur de Duluth, to build a fort along Lake Huron. In 1686 Duluth built Fort St. Joseph near the present city of Port Huron. The fort was abandoned by the French, however, within two years.

The most important center of activity in the Michigan area during the late 1600s was at St. Ignace along the Straits of Mackinac. Along with the mission established by Father Marquette, there were Ottawa and Huron settlements whose ideal location made them a natural center for the fur trade. Although the priests referred to the area as St. Ignace, the traders and Indians called it Michilimackinac. In 1690, French officials decided to build a fort in the area. Although it was named Fort De Buade, most referred to it as Michilimackinac.

For a few years Michilimackinac and the St. Ignace mission made up the most important French settlement in the western Great Lakes area. It was a Jesuit headquarters as well as the military headquarters for the French forces commanded by Antoine de la Mothe Cadillac. About sixty houses occupied by the French surrounded the fort, in addition to the mission and several Indian towns. During the summer months hundreds of traders and thousands of Indians flocked to the settlement with their furs, expanding the population even further.

The activity at Fort De Buade did not last. King Louis XIV of France issued an order withdrawing all French traders, soldiers, and settlers from the "west," which included the Michigan area. The order came because of an economic problem. Too many furs had been sent to Europe, and prices were rapidly dropping. Businessmen could not continue to make money unless the supply was cut back. The answer seemed obvious. Stop the trading in the western Great Lakes area, where the Jesuits were also up in arms. Traders, they complained, were ruining the Indians by sup-

Fort De Buade may have looked like this artist's sketch recreated from an old engineering drawing.

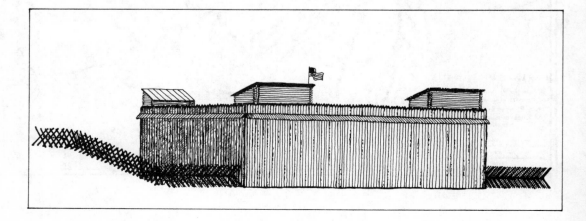

plying them with alcohol. And the Jesuits' complaints were important to King Louis XIV.

Cadillac builds a fort

One of the people most upset by the king's decree was Cadillac, the military commander at Michilimackinac. Although he had made a great deal of money from the fur trade there, he realized that there was more than a loss of his own money at stake. Without Fort De Buade, France's western territory would be unprotected. To prevent this from happening, Cadillac traveled to France hoping to convince the king's advisers to build a new fort.

Cadillac's plan consisted of building a fort somewhere along "Le Detroit." This was the French name for the present-day Detroit and St. Clair rivers as well as Lake St. Clair, all of which they considered to make up one waterway. At this point, Cadillac argued, the French could prevent the British from entering the western Great Lakes area. Cadillac planned that the fort would be an important fur-trading post, but he insisted that the area be a permanent French settlement. He proposed that he be the land-

Cadillac built a French fort and colony along the Detroit River. Although his plans for the area were quite successful and the fur trade prospered there, his enemies worked against him and he was reassigned to Louisiana.

lord of the entire area, and that several Indian tribes also be invited to live there, gradually being introduced to the French way of life.

Cadillac received permission from Count Pontchartrain, a French government official, to build the fort he had planned. On July 24, 1701, Cadillac and his party chose a site that is now part of the city of Detroit. For Cadillac it seemed like an ideal location. From the high bank they could overlook the river, which was narrow enough there so that an enemy ship could be hit by the fort's cannons. There was a rushing stream in the area and meadows thick with grass. There were many fruit trees, and when Cadillac later wrote to Pontchartrain he described the area as "the earthly paradise of North America."

The French soldiers and the Indians who accompanied Cadillac quickly began work on the fort. They built the walls of the fort from logs placed in an upright position. Inside these walls, called palisades, they constructed houses, again placing the logs in an upright position and covering them with grass roofs. They also built a church and named it St. Anne's. The fort itself was named for the Frenchman who had approved Cadillac's plan, Count Pontchartrain.

The layout of Fort Pontchartrain shows each street (rue) within the palisades. In addition to the commander's quarters and church there were shops and houses.

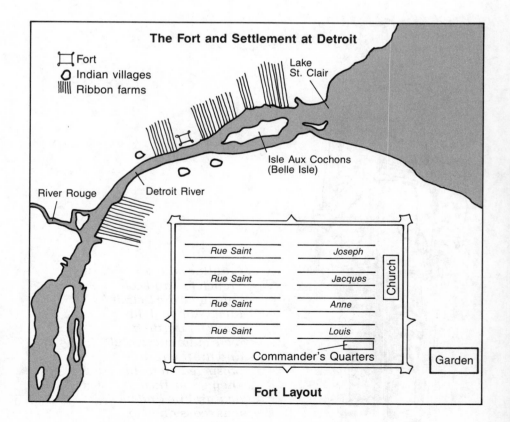

To convince everyone that this fort in the western wilderness was to be a permanent settlement, Cadillac sent for his family within weeks after his own arrival. Peace had recently been made between the Iroquois and the French, allowing Madame Cadillac's party to canoe safely across Lake Ontario and Lake Erie. When they arrived at Fort Ponchartrain, Madame Cadillac, her youngest son, and Madame Tonty, the wife of Cadillac's assistant, Alphonse de Tonty, were greeted warmly. It was simply unheard of for European women of such high social standing to journey this far from the eastern settlements. Some Iroquois men who were at Detroit at the time were especially impressed. Cadillac later wrote about their reaction:

> It is certain that nothing [ever] astonished the Iroquois as greatly as when they saw them. You could not believe how many caresses they offered them, and particularly the Iroquois who kissed their hands and wept for joy, saying that French women had never been seen coming willingly to their country. It was that which made the Iroquois also say that they well knew that the general peace . . . was indeed sincere, and that they could no longer doubt it since women of this rank came amongst them with so much confidence.

This old engraving of Fort Pontchartrain is very romantic and probably inaccurate in a number of ways. Old historic accounts and drawings cannot always be relied upon as true pictures of the past.

Cadillac brought old European customs to his fort and settlement on *Le Detroit.* In addition to being a military commander, he was a landlord of the entire area, something similar to a feudal lord of medieval times in Europe. French settlers were granted a tract of land, but they had to pay him a fee each year. They had to work a certain number of days on his farm, and the grain that they raised on their own land had to be ground in his mill. A portion of that grain, of course, had to be given to Cadillac.

The tracts of land given to French settlers in the Detroit area were as strange as the contracts by which these people lived and worked. The properties were narrow, perhaps two to three hundred feet wide, with frontage along the river. The lots were extremely long, however, extending two to three miles deep into the wooded shore. This arrangement of property allowed each farmer to have easy access to the river, since roads were only trails through the forest. Houses of the community were built close together along the riverfront so that families could visit and help one another. The farms, called ribbon farms, were similar to the French farms along the St. Lawrence River.

The settlement at Detroit did not grow as rapidly as Cadillac had hoped. Cadillac himself was a difficult man for settlers to work with, since he charged high prices and had little compassion in his business dealings. He also had enemies throughout New France who were more than willing to spread news about the settlement's shortcomings. Traders in other areas were angry because he was able to take away much of their business. The Jesuit priests accused Cadillac of using the Indians and giving them alcohol in exchange for furs. Added to these problems was the fact that the French simply were not as interested in settling down and farming or building towns as were people in the British colonies.

Among the Indian people, however, Cadillac had few enemies. Bands of Huron, Miami, Ottawa, and Ojibwa accepted his invitation to build villages near the fort. He treated chiefs with great respect, inviting them to his home and presenting them with gifts. Within four years so many Indians had come to Cadillac's settlement from the Michilimackinac area that the St. Ignace mission was abandoned.

Cadillac's command at Fort Ponchartrain lasted for nine years. He was then sent to govern a French colony in Louisiana, and finally returned to France, where he spent the rest of his life. Although Cadillac had been a difficult leader at the settlement, his absence from Detroit did not spur new progress. The French were interested only in the fur trade, not farms and towns. Food and other supplies had to be shipped to the Michigan area and other western regions. A French colony like the first thirteen British colonies on the eastern coast which grew their own food and manufactured many of their own goods was simply not destined to be a part of Michigan's history.

Signs of war

For more than thirty years during the 1700s the French, Indians, and British generally remained at peace in North America. But the French were not taking chances with their western territories. A new fort was built on the southern side of the Straits of Mackinac at present-day Mackinaw City. It, too, was called Michilimackinac. French soldiers also occupied Fort St. Joseph, which had been built near the mission on the St. Joseph River, as well as Fort Pontchartrain.

During the years of peace one of the major problems of the French was to keep Indians in the west from trading with the British. This had become more difficult because of the location of Fort Pontchartrain. It was now easier for the many Indians who had moved to the Detroit area to travel eastward and trade with the Iroquois and the British, who offered more trade goods in return for furs.

Value of the Beaver

2 Otters	≈ 1 Beaver
1 Moose	≈ 2 Beaver
2 Deerskins	≈ 1 Beaver
1 Wolf	≈ 1 Beaver
1 Black Bear	≈ 2 Beaver
Beads, colored	~ 3/4 lb. for 1 Beaver
Gun-powder	~ 1 1/2 lb. for 1 Beaver
Shot	~ 5 lb. for 1 Beaver
Sugar	~ 2 lb. for 1 Beaver
Brandy	~ 1 gal. for 4 Beaver
Blankets	~ 1 for 6 Beaver
Buttons	~ 12 doz. for 1 Beaver
Knives	~ 8 for 1 Beaver
Fish Hooks	~ 20 for 1 Beaver
Guns	~ 1 for 10-12 Beaver
Needles	~ 12 for 1 Beaver
Kettles	~ 1 for 1 Beaver

Beaver skins were the measure of value in the fur trade. Like today, however, prices changed from time to time. Prices set by the French, British, and later, American traders also varied.

Another major problem of the French was that of land claims. French leaders became more and more alarmed by the English fur traders who were moving westward from the Allegheny Mountains. This territory south of Lake Erie, known as the Ohio River valley, had been claimed for the King of France during the Pageant of the Sault. The King of England, however, had claimed the land even before St. Lusson had, declaring that the English owned it from the Virginia area "throughout from Sea to Sea, West and Northwest."

As alarming to the French as the invasion of British fur traders were the English settlers who were moving westward with their families to the rich farmlands of the Ohio valley. The French were traders, and the whole economy of New France depended upon furs. At least the British fur traders had the same goals as the French: keeping the land as wilderness so that hunting and trapping could continue. Farms would ruin the wilderness and bring a whole new way of life to the area.

To show their power and ownership of the land, the French made several moves. They sent soldiers into the Ohio Valley to talk to Indian tribes and convince them to be loyal to France. As they traveled, they put markers into the ground to claim the land as French territory. A small fort was also constructed at Sault Ste. Marie to stop northern Indians from traveling into the lower Great Lakes and trading with the British. Most important, the French attacked a large village of Miami Indians who were living in what is now western Ohio and trading freely with the British. The village was destroyed and several British fur traders were taken captive. Commanding the French forces was Charles Langlade, a fur trader in the Michigan area who was part Indian and part French. His men would soon strike fear in the hearts of people living in the British colonies.

The French and Indian War

The fight over the fur trade and the Ohio Valley led the French and British into a war that would settle a much bigger question: who would win the land, the great North American continent? The English colonists called it the French and Indian War, named for the people who blocked their movement into the Ohio Valley. On a larger scale, it was only one war in a series of wars that the French and British had been fighting for nearly a century in Europe.

From today's viewpoint, the French were already in a losing position at the war's beginning in 1754. The success of the Hudson's Bay Company and problems within the French fur trading system had put the English ahead of the French in the business.

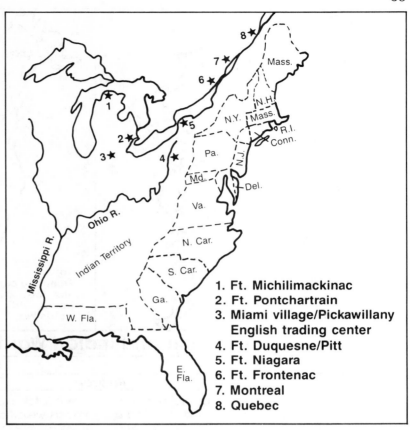

1. Ft. Michilimackinac
2. Ft. Pontchartrain
3. Miami village/Pickawillany English trading center
4. Ft. Duquesne/Pitt
5. Ft. Niagara
6. Ft. Frontenac
7. Montreal
8. Quebec

Most of the major forts in the French and Indian War were located along the Great Lakes waterway. Here French and British interests in North America met head-on.

The French were also greatly outnumbered by the English on the North American continent. While there were well over a million people in the British colonies, there were only about eighty thousand in the French territory.

Still, the French had some important advantages. The governor of New France could quickly call his forces together and prepare them to fight. The English colonies had many governors and a much more difficult time organizing fighting units. The French also had an excellent commander, the Marquis de Montcalm, who was able to bring victories to the French for the first few years of the war.

For a time it seemed as if France would win the war. Then in 1757 new leadership in England helped to turn the tide. British army and navy officers were changed, and the British began to achieve victories. They conquered Fort Frontenac and cut France's route from the St. Lawrence River westward on Lakes Ontario and Erie to Detroit. The British also captured Fort Duquesne, which the French had built at the site of present-day Pittsburgh, Pennsylvania. This important fort gave the British

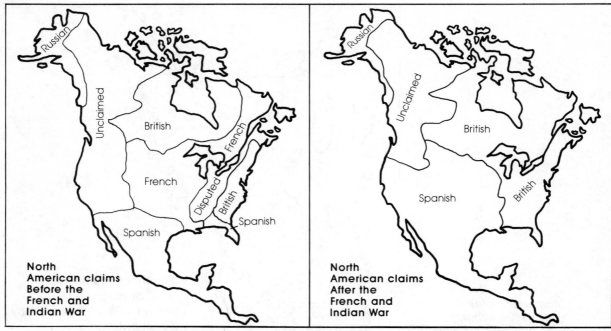

North American claims Before the French and Indian War

North American claims After the French and Indian War

The French and Indian War 1754-1763

FRANCE	GREAT BRITAIN
### Reasons	
The French wanted permanent control of the St. Lawrence River, the Great Lakes, and the Mississippi River to the Gulf of Mexico. They hoped to keep Great Britain east of the Allegheny Mountains and out of the Ohio Valley.	Great Britain claimed the Ohio Valley. British fur traders were trading there, and English settlers were anxious to move there. Britain and France had long been rivals and had been fighting each other in Europe for nearly 100 years.
### Leaders	
Charles Langlade Marquis de Montcalm Coulon de Villiers Hyacinth de Beaujeu Marquis Duquesne (governor of New France)	Edward Braddock James Wolfe George Washington William Johnson Jeffrey Amherst Robert Rogers William Pitt (English prime minister)
### Allies	
Ottawa Potawatomi Algonkin Sauk Wyandot Shawnee Nipissing Seneca Ojibwa Delawares Choctaws Creeks (some)	Cherokees (some) Mohawks Chickasaws Creeks (some)
### Advantages	
Strong central government; outstanding leaders; many Indian allies	Large population with many ways of earning a living
### Disadvantages	
Small, scattered population concerned mainly with the fur trade	Disunited colonial governments; military leaders unskilled in American warfare; few Indian allies
### Outcome	
Lost all major claims in North America	Gained territory to the Mississippi, including parts of Canada

control of the movement of settlers and traders into the Ohio valley.

One of the last major battles of the war took place at Quebec. This fort, high on the banks of the St. Lawrence, had been under siege by British troops for many weeks. The British general, James Wolfe, then discovered a way to enter the fort. In the dead of night hundreds of British soldiers made their way up to the fort on a hidden path used by women to wash their clothes in the river. The British were quickly able to defeat the French, but both Wolfe and the French commander, Montcalm, were killed in the battle. A year later, in 1760, Montreal was taken by the British, ending the war.

Although none of the fighting of the war took place on Michigan soil, and the forts in Michigan were still in the hands of the French at the end of the war, Indians and French traders and soldiers from the area played important parts in the battles. Charles Langlade led the Indian forces from Michigan in an early victory over the British General Edward Braddock at Fort Duquesne. He returned a year later with forces of Indians and fur traders and destroyed outlying settlements in Pennsylvania, Maryland, and Virginia. Langlade was also present at Quebec when the French received their most serious defeat. He later returned to Michilimackinac to tell the soldiers there about the French surrender.

Although Indians from Michigan traveled east during the war to fight against the British with Langlade and other French officers, most of them returned home each fall. To them the fall was the time to hunt and gather food, a very practical Indian custom that no doubt upset French military plans. Some Indians became even more practical as the French drew nearer to defeat. These Indians smoked the peace pipe with British military leaders. The British, after all, usually offered more trade goods for the Indians' furs. Perhaps life with the British would be better.

Although the war ended in 1760, the final peace treaty was not signed until 1763. The British won the North American lands west to the Mississippi River, leaving France with only two tiny islands near the mouth of the St. Lawrence River. By the time of the treaty the French soldiers had already left Michigan's forts. But the French influence in Michigan was not gone. The French inhabitants of Detroit remained, making them Michigan's first pioneer families of European descent. French place names still dot the Michigan map, and stories of the fur trade, the voyageurs, and the *coureurs de bois* make up a colorful chapter in Michigan's past.

M I C H I G A N

I·N T·I·M·E

Date	In Michigan	Outside Michigan
1760	British take command of Fort Pontchartrain (1760) Pontiac leads seige at Fort Detroit (1763) Indians attack British soldiers at Fort Michilimackinac (1763) Dalyell & British soldiers killed in the battle at Parent's Creek (1763)	British forbid settlement west of the Alleghenies in the Proclamation of 1763 British begin new taxes in the American colonies to help support their newly won territory (1764) Daniel Boone explores in Kentucky (1769)
1770	Michigan becomes part of the Quebec territory (Quebec Act, 1774) Henry Hamilton becomes leader at Detroit (1775) British build Fort Lernoult in Detroit (1779)	Boston Tea Party (1773) Colonies declare the Quebec Act intolerable (1774) American Revolution begins (1775) Declaration of Independence is written (1776) Clark defeats Hamilton at Vincennes (1779)
1780	British move Fort Michilimackinac to Mackinac Island (1780) Spanish take over Fort St. Joseph for one day (1781) Michigan becomes part of the American Northwest Territory (Treaty of Paris, 1783)	British surrender to Americans (1781) Treaty of Paris formally ends the Revolutionary War (1783) U.S. Constitution is written (1787) George Washington becomes the nation's first president (1789)
1790	Treaty of Greenville gives some Indian lands in Michigan to the U.S. (1795) British leave American forts in Michigan (Jay Treaty, 1796)	Indians attack settlements in the Northwest Territory (1791) General Wayne defeats Indians in the Battle of Fallen Timbers (1794) Treaty of Greenville brings Indian/American peace (1795) John Adams becomes U.S. President (1797)

Chapter 5

Englishman, although you have conquered the French, you have not conquered us! We are not your slaves. These lakes, these woods and mountains, were left to us by our ancestors. They are our inheritance; and we will part with them to none.

Minavavana, Ojibwa chief

The British Rule Michigan

On a chill November morning in 1760, a bold, strong British officer, Major Robert Rogers, approached Fort Pontchartrain with 275 soldiers. They had come across Lake Erie and up the Detroit River in whaleboats, or long, narrow rowboats. They were moving in to take over the command of Fort Pontchartrain from the French. Captain Bellestre, the French commander, had received word of France's surrender at Montreal and was prepared to give up the post.

Major Rogers and his company, called Rogers' Rangers, were famous in the British colonies as Indian fighters, men skilled in wilderness warfare. Instead of the usual British uniforms, they wore green coats, buckskin pants, and carried both rifles and tomahawks. With them was a company of Royal American regulars commanded by a British officer, Captain Donald Campbell.

As they waited for the peaceful surrender, a crowd gathered outside the wooden walls of the fort. The British soldiers eyed them with great curiosity. There were rugged fur traders, French farmers and their families, and Indians who made their homes along the river and in the surrounding forests. They, too, watched the soldiers with curiosity, wondering how the takeover would change their lives.

Fort Ponchartrain looked promising to the British commanders. For a fort of that time, the high, sturdy palisade seemed to enclose a large area. They could see the steeple of Ste. Anne's Church and the pointed rooftops of the houses and shops. After years of battles and the long trip into the western wilderness, Fort Pontchartrain was indeed a pleasant sight.

At noon the west gate of the fort swung open. A French officer walked out proudly and signaled to the British. In true military style, Major Rogers ordered a drum roll, and thirty-six of his troops marched briskly into the fort, carrying the red and blue flag of Great Britain. On a small parade ground within the fort stood Captain Bellestre, along with the several French officers, traders, and merchants who lived there. Bellestre surrendered the French arms. Then the flag of France was lowered and the British Cross of St. George raised. There were shouts from the Indians watching beyond the walls and cheers from Rogers' Rangers.

And so with great ceremony and high hopes, the British began their rule in Michigan. Their occupation of this fort was to last for thirty-six years. But they were to be years of trouble and trial for all who lived there.

Expectations

The ruling British, the French inhabitants, and the Indian tribes of the region held very different ideas of what the new peace would bring. Perhaps it mattered least to the French settlers. Although records disagree on how many French lived in or near the fort in 1760 (figures vary from two hundred to two thousand people), the settlers had gained a reputation for being easygoing and fun-loving. They seemed happy with their day-to-day chores, working hard, worshipping regularly at Ste. Anne's Church, and enjoying parties, dances, and sports such as ice skating. They seemed to have little interest in governing themselves or expanding their settlement. For the most part, their relationships with their Indian neighbors were friendly ones.

The lives of the Indians living near the fort had changed greatly from those of the generations before them. They now depended on the fur trade to provide them with knives, utensils, blankets, and clothing. Many of the skills they had learned from their ancestors were lost. Instead of killing only the animals they needed for food and clothing, they hunted and trapped as much as possible to secure the furs they needed for trading. But most destructive of all were the rum and other liquors the Indian people obtained through the fur trade. Fighting, stealing, and other problems that had never been present in their villages had now become common.

In many ways the Indian people had not been threatened by the rule of the French and had generally lived in friendship with them. The Indians had often shared their hunting grounds with French traders, but had given up little or no land to them. Many Indians hoped that the British rule might be better for them, simply because the English offered cheaper trade goods. But some Indian leaders knew otherwise. They understood that the British wanted more than furs. They wanted land for their settlers, land for farms and towns. It was a new and very real threat.

And, of course, control of the land was exactly what the British leaders did expect. They believed they had won the right to these lands. While they knew that it would be difficult to settle and govern this vast region beyond the Allegheny Mountains, they never thought that the Indians had rights to this territory. They might bargain with the Indians to make their plans work more smoothly. But whether they bargained for the lands or simply took them, it was clear that this new territory would be developed to serve British needs.

To help ease the change of command, the British sent George Croghan with Rogers and Campbell. Croghan, an Indian agent, had been a fur trader and was skillful in dealing with the Indian people. He met with Huron, Ottawa, Potawatomi, and Ojibwa leaders in the Detroit area and assured them that the British wanted good relations with them. He promised the Indians guns, ammunition, and the use of a doctor and gunsmith in exchange for furs and a promise of cooperation. Then Croghan, like Rogers and his Rangers, returned to the East. In spite of all the talk and

When the British took over the fort at Detroit, they were surprised to find such a civilized settlement there.

high hopes, conflict between the Indians and the British began almost immediately.

Taking command

At the departure of Major Rogers and his Rangers, Captain Campbell and his men set about to live and work peaceably at Fort Detroit, the new name given Fort Pontchartrain. Campbell, rather heavyset and slowmoving, was an intelligent, adaptable leader. He spoke French well and was friendly to the local French merchants and farmers.

The town inside the fort was a surprise to the British. Its four streets were lined with stores and houses. Instead of rough log cabins, they found houses that had been covered with white-washed planks, giving the community a very civilized look. Inside the homes were plastered walls, another feature rarely found on the frontier.

These comforts, as well as the friendliness of the French people, made the winter pass quickly. There were races, dances, card games, and parties. Campbell and his men fit easily into this atmosphere and were soon entertaining the French in their homes.

The problem of Indian relations

Although Campbell was able to work with the Indians, he quickly became aware of growing problems. Croghan had promised gifts for the Indians not only at Fort Detroit, but also at other forts in the west. The commander of the British troops stationed in the East, General Jeffrey Amherst, had different ideas. Unfamiliar with life at frontier posts and unaccustomed to dealing with the Indians, Amherst ordered the gifts stopped. The cost of the French and Indian War had left the British government heavily in debt, and Amherst's solution was to tighten the purse strings. He sent orders to Campbell and other western commanders to stop the gifts. The Indians, he said, were not to be indulged. In spite of the protests from his officers, Amherst refused to change his mind.

General Amherst made other policies which added to the unrest among Indians from the Ohio Valley west to the Mississippi River, including those in Detroit and the entire Michigan area. To gain more control of the fur trade, he ordered traders to stop going to Indian villages. Instead, the Indians were instructed to bring furs to the British forts. This made the Indians unhappy, since it involved more work for them. They also had to put up with insults from smug British officers.

Since there was no longer competition from French traders, the British raised their prices for trade goods. A blanket that once had cost an Indian trader two beaver skins now cost three skins. The goods that British traders provided for the Indians were also of a lower quality than they had been in the past. Most irritating of all to the Indians was the fact that the British refused to give them rum or ammunition for hunting as they had in the past.

The general breakdown of relations between the Indians and their new British rulers was encouraged by the French who remained in America. They told the Indians that the French king was "asleep." This meant that since France was still at war with England in Europe, he had no time, energy, or money to give to problems in North America. They assured the Indians that when he "awoke," he would rush to the aid of his Indian friends. Indians throughout the western territory began to pass wampum belts among the tribes. These belts made of shells were used as a sign of a treaty or pledge. In this case a belt stood for a tribe's dislike of the new British leaders and the promise that it would join forces with the French king when he sent his troops to oust the British.

Once the British controlled the fur trade in the Great Lakes area, they treated the Indians differently than in the past. British traders demanded more furs for trade goods of a lower quality.

Captain Campbell became increasingly worried about the situation he saw developing. He wrote to another British officer in the east and complained: "The general [Amherst] says the Crown is to be no longer at the expense of maintaining the Indians, that they may very well live by their hunting, and desires to keep them scarce of powder. . . . I am certain if the Indians in this country had the least hint that we intended to prevent them from the use of ammunition, it would be impossible to keep them quiet."

Campbell also understood that the Indians expected the French to return to Quebec and were spreading that rumor from village to village. He wrote ". . . this goes from one nation to another, and it is impossible to prevent it. I assure you they only want a good opportunity to fall upon us if they had any encouragement from an enemy."

In spite of warnings, General Amherst continued to ignore the seriousness of Indian relations. He sent Major Henry Gladwin to Fort Detroit and appointed Campbell to command the fort at Sault Ste. Marie. Gladwin, however, realized that Campbell would be much more helpful at Detroit and kept the captain on to help him solve the problems there.

An emerging leader

Among the Ottawa Indians was a man who had begun to distrust the British soon after they had taken over Fort Detroit. That man was Pontiac, a chief who was known as a firm, intelligent leader and an outstanding orator. Pontiac did more than warn his own people about the dangers of British control. He began speaking to many tribes outside of the Michigan area, including the Shawnee, the Seneca, the Delaware, and the Kickapoo.

Pontiac believed that even though the French could not help them now, the Indian people had to continue the war against the British. It seemed clear to him that the British did not plan to live side by side with them as the French had. Instead these new rulers wanted to control Indian lands and hunting grounds by allowing settlers to live there. Wasn't it true that the British would destroy the Indians' means of earning a living? Hadn't they been withholding ammunition that the Indians needed for hunting? Pontiac preached that it was only a matter of time before the French troops would return to their lands and reclaim their command of the west.

Other Indian people understood Pontiac's distrust and anger and were encouraged by his words to strike back at the British. They believed that the British forts west of the Allegheny Mountains should be destroyed. They also felt that settlers should be

At the peak of the uprising, Pontiac commanded nearly 900 men. Still, he would not consider storming the fort at Detroit and risking many Indian lives.

driven from Indian hunting grounds. By the spring of 1763, wampum belts that stood for war had been sent from tribe to tribe. Although there was no overall plan or uniting of tribes, a number of uprisings began to take place in the Ohio valley and west to Wisconsin.

The siege of Detroit

On the morning of May 7, 1763, a drama began to unfold in Detroit. Pontiac and sixty of his warriors entered Fort Detroit for a grand council with Major Gladwin. Under their blankets were sawed-off muskets, knives, and tomahawks. Behind them were other members of the tribe, including women, who also had hidden weapons. Members from Huron and Potawatomi tribes remained outside the fort, pretending to be interested in the meeting.

As Pontiac entered the fort with his people, he noticed that Gladwin's troops were lined up and armed. Gladwin and Campbell were also wearing swords and guns. Pontiac quickly realized that his secret plan for a surprise attack on the fort had been discovered! Still, he proceeded with the meeting as if nothing were wrong. When it came time to hand Gladwin a wampum belt, a signal to his warriors whether to attack or hold their fire, he displayed the belt's white side, a signal not to attack. He and his people left the fort in anger, knowing they had been betrayed!

Just how the plan was revealed to the British is still unclear. Perhaps an Indian passed the secret to Gladwin, or a French inhabitant had learned of the Indians' preparations for the attack. At any rate, the surprise had failed, and the Indians were frustrated and eager for an attack. Pontiac decided to try once again to enter the fort for talks, but Gladwin refused to let him visit with his Indian warriors. Furious because another plan had failed, Pontiac ordered an attack on British families who lived on farms outside the fort. Then, in fury, the Indians turned their anger on the fort itself.

Pontiac's warriors moved into the houses and barns of the French who either remained neutral or sided with the Indians. Inside the fort British soldiers felt well-protected, although they had not received their first supplies of food and ammunition from Fort Niagara. Outside the fort two British ships were anchored in the harbor, protecting the fort from an attack by way of the river.

Pontiac planned to keep the fort under siege for as long as necessary to force the British to surrender. First, however, he demanded talks with Captain Campbell. When Campbell and another officer arrived at a French home for a meeting with the Ottawa chief, they were taken hostage. Pontiac sent messengers to Gladwin saying that he would hold the officers until his terms for surrender were accepted. Gladwin, however, refused to be blackmailed. He replied that he would have no further dealings with the Indians until his men were returned. It was a battle of wills which was to last for five months.

For five months Indian warriors held the Fort Detroit under siege in hopes of driving the British from the Great Lakes area.

The conflict spreads

Although the siege of Detroit was at a standstill, Pontiac sent messengers to other tribes in the Midwest. The cry went out that

Fort Detroit had been attacked and that other tribes should take up the fight in their regions. During that spring and the summer that followed, Indian wars blazed from the Alleghenies to the western Great Lakes. At Fort St. Joseph a band of Potawatomi defeated the British, and there were similar Indian victories at forts in Indiana and Ohio.

One of the most violent outbreaks occurred at Fort Michilimackinac. There, on June 2, the British soldiers and traders were relaxing and celebrating the birthday of the English king. Just outside the open gates of the wooden stockade, a band of Ojibwa, called Chippewa by the British, were playing a game of lacrosse with a visiting Sauk band from Wisconsin. The soldiers and traders calmly watched the game and enjoyed the spring sunshine. Their commander, Captain Etherington, had been warned about the Indians, but he apparently ignored the warning. It is also possible that he had not heard of the Indian attacks in other areas.

As the game grew more active, a group of Indian women drifted near the gate. Although the sun was warm, they wore blankets that hid an assortment of weapons. Suddenly, one of the players sent the ball flying across the stockade and into the fort. As if to retrieve it, the players rushed into the fort, grabbing weapons from the women as they passed. The soldiers, most of whom were unarmed, were taken by surprise. In the short fight that followed, many of them were killed, and others were taken prisoner. The French who lived at the fort, however, were not injured. These included Charles Langlade, who had led the Indians against the British during the French and Indian War. Alexander Henry, an English trader who hid in Langlade's house, also escaped death and later wrote about the attack and had his story published in New York.

The continuing siege

News from the Great Lakes area traveled slowly to the British command in the East, but each letter to General Amherst convinced him that the Indians were more united than he had imagined. Since many of his forts had been taken over by the Indians, he decided to strengthen the forces at Detroit. In late June he sent Captain James Dalyell to gather troops and head westward to Fort Detroit, a trip that took over a month.

Captain Dalyell arrived in Detroit eager to end the siege and please General Amherst. He planned a surprise attack on Pontiac's camp several miles upstream. Gladwin, knowing the Indians better than Dalyell, knew a surprise was not possible. But Dalyell insisted. Although he knew little about Pontiac's fighting

An Indian game of lacrosse turned into a well-planned attack at Fort Michilimackinac.

skills and nothing about the territory, Dalyell and 247 soldiers marched out of the fort early one morning in late July wearing swords and carrying muskets.

As Gladwin had feared, Pontiac's warriors were waiting. Near the banks of a small stream called Parent's Creek the Indians fired on the long line of British soldiers. A battle followed, but the confused British fighting in the dark were no match for the local tribes. By daybreak, Captain Dalyell and nineteen of his men were dead, and many others were wounded. Parent's Creek was so red with the blood of fallen soldiers it became known as Bloody Run.

Indian problems

Despite the loss of British soldiers in the battle of Bloody Run, the tide of the siege slowly began to change. Four months had passed, and many of the tribes were losing interest in the continuing struggle. Major Gladwin sensed that waiting was to his advantage. He and his men had been able to withstand the Indian attacks, which were usually short. It was simply not the Indian way to approach the fort and enter into a full-scale battle

Charles Langlade

One of Michigan's early war heroes was born at Michilimackinac in 1732. Charles Langlade was the son of a Frenchman who had come to America hoping to make his once-wealthy family wealthy again. Charles's mother was an Ottawa Indian woman.

The Indians of northern Michigan felt Charles Langlade was special. As a little boy, he was taken into battle by his Indian uncle who believed that this was an order from the Great Spirit. When the Ottawas won the battle, they credited Charles with the victory. Surely he had special powers!

As a grown man Charles Langlade went on to prove his talents as a military leader. His background enabled him to gather and lead Indian forces better than other Frenchman. Accustomed to Indian battles, Langlade and his forces made guerila-style attacks upon the British, leaving them with great losses. Some years later, the British persuaded him to fight against the Americans in the Revolutionary War. Again Langlade proved himself an outstanding military leader.

Langlade was not only a great fighter, however. He was also a fur trader. After the French and Indian War he settled in an area north of Green Bay, Wisconsin. He is sometimes referred to as the "father of Wisconsin," and both a city and a county in that state are named in his honor.

in which many of their warriors would certainly be killed. In addition, British ships had been able to reach the fort on several occasions, bringing food and gunpowder to the soldiers.

Pontiac's influence also began to weaken as the siege wore on. French soldiers had not returned to aid the Indians as Pontiac had predicted. But most important, the Indian tribes were not used to working together under one leader. Each band made its own decisions and demands. When a nephew of an Ojibwa chief was killed and scalped by a British soldier, for example, the angry chief demanded that Pontiac give him Captain Campbell for revenge. Pontiac, wanting to keep peace among his allies, reluctantly turned Campbell over to the chief. Shortly after, Campbell was killed by the Ojibwa chief, an act that angered the British and brought more help from General Amherst.

During the fall of 1763, various Indian bands began giving up the siege and returning home to hunt and prepare for winter with their families. The Potawatomi, several bands of Ojibwa, and even some of Pontiac's own tribe left to gather food and hunt. The first hard frost hit late in October, followed by a huge snowstorm.

But it was more than the early arrival of winter that brought an end to the siege. A French messenger from an Illinois fort brought word to Pontiac that the French and British had made peace in Europe. The French king, the messenger said, wanted his Indian brothers to make peace with the British. The translated message read: "Leave off spilling the blood of your brethren, the English; our hearts are now one. . . ." With this, Pontiac's dream was finished.

Crushed with disappointment, Pontiac sent a message of peace to Gladwin. When the major replied that he would have to wait for permission from General Amherst, Pontiac simply left the Detroit area and never returned. For a time he traveled and again tried to unite tribes for another uprising. His efforts failed, however, and in 1766 he agreed to sign a treaty and to work for peace between the Indians and the British. He was later murdered by an Indian from a band that hated him for his new peace-keeping efforts.

The siege of Detroit, along with uprisings at the other British forts, was an important turning point in the lives of the Indian people in the Great Lakes region. Their way of life in their native land was being destroyed. The fight would continue for another century, but they had lost their major battle to resist the changes that were taking place in their world.

Legend says that Major Henry Gladwin, commander at Fort Detroit, was warned about Pontiac's plan by an Indian woman who loved him. But Gladwin never revealed how he learned about the attack.

Improved Indian relations

The ten years that followed the Indian uprisings were more peaceful ones in Michigan's forts, forests, and fur-trading posts. The British at last understood the importance of their relations with the Indians and made efforts to earn the trust of the tribes. British leaders in London saw the fur trade as the most important activity in their western territories. They knew that friendly relations with the Indians were absolutely necessary for the trade.

In the fall of 1763, the British government issued a policy designed to satisfy the Indians. This policy, called the Proclamation of 1763, was aimed at keeping the territories west of the Allegheny Mountains unsettled and open for Indian hunting and trade. Americans living in the colonies could not trade with the Indians or buy any of their lands without acting through a British official.

British officials knew the proclamation was only a temporary solution to the Indian problems in the west. But the people in the colonies were angered. Some colonies had claims to the territories that the British government was now making off-limits to settlers. For example, Virginia, Connecticut, and Massachusetts all claimed parts of the Ohio Valley. Their citizens resented this sudden loss of their right to settle there.

Britain and the colonies

Although the Proclamation of 1763 helped to reduce tension between the British and the Indians, it marked the beginning of serious problems between Britain and the American colonies. During the long years of war with France, Britain had allowed the colonies to develop on their own. This policy had helped them create a strong sense of self-reliance. Now the British suddenly turned their attention to the American colonies. And the colonists began to balk at the British government's demands on their daily lives.

Britain's new concern with the American colonies was based largely on a need for money. The long wars with France had left Britain short of funds. It was also costly to govern the colonies and maintain forts to protect the fur trade. After much disagreement, British leaders decided that the colonies must help pay for these expenses through higher taxes.

The colonists, of course, were unhappy. They could see no reason for Britain to burden them with the expenses of maintaining forts in the west and dealing with the Indians if they could not settle there. To make matters worse, they received no benefits from the fur trade, since profits passed through Montreal to London.

In 1774 the British government passed an act that increased the tension in the colonies. This was the Quebec Act which was meant to organize Canada and the western lands gained by the British in the French and Indian War. The territory, called Quebec, was extended to the Ohio Valley and west to the Mississippi River, including Michigan. Assistant governors were put in charge of activities at Detroit, Michilimackinac, and several other posts in the west. The act also gave the French people living in the region the right to practice their Catholic faith.

The Quebec Act created some immediate changes in Michigan. Henry Hamilton was named lieutenant governor at Detroit and Colonel Arent Schuyler de Peyster was sent to Michilimackinac. For the first time the people of Michigan were to be under civil law. Instead of military leaders handling arguments and disputes, courts were established at the two forts. Citizens now had a right to a trial and could possibly take their cases beyond the local courts to higher courts in Quebec and Montreal. Although

The Maple Sugar Makers

I'll sing my papoo's cradle, said Kitchenegoe's Meg
With kettle, bowl, and ladle, and scoutawaba keg.
  A sug'ring I will go, will go, will go,
    A sug'ring I will go.

In kettles we will boil it, on fires between the rocks,
And lest the snow should spoil it, there tramp it in mococks,
  A sug'ring I will go, will go, will go,
    A sug'ring I will go.

Of all our occupations, sweet sug'ring is the best,
Then girls and their relations can give their lovers rest,
  A sug'ring I will go, will go, will go,
    A sug'ring I will go.

But when the season's over, it will not be amiss,
That I should give my lover a sissobaquet (sugar) kiss,
  A sug'ring I will go, will go, will go,
    A sug'ring I will go.

In the summer of 1774 Captain Arent Schuyler De Peyster took command of Fort Michilimackinac. In his spare time De Peyster wrote poetry about life at the fort.

on a small scale, it was the beginning of civil government in Michigan.

The Quebec Act upset and frightened the American colonial leaders. It raised the old angers that had been created by the Proclamation of 1763. Many colonists feared the Catholic religion. If the British officials were taking a stand on religion in Quebec, would they also try to interfere with religion in the colonies? The act threatened the colonists so much that in 1776 the writers of the Declaration of Independence quoted directly from it when they proclaimed their break from the British.

The frontier and the Revolution

In an age of radio and television, it is hard to imagine the isolation and lack of information that were part of life on the western frontier. Poor communication made life especially hard during the Americans' struggle for independence. Messages from the colonies in the East sometimes took months to reach the forts in the Michigan area. Local battles seemed almost unrelated to the larger war for independence, and it was difficult to unite people for a common goal. In short, fighting on the frontier took extra patience and determination.

One frontier man with a particular gift for uniting soldiers and making battle plans was George Rogers Clark, a Virginian who had lived on the Kentucky frontier for several years. Clark was appointed by the governor of Virginia to gather an army and march into Illinois country and protect settlers from Indian attacks. But there was a secret plan involved in these orders, a plan masterminded by Clark himself. He would go farther west and take over Fort Kaskaskia along the Mississippi River. There he hoped to win the support of Indian tribes and gain enough strength to lead an attack against Fort Detroit.

With skillful planning, Clark and his enthusiastic band of soldiers captured the French fort at Kaskaskia without a battle. He soon won the loyalty of the French villagers by telling them that the French king had sent forces to help Americans in their fight for freedom. He also helped spark their hatred toward Hamilton, the lieutenant governor stationed at Detroit. Hamilton was known as the "hair buyer," and it was said that he paid Indians for bringing settlers' scalps to the Detroit fort. In reality Hamilton seemed to dislike·this policy which was given to him from higher officials, and offered Indians more for prisoners than for scalps.

In spite of poor communications, Clark's march into Illinois country was not a secret for long. Hamilton, who was greatly alarmed, marched his troops and Indian allies westward to Fort Sackville at Vincennes in what is now Indiana. There he surprised the Americans in charge and quickly took command of the fort. Since winter was approaching and food was in short supply, he sent many soldiers and Indians back to Detroit.

Although it was risky and unusual to attack in winter, Clark decided that his only chance to triumph over Hamilton was to take him by surprise. Early in February, 1779, Clark and his men began their 180-mile march from Kaskaskia to Vincennes. An early thaw had swelled rivers and streams and soaked the fields. For days they marched, dressed in buckskin and carrying their rifles and other gear. At night they cooked game and sang songs, led by the French trappers among them.

About twenty miles from Vincennes, at the flooded Little Wabash River, their problems mounted. The two branches of the river had swollen into a single channel five miles wide. Clark ordered his men to build canoes and continue their journey. With food scarce and travel difficult, the French volunteers talked of quitting. But Clark humored them, allowing time for hunting and rest.

Finally, within a few miles of the fort, Clark's forces faced their greatest challenge. Before them lay Horse Shoe Plain, covered with water so deep that only the tallest men could get through it on foot. Bravely, Clark plunged into the freezing water, leading the strongest and tallest of the men. Others, barely strong enough

The battle at Vincennes, though far from the American colonies, was an important victory for the Americans during the Revolutionary War.

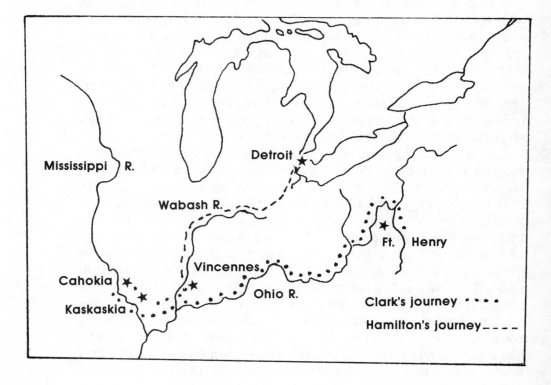

to continue, followed in canoes. Finally, they reached dry ground and were met by Indians, who kindly supplied them with food.

Meanwhile, Hamilton waited inside Fort Sackville, certain that he and his men were safe until spring. He was unaware of Clark's approach until he heard the sound of guns. By then it was too late. Clark's men kept firing until they forced Hamilton to give up.

Clark's success was a great victory for the Americans. Everywhere the story was told, it gave new strength to the American cause. The Indians, who had sided with the British in their struggle against the Americans, began to fear that they had once again chosen the losing side. Britain's grip in the west was slipping.

Henry Hamilton surrendered to George Rogers Clark at Fort Sackville in February of 1779. Clark's victory made Great Lakes Indians wonder if they should continue to support the British.

GREAT BRITAIN		THE AMERICAN COLONIES	
Reasons			
Great Britain wanted the colonies to carry a greater load in the new expenses of the western territories obtained from France. Great Britain had many strict rules about trade and wanted the colonies only to supply them with raw materials. Government leaders restricted manufacturing in the colonies.		Colonists were not allowed to buy, sell, or settle on land in the western territories. The colonists objected to Britain's many taxes and strict trade policies. The colonists did not want to maintain a British army in America. Time and distance had weakened the colonists' ties to Great Britain. The colonists wanted more home rule.	
Leaders			
Thomas Gage	Henry Clinton	George Washington	Ethan Allen
William Howe	John Burgoyne	John Stark	George Rogers Clark
Lord Cornwallis		John Paul Jones	Nathaniel Greene
		Anthony Wayne	
Allies			
Nearly all Indian tribes and the Hessians (a hired foreign army)		France	
Advantages			
More money and a greater army		Firm, patriotic leaders; some help from the French	
Disadvantages			
Poor use of Indian allies; overconfident leadership; far from home supply base		Lack of government funds; soldiers often deserted; inexperienced army; conflict of interest between colonies	
Outcome			
The British lost a large section of North America they had won from France. (see map on page 70).		The new republic gained the territory from the Atlantic Ocean to the Mississippi River and from the Great Lakes to Florida.	

Fortifying Michigan

Fearing other attacks by Clark, the British decided to strengthen their forts in Michigan. Captain Richard Lernoult, who had taken command of Fort Detroit for Hamilton, ordered a new fort built at Detroit on higher ground behind the village. This gave the British a better position from which to defend the growing town than the old fort on the riverfront had provided. The new fort was named Lernoult.

A new commander at Fort Michilimackinac, Major Patrick Sinclair, decided to improve the British position there. He ordered the fort moved to an offshore island in the straits between Lake Michigan and Lake Huron. The project was begun in the winter of 1780, and some of the buildings from the old fort were towed across the frozen straits to the island. The rest of the old buildings were burned to the ground.

By the spring of 1781, the large stone buildings of the new fort were ready for use. The main British fur-trading operations were also moved to a building in the town, just below the fort. Although the fort was still called Michilimackinac by the British, the island came to be known as Mackinac Island. Major Sinclair kept his fort ready for attack and even sent troops south along Lake Michigan to head off an American march. Clark's soldiers never reached Michigan territory, however, and no battle was fought at the new Michilimackinac fort during the war for independence.

The only Michigan fort to be taken during the Revolution was Fort St. Joseph on the St. Joseph River. In 1781 a force of Spanish soldiers, who occupied land west of the Mississippi River, joined with French soldiers and Indians and marched into the fort. At the time of the takeover, however, Fort St. Joseph was occupied only by fur traders who were not officially in the British army or government. Just why the Spanish troops marched so far to take such a small post is unclear. Nevertheless, the Spanish raised their flag over the fort for one day, captured the furs and trade goods from the local traders, and then marched back to their post in St. Louis. The event later made the city of Niles famous for being ruled by four different nations at various times in its history. It also left historians arguing about why the event took place.

The American victory

In the autumn of 1781, General George Washington's troops defeated the British at Yorktown, Virginia, marking victory and independence for the American people. For the next several years, the British and the Americans worked out terms for peace as well as a boundary between Canada and the new American territory. One of the dividing lines they discussed was the 45th parallel, which cut across the northern part of Michigan's Lower Peninsula. This would have given the Americans full control of Lake Erie and Lake Ontario and made the entire Upper Peninsula of Michigan a part of Canada. The other choice was to run the boundary line through the center of the Great Lakes. This would give each country use of all the Great Lakes except Lake Michigan, which would be completely in American territory.

The boundary decision, of course, was to divide the Great Lakes. The peace treaty also established the Mississippi River as the western boundary of the American territory. This large region, from the Allegheny Mountains to the Mississippi River, including Michigan, was a great gain for the American nation. It was called the Northwest Territory, and the American settlers spent the next

The British moved Fort Michilimackinac to Mackinac Island in 1780. This old engraving shows the ruins at Michilimackinac looking across the Straits to St. Ignace and Mackinac Island.

century taming and developing its rich farmlands, vast forests, and beautiful lakes and rivers.

The British stay in Michigan

The British officially gave up their claim to the Northwest Territory by the Treaty of Paris in 1783. But they continued to control the Michigan forts for thirteen more years before turning them over to the Americans. The British were in no hurry to leave. The fur trade kept British traders and London merchants wealthy. During those years, a British company called the Northwest Fur Trading Company was established on Mackinac Island. It was the first trading company in this part of the Great Lakes region to control the fur trade.

It seems unusual today that the British could have continued to hold the Michigan forts which they had lost in the Treaty of 1783. But the Americans were busy establishing a new government. The forts and fur trade at Detroit and Michilimackinac seemed far away and unimportant to the statesmen who were struggling with more urgent problems.

The British realized their advantage and tried to stall the Americans in their takeover of the forts as long as possible. When

Michigan and its Forts

1. FORT DE BAUDE was established by the French at St. Ignace in 1690 and was an important fur trading center for several years. It was usually referred to as the fort at Michilimackinac instead of Fort De Baude. In 1696 French troops were withdrawn by the French king who decided to close trading posts in the western Great Lakes area.

2. FORT MICHILIMACKINAC was built by the French on the southern side of the Straits of Mackinac when they decided to reestablish trading posts in the western Great Lakes area. It is believed to have been constructed around 1715 and stood until 1780 when the British decided to change the fort location to Mackinac Island.

3. FORT MIAMI was established by La Salle in 1679, but abandoned shortly after.

4. FORT ST. JOSEPH near the present-day Niles was built by the French in 1691 and then rebuilt by the British during the American Revolution. It was briefly captured by Spanish soldiers in 1781, giving Michigan the distinction of being occupied by four different countries.

5. FORT ST. JOSEPH was a temporary French fort established by the explorer Duluth. It was intended to protect the French fur trade and keep the British from moving further northward into the Straits area. In the War of 1812 FORT GRATIOT was built near the same site.

6. FORT PONTCHARTRAIN was the concept of Antoine de la Cadillac and the beginning of Detroit. Cadillac established the fort in 1701 and worked to bring French families to the area. When the fort was taken by the British in 1760, they renamed it FORT DETROIT. In 1813, the Americans changed its name to FORT SHELBY. The fort was abandoned in 1825.

7. FORT LERNOULT was constructed in Detroit by the British during the American Revolution in 1779. Built on a hill instead of along the river like Fort Pontchartrain, they believed the new fort would give them better protection. Americans later renamed it FORT DETROIT.

8. FORT WAYNE was built along the Detroit River in 1851 to guard against possible attacks from the British in Canada.

9. FORT MICHILIMACKINAC at Mackinac Island was built by the British between 1779 and 1781. By the War of 1812 it was referred to as Fort Mackinac. During the war it was recaptured by the British and occupied by them for over two years.

10. FORT BRADY was built at Sault Ste. Marie in 1822. The Americans felt the fort would protect their borders and help control the Indians and the fur trade.

11. FORT WILKINS at the tip of the Keweenaw Peninsula was built in 1844 to help keep peace between the Indians and the copper miners. Troops were withdrawn in 1846.

the Americans sent a small group of men to Fort Detroit, the British commander refused to let them stay. He told them he could not give up control until he was ordered to do so by officials in London. The Americans, having no troops with them nor the spirit to fight, went away to await further news.

The matter of the Michigan forts was settled at last in 1796. John Jay, a special representative of the United States sent to Britain, made a treaty with the British to end their occupation of forts in Michigan. It was decided that the fur trade could continue if the British traders paid duties, or taxes, at the borders. Thirty-six years after their soldiers had claimed the fort at Detroit, the British now peacefully turned it over to the Americans. More than one hundred American soldiers also took control of Fort Michilimackinac. A new era was beginning. The young American nation was preparing to bring the distant lands of the Northwest Territory into the experiment called democracy.

The Indian struggle

While the Americans were making treaties with the British, the Indians continued their struggle to save their land from the Americans. At the time George Washington took office as President of the United States, the Northwest Territory was filled with violence and frustration. The Indians, seeing their hunting grounds and way of life upset once again, battled against the settlers who built farms and homes in the areas of Ohio, Kentucky, and Indiana. The British encouraged the Indians in their struggle, and provided them with ammunition and supplies from the fort in Detroit.

For several years the American troops sent to the Northwest Territory were badly defeated by the Indians. The seriousness of the situation forced President Washington to turn to one of his well-known commanders from the Revolutionary War, General Anthony Wayne. Because of his recklessness and daring, Wayne had been nicknamed "Mad Anthony."

After training his forces for a year, General Wayne marched westward. Then, in the summer of 1794, a showdown between the Indians and the American troops occurred on the banks of the Maumee River south of the present city of Toledo, Ohio. In the Battle of the Fallen Timbers, an area where a tornado had uprooted many big trees, Wayne and his troops soundly defeated a large force of Indians led by a chief named Blue Jacket. The Indians who retreated were refused help at the British forts, and their villages were burned by Wayne. For the Americans, the battle was a great victory, opening at last the rich lands they wanted so

badly. For the Indians, it was a huge loss that would force them from their homes and hunting grounds.

Their loss at the Battle of Fallen Timbers forced Indian leaders to sign a treaty and give up their hold on much of the Ohio region as well as a section in Indiana. This Treaty of Greenville, signed in 1795, also gave Indian lands in Michigan to the United States. This included a strip of land along the Detroit River between Lake St. Clair and the River Raisin. In the north, Indians gave up Mackinac Island and the areas on either side of the Straits of Mackinac to the United States. In exchange, they received $20,000 and a promise of yearly payments of $9,500 in goods forever.

By the end of the 1700s, the United States claimed all of the area that is now Michigan. But the American government would still have to make purchases and treaties with Michigan's Indian people. And the British did not move far away. They built posts on an island in the St. Marys River and along the east side of the Detroit River. Another war loomed in the not-so-distant future that would again bring the British to Michigan.

At the Treaty of Greenville, an Ojibwa chief named Matchekewis spoke for his tribe as well as the Ottawa and Potawatomi, and made peace with General Anthony Wayne and the Americans.

M I C H I G A N

I·N T·I·M·E

Date	In Michigan	Outside Michigan
1780		Land Ordinance outlines ways to divide land in the Northwest Territory (1785) Northwest Ordinance outlines ways territories can become states (1787)
1790	Gen. Anthony Wayne visits Michigan (1796) Michigan area called Wayne County (1796) Solomon Sibley is first to be elected representative to the Northwest Territory legislature (1798)	U.S. Post Office Department formed (1795) Peace with Indians spurs settlement in Northwest Territory (1796) First Northwest Territory legislature meets in Cincinnati (1798)
1800	Detroit becomes incorporated (1802) Michigan becomes part of the Indiana Territory (1803) Detroit is destroyed by fire (1805) Michigan Territory is created (1805) William Hull is first territorial governor (1805) Woodward's plan for Detroit is adopted (1807) Father Richard brings a printing press to Michigan (1809)	Thomas Jefferson becomes President of the U.S. (1801) Ohio becomes a state (1803) Louisiana Purchase (1803) Lewis & Clark expedition (1804) Astor forms the American Fur Company (1808) First successful steamboat is tested (1809) James Madison becomes U.S. President (1809)
1810	British take over the fort on Mackinac Island (1812) Hull surrenders Detroit to the British (1812) Battle at River Raisin (1813) Lewis Cass named governor of Michigan Territory (1813) Fort Detroit reclaimed by Americans & renamed Shelby (1813) Americans regain Fort Mackinac (1815)	Harrison wins Battle of Tippicanoe (1811) War of 1812 begins (1812) Perry wins on Lake Erie (1813) Tecumseh & British defeated in Battle of the Thames (1813) Treaty of Ghent ends War of 1812 (1814) James Monroe becomes U.S. President (1817)

Chapter 6

Wilderness, once the chosen residence of solitude or savageness, converted into populous cities, smiling villages, beautiful farms and plantations! . . . What a scene—how beautiful, how grand!—yet not ideal: another century will realize it.

from an Ohio newspaper editorial, 1817

Michigan Territory: The Early Years

America's leaders did not look at the fertile, sprawling lands known as the Northwest Territory simply as the rich spoils of war. The vast area came with a long list of problems. To begin with, the territory was mostly a wilderness without roads or ways of communicating. Its population was made up of angry Indian tribes, indifferent French inhabitants, and a few hostile British farmers and merchants. Mixing with these were the eager bands of American settlers from the east. The presence of British soldiers in several frontier forts, especially at Detroit, made matters worse.

Gaining the Northwest Territory added to the list of important decisions that the American government had to make in its early years. Who really owned the new territory? How would it be governed? The questions to be decided were almost endless.

Claims to the Northwest Territory

Very early in the Revolutionary War, the Continental Congress worked to set up principles for government on which the new union of states could agree. One of the major arguments concerned the control of the lands in the Northwest Territory. Massachusetts, Connecticut, and Virginia all had claims to parts of the territory because of the wording of their charters. New York and Pennsylvania also claimed rights to some of the same territory because of their agreements with the Indians.

In 1777 the Continental Congress proposed the Articles of Confederation and sent them to the individual states for approval. Maryland, which made no claim to any of the Northwest Territory, refused to agree to the Articles unless these western lands were placed under the control of the central government. This would enable all states to benefit from the sale of lands in the territory.

Other states soon joined Maryland in its demand, and by 1780 the Continental Congress made a historic decision. It proposed that separate states be formed from the Northwest Territory and that citizens in those states be given the same rights as people in the eastern states. Although it took six years for all of the states to give up their claims in the territory, the decision made in 1780 was the basis for the future statehood of Michigan and its neighbors.

As the eastern states gave up their claims to the Northwest Territory, Massachusetts made a special agreement with New York that eventually affected Michigan. Most of western New York State was owned by Massachusetts, but governed by New York. In the agreement, Massachusetts was given the right to sell this land to settlers, most of whom were New Englanders. Years later, these settlers moved on into Michigan. Their New England attitudes and background influenced Michigan's early development as a state.

The Northwest Territory included all the area shown on the map and was gradually carved into states.

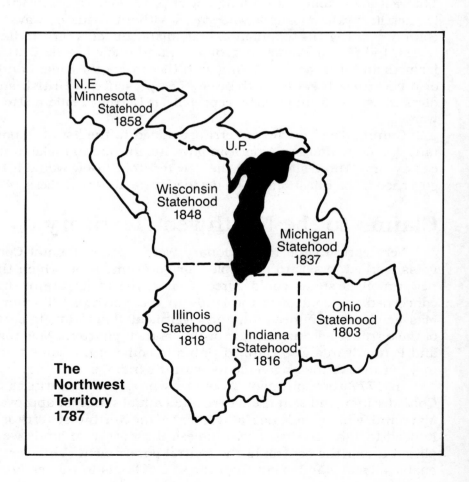

Dividing and governing the new territory

Once control of the Northwest Territory was in the hands of the American government, plans had to be made to divide the land. Congress (now the Congress of the Confederation) had to decide whether these lands should be sold at high prices to help build the national treasury, or sold on easy terms to benefit the thousands of settlers pushing westward. After a long debate, the lawmakers came to a compromise in an act known as the Land Ordinance of 1785.

The Land Ordinance of 1785 divided the new territory into townships that were six miles square, each with thirty-six sections one mile square. Those who bought the land had to purchase at least one section, which consisted of 640 acres, at a minimum price of one dollar an acre. The ordinance also said that each township had to set aside one section for the establishment of schools.

The first people to buy property in the territory were land speculators. They made money by buying the land sight unseen and in turn selling smaller pieces to settlers. These pieces had to be divided in a uniform way that was outlined by the ordinance.

To give some framework of government to the new lands, Congress passed the Northwest Ordinance of 1787. This act not only provided an immediate government for the territory but also outlined the stages for becoming a state. Although it set some boundaries for future states, it also allowed room for change by declaring that the territory should become not more than five but not less than three states. The ordinance also promised the basic rights and freedoms of American citizenship to the people of the region.

The Northwest Ordinance of 1787 stated that the new territory should be governed by five people selected by Congress. (Later they were selected by the President of the United States). These included a governor, a secretary (who would act in the governor's absence), and three judges. When the population of the territory reached five thousand free adult males, a form of self-government could begin. The qualified voters of the territory, which in those days meant male inhabitants who owned at least fifty acres of land, could elect members of a House of Representatives that would make laws. Political leaders in the eastern states would continue their control, however, with a Legislative Council chosen by Congress. The first capital of the Northwest Territory was established at Marietta, a town located on the Ohio River.

One township – 36 sections

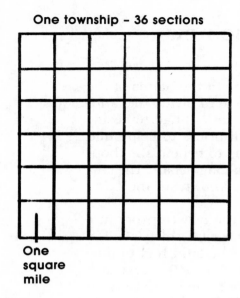

One
square
mile

One section – 640 acres

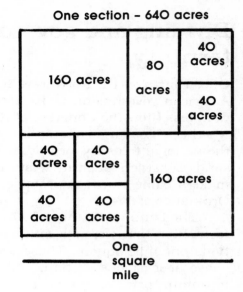

One
square
mile

The Land Ordinance of 1785 divided the Northwest Territory into townships that were six miles square. Each township was made up of thirty-six sections which could be divided in various ways.

Detroit becomes American

After the British gave up the Michigan forts, American troops moved in with the plan of expanding their new democracy into the Northwest Territory. On July 11, 1796, Captain Moses Porter led a small unit of men to Fort Lernoult, which was quickly renamed Fort Detroit by the Americans. He was followed by Lieutenant Colonel John Francis Hamtramck and his unit of four hundred soldiers. In August they were joined by the famous General Anthony Wayne who was to help make a treaty with the Indians.

In 1796 Detroit's population inside the stockade was approximately five hundred people. Another two thousand lived on farms along the river. General Wayne was favorably impressed with the town and surprised by its many cultured citizens. In a letter he wrote that there were ". . . people from almost all nations, among whom are a number of wealthy & well informed Merchants & Gentlemen & fashionable well bred Women." He described streets lined with well-kept houses and was especially interested in the lively traffic on the river. "Here in the center of a wilderness," he wrote, "you see Ships or large vessels of War & Merchantmen laying at the wharf or sailing up & down a pleasant river of about one mile wide as if passing and repassing to & from the ocean."

With General Wayne was the Secretary of the Northwest Territory, Winthrop Sargeant, who set about to establish some form of civil government. This was a difficult task for an outsider to do. Sargeant discovered that the local French were not interested in taking on leadership roles. Many of the British citizens were so unhappy about the American takeover that they had moved across the river to Windsor, Sandwich, and Amherstburg in Canada. Those that remained were still so linked to their British friends that they were not good candidates for holding office in the new American government. As a result, Peter Audrain, an American who had accompanied Wayne to Detroit, was given four offices of leadership, since he was one of only a few people who could speak both French and English and had proven himself to be a loyal American.

Secretary Sargeant made other decisions during his stay. He appointed judges and a sheriff and organized courts. He also established Michigan's lower peninsula and parts of Ohio, Indiana, Illinois, and Wisconsin as a division of the Northwest Territory named Wayne County. This honor to General Wayne was a timely move, for he died on his trip home to Pennsylvania. After setting up the government at Detroit, Sargeant traveled to Michilimackinac to appoint officers there before returning to Ohio.

The trials of self-government

By 1798 the Northwest Territory had enough voting male citizens to elect a House of Representatives. At the time, Detroit and Wayne County had only enough people for one elected representative. The election was held at John Dodemead's tavern in Detroit. Since a secret ballot was unheard of in the frontier town, voters had to appear before two judges and publicly announce their choice of candidates. This lack of privacy led to problems. The winning candidate, a young lawyer named Solomon Sibley, was said to have bribed and harassed voters. Sibley did not seem bothered by the complaints, however, and set out for Cincinnati where the legislature was to meet.

One of the early acts proposed by Sibley and passed by the legislature made it possible for Detroit to become incorporated as a town with trustees, police, and a tax collector. The people of Detroit found the new rules difficult to live with, and they broke them often. The fines collected from lawbreaking citizens became the main source of income for the town's treasury.

One of the first sets of laws established by the trustees were fire regulations, since fire was a serious threat to Detroit's crowded, narrow streets. New laws demanded that all citizens help fight fires and keep barrels of water handy. Each property owner also had to have ladders and buckets to use for fire fighting. Early records show that even some of the original board of trustees paid fines for not keeping their places properly fireproofed!

Other unusual laws were passed as the people of Detroit learned to govern their own town. One rule was a rather practical ban on horseracing in the town streets. Other laws set the price for certain products. For instance, bakers had to obey laws on the weight and price of their loaves of bread and had to stamp their initials on every loaf they sold.

Territorial changes

It was not long after Congress passed the Northwest Ordinance of 1787 that Ohio officially became a state. Settlers flocked to the Ohio River basin and the rich plains south of Lake Erie. By 1803 the people there had already met the requirements for statehood.

The boundaries of Ohio, which were set by Congress, were disturbing to people in the Michigan area. Detroit was not to be

The Detroit fire was a great setback to the settlement's beginning under American rule.

part of Ohio, but instead Wayne County was to be part of the newly formed Indiana Territory. The capital of the Indiana Territory was Vincennes on the Wabash River, hundreds of miles from Detroit. Even more discouraging than the distance was the fact that Detroit would have no representatives. The area would be governed by officials living miles away and understanding very little about Detroit's needs.

Local leaders in Detroit were very unhappy with these new arrangements. Immediately they began pressing for a census count to determine the total Wayne County population. Their goal was to convince the United States Congress that Wayne County should become a separate territory called Michigan and that Detroit should be its capital. Finally, on January 11, 1805, President Thomas Jefferson signed an act which created the Territory of Michigan.

The borders listed in the Northwest Ordinance of 1787 helped set the boundaries for the new Territory of Michigan. The western border was a line drawn from the southern end of Lake Michigan through the center of the lake northward to the Canadian border. Only a small part of the present Upper Peninsula was included at the time. This was the area around St. Ignace and the settlements at Mackinac Island and the Sault.

Most of the men chosen to lead the new territory were from the East. The governorship was given to a Massachusetts war hero named William Hull. As a lawyer and a military leader, Hull had proven his leadership skills, although he was not familiar with the problems of frontier life. The position of territorial secretary was given to Stanley Griswold, a Connecticut native who immediately angered local citizens with his strong opinions and difficult nature. The three appointed judges were Augustus Woodward, a Virginia lawyer and close friend to President Jefferson; Frederick Bates, the only Michigan resident in the group; and Samuel Huntington, an Ohio official who refused the Michigan appointment, leaving the position open for some time.

A disastrous beginning

Just before the new territorial officers arrived in the capital, Detroit was hit by a terrible fire. Early on the windy morning of June 11, 1805, a baker named John Harvey went to his barn to hitch up his pony and wagon for a trip to the mill. As he entered the barn, a gust of wind lifted the burning tobacco from his pipe and blew it into a pile of hay just inside the door. In an instant, the dry heap burst into flame. Fanned by winds outside, the fire spread rapidly through the barn and was soon threatening to spread to other buildings. Harvey's cries for help were quickly answered by the neighbors, but a major blaze had already begun.

Even the local fire laws were not enough to protect the town in the hours that followed. In spite of the water barrels, ladders, and the help of citizens and soldiers, the dry frame houses were soon lost in flames. All efforts to stop the fire's spread failed miserably, and by evening all but a few buildings along the waterfront and the fort on the hill were in smoking ruins.

Fortunately, no one died in the disaster, but those who met in the smoke-filled square that evening were stunned and shaken. Many wanted to begin rebuilding immediately, but the newly appointed Judge Bates urged them to wait until the governor and other leaders arrived to advise them. Some felt that the log stockade had kept the town from growing, and the fire had given them the chance to plan the town in a new way.

When Governor Hull arrived in Detroit, he was shocked to find the community that had so impressed General Wayne in ruins. Like the other citizens who had lost their homes, Hull had to live with a farm family until a new house was built. In spite of everything, Hull arranged to install the local judges. On July 2, 1805, the citizens of Detroit gathered to watch the ceremony. A cannon fired from the fort announced that Michigan was now an official Territory of the United States.

Recovery and planning

The problems of rebuilding Detroit were made worse by the confusion over property claims. To help settle the disputes, Congress made two important decisions. It gave Detroit ten thousand acres of land outside of the original town, and it created a board to listen to land ownership problems. Within the town, land owners were given a piece of property the same size as the one they had once had. Outside the town, people could remain on their

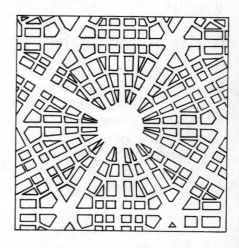

Augustus Woodward's plan for rebuilding Detroit was modeled after the layout of Washington, D.C. A circular park was at the city's center.

property if they held the land grants from earlier years. Since the importance of Detroit was increasing, so was the value of land, and the claims often caused serious disputes.

Judge Woodward, who was known to be a creative thinker, came up with a grand city layout. The Woodward plan was modeled after Washington, D.C. The city was to be shaped like a hexagon, with six sides. From a circular park in the center of the city, streets were to branch out like the spokes of a wheel. Woodward wanted the city to have broad avenues two hundred feet wide and lesser streets over one hundred feet wide.

To citizens of a burned frontier town, the plan seemed incredible. People who worked with Woodward wondered if the plan was practical. Although they agreed to go ahead with the first stages of his plan, they made many changes. They decided the streets were too wide, and added many smaller streets. A four-sided pattern gradually replaced the hexagonal design. Woodward complained that his grand plan had been ruined. In dramatic and colorful language he wrote:

Father Gabriel Richard

Father Gabriel Richard was a Catholic priest who made great contributions to the people of the Michigan Territory. Sent to serve the parish of St. Anne's Church, Father Richard was soon spending his time and energy on education. From 1804 to 1812 he started schools in Detroit and the surrounding area and trained teachers to work in them. One of his schools included Indian children whom Richard hoped would begin to live and work in the same way as the white people.

It was Father Richard's belief that schools on the frontier needed to teach practical skills in addition to regular courses. As a result, his teachers taught carpentry, printing, weaving, sewing, farming, and other useful subjects. Richard supplied students with study materials by bringing a printing press to the area. The first book produced was called *The Child's Spelling Book and Michigan Instructor.*

A caring and sensitive pioneer, Father Richard continued to make important contributions to the territory after the War of 1812 closed his schools. He served in Congress and became vice president of the school that was to become the University of Michigan.

Nature has destined the city of Detroit to be a great interior emporium, equal, if not superior to any other on the surface of the terraqueous globe. . . . A proper and prudent foresight can alone give to a great city its fair development. Order, regularity, beauty must characterize its original ground plan. No petty interests ought to be permitted to enter into collision with its permanent welfare. Uniformity of plan, amplitude of avenue, of square, of plan, of space, of circus . . . are not to be hoped for if one age shall determine on its limited and contracted view of things that a city can never reach beyond a certain limit.

Woodward was a man ahead of his time.

While the new leaders worked to establish the city, they also had to give time to the needs of the great wilderness they were also governing. Hull divided the territory into four districts to make the job easier. The Detroit district was a ten-mile strip along the riverfront. The district of Erie included land south of Detroit. All the territory north of Saginaw Bay was known as Michilimackinac. The remaining areas made up the Huron district.

William Hull, governor of the Michigan Territory, made decisions that were often impractical for a town on the frontier. He lost the respect of the people both with his actions as governor and later as commander of the army.

Discord and conflict

The differences in political views among the new officials of the Michigan Territory kept Detroit and the territorial government in a state of unrest for the next few years. Hull and Woodward quarreled openly, and in 1808 Secretary Griswold was removed from office because of his unpleasant nature. The most respected and trusted official, Judge Bates, left Detroit to become the Secretary of the Louisiana Territory.

Although he made some good decisions during his career, Governor Hull was not well liked. Many of his ideas were not suited to life on the frontier. For example, he required that the local militia wear fancy uniforms. He also insisted that each soldier pay for his own outfit, which included coats, capes, hats with feathers, and other decorations that would be changed with the season. This demand was nearly impossible for the poorly paid army of a frontier town. When it was found that Hull himself had purchased the materials to sell to the soldiers, people were angry that he had tried to make money on the uniforms.

Hull gave the job of making laws for the Michigan Territory to Judge Woodward. Unfortunately the judge's thinking was also out of touch with the simple life of the local citizens. The laws shaped by Woodward were complicated and in some cases unnecessary for a frontier town. Detroiters were upset that Woodward planned a courthouse and jail that cost $20,000, a huge amount of money for that time. Woodward and Hull also promoted and directed a bank for the territory. The bank failed, and although the pair were finally cleared of any wrongdoing, citizens lost faith in their leaders.

The continuing fur trade

Although the British had left the forts in Michigan, they still had a strong grip on the fur trade. The North West Company, owned by British and Scottish businessmen, continued to control most of the fur trading at Mackinac Island. The bulk of the fur trade at Detroit had moved with the British across the river to Fort Malden in Amherstburg, Canada.

To help break the British hold on the trade, the United States Congress required that stores called factories be opened at all important fur-trading posts. The factories supplied American goods at their actual cost to the Indians in exchange for furs. The factory system did little to lessen the British control of the trade, however. The Indians complained that American goods were not as good as British products, and they resented the American ban on liquor. In addition, British traders carried their goods to In-

The fur post established on Mackinac Island by John Jacob Astor's American Fur Company still stands today.

dian settlements. This made it easier for the Indians to trade with them than to carry their furs to the American factories.

In 1808 serious competition to the North West Company finally arose with the leadership of John Jacob Astor. This young German immigrant established the American Fur Company and opened a business at Michilimackinac, much to the distress of the British traders. Competition between Astor's company, the North West Company, and the Mackinac Company, which was the American factory in that area, was intense. Finally, in 1811, the companies agreed to a truce. Astor convinced the North West Company to keep its trade in the Canadian territories. The Mackinac Company became part of the American Fur Company.

Threats of War

Although the Americans had won their independence from the British, the two had still not become good neighbors by the beginning of the 1800s. The British who lived along the American borders encouraged the Indians to rebel against the Americans.

British officers at Fort Malden and at their fort on St. Joseph Island in the St. Marys River supplied the Indians with gunpowder and liquor.

In the East, feelings against the British were even stronger. The British navy had been seizing American trading ships at sea and forcing American sailors into the British navy. President Jefferson, wanting to avoid war, convinced Congress to pass the Embargo Act. This act kept American ships from sailing into foreign ports. Unfortunately it hurt American traders more than it hurt European merchants. A few years later American ships began trading only with France, adding more tension between the United States and Great Britain.

On the western frontiers of Ohio, Indiana, and Michigan, problems between the Indians and the Americans were also increasing. For more than a decade, Americans had settled as squatters on Indian lands. One of the Indian leaders who was especially angered by the squatters and the American wish to take over Indian lands was a Shawnee chief named Tecumseh. Like Pontiac before him, Tecumseh began a move to unite Indian tribes against the Americans. His powerful speeches and keen understanding of the problems that faced his people made him one of the most powerful Indian leaders of all time.

From his village on the shores of the Tippecanoe River in the Indiana Territory, Tecumseh traveled throughout the Northwest Territory and even into the southern states. He talked to many tribes, urging them to work together and turn back the Americans. While he was away, Governor William Henry Harrison of the Indiana Territory invited several older Indian leaders to meet with him and discuss the problems of settlers on their lands. After several rounds of drinks, the Indians signed an agreement to sell three million acres of land.

When Tecumseh returned and learned of Harrison's treaty with the Indians, he was furious. "Sell a country," Tecumseh is recorded as saying to Harrison, "why not sell the air, the clouds and the great sea, as well as the earth? Did not the Great Spirit make them all for the use of his children?"

Tecumseh's brother Tenskwatawa, often called the Prophet, also urged the Indians to unite against the Americans. Tenskwatawa preached that the Indians must return to the ways of their ancestors and reject the ways of the white intruders. Many Indian people believed that Tenskwatawa had magical powers and were strongly influenced by him. They were stirred by his hatred of Americans and began to attack settlers, particularly in the Indiana Territory.

In November of 1811, while Tecumseh was traveling in the South, Governor Harrison led a large army against the Shawnees near the present city of Lafayette, Indiana. Although Tenskwatawa had been warned by Tecumseh not to start a fight at this time, the Prophet ignored his brother's advice and urged his warriors to attack the Americans. Harrison's troops drove the Indians back and then burned their village which was located near Tippecanoe Creek. Harrison became famous as an Indian fighter because of the battle. Almost thirty years later he ran for presidency and used the slogan, "Tippecanoe and Tyler too." Harrison and his running mate, John Tyler, won the election.

Tecumseh was so upset with William Henry Harrison's scheme to get Indians to sell their land that he could hardly control his anger.

Angry with his brother and broken in spirit, Tecumseh decided to stand firm against the Americans. He traveled to Canada, where he was made a brigadier general in the British army. He and his troops were to play an important role in the upcoming war between Great Britain and the United States.

Michigan and the War of 1812

For the first time in the long struggle to control the North American continent, Michigan became a battlefield—in the War of 1812. It was the setting for some discouraging defeats for the Americans. And its strongholds at Detroit and Mackinac Island were again seized by British troops.

Shortly before the war's beginnings in June of 1812, Governor Hull of Michigan was made commander of America's western forces in addition to his role as the leader of the Michigan Territory. Hull was not happy about this appointment, for he felt that the forces in the area were quite unprepared to face the British. Now nearly sixty years old, he perhaps did not like the idea of leading soldiers in battle. Still, he accepted the job that was to ruin his career.

The Voice of the Ottawa

In 1818 an Ottawa chief named Okactau presented the British with wampum belts and related the long history of the tribe. In this selection he describes the Ottawas' attitude toward the War of 1812. He addresses the British commander, Major William McKay, as "father."

Father. Listen with attention to what I tell you. It is the voice of my chiefs and the Ottawa nation. Not long ago you sent for us to St. Josephs (island) and spoke to us with a strong voice. We never till that moment hesitated to obey your orders. But, my father, something whispered in our ears that it would be a good policy for us to sleep during the War and cultivate our lands for the support and comfort of our families. But, my father, when one of your warriors told us it was for our good, and that you would never make peace with the Americans till you would drive them over the Mississippi, and that then you would make a large road (boundary line) that would divide them from us. That they never should be allowed to step over it and that when you would make peace all your Red Children that would join you should be consulted and included as your sincerest friends. At the same time that you implored our assistance you won the influence of our sensible chiefs who talked to us incessantly till with one voice we raised the hatchet and made the Americans run out of their fort (Mackinac Island, 1812).

Father. We were not anxious to raise the hatchet for fear the Americans should be too strong for you and in that case we should lose your support and be obliged to fight them ourselves in defense of our Women and Children and prevent their taking from us the Lands that the Great Master of Life planted us on. But knowing your words to be the breath of truth, we seized the hatchet, painted our faces and made the woods echo with the War Song.

News of America's declaration of war against Great Britain did not reach Detroit until two weeks after the war had begun. Hull received orders to cross the Detroit River and capture the British Fort Malden. But Hull did not jump into action. Instead he moved his troops across the Detroit River to a community called Sandwich. Although this was British territory, he landed without resistance and moved his headquarters into a farmhouse there. One of the community's citizens recorded in his diary that Hull and his troops were polite to the local people. Hull seemed far more interested in encouraging the British there to become American citizens than in treating them as enemies.

Instead of pressing on to Fort Malden and attacking that small post, Hull settled in and waited. He seemed unsure that his troops could win a battle against the British. He was also afraid that the three British ships anchored in the river would fire on his men as they stormed the fort. Some historians believe that his job as governor interfered with his decisions as a military leader. He knew that many Detroiters had relatives in Canada and that a war with the British would destroy families and friendships. His concern for these people seemed to weigh heavily on him as he considered his choices.

At the end of July, Hull and his troops were still waiting several miles from Fort Malden. He then received word that the British had captured Fort Michilimackinac without a fight. Hull now feared that a large company of British and Indians would sweep down from the north to attack Detroit.

Hull continued to wait, although by now his troops were restless. While he waited he sent a unit southward to meet a large number of soldiers who were marching north from Ohio. But on their way, Hull's men were ambushed by Tecumseh and a group of his warriors. The Americans lost eighteen men, six of whom were officers. It was a heavy blow for Hull, who now ordered his troops back to Detroit.

A disgraceful surrender

While Hull had stalled, the British had managed to move more troops into Fort Malden. The British leader, General Isaac Brock, sent a message to Hull asking for surrender so that bloodshed could be avoided. He stated that once a battle had begun, he would be unable to prevent the Indian tribes from destroying lives and property. Although Hull was afraid of battling the Indians, he told Brock that the Americans were ready to meet any attack. Then surprisingly, when British troops crossed the river and marched to the fort, General Hull surrendered without a battle.

Much to the dismay of Detroit residents, Commander Hull surrendered the fort to the British without a fight in the War of 1812.

Hull's troops as well as the people of Detroit were angered by Hull's action. A Detroit resident named Mrs. M. McCarty, daughter of Detroit leader Peter Audrain, later wrote about the surrender:

> There was one universal burst of indignation from officers, soldiers, and inhabitants, at this disgraceful surrender, this stain on our national honor. General Hull's son, more brave than his father, raved and swore most fearfully. My father saw many of the officers break their swords, and weep over their disgrace like little children.

Hull's action, or lack of action, brought serious consequences. In a military trial that took place after the war, he was found guilty of being a coward, neglecting his duty, and not acting as an officer should. He was actually sentenced to death, but then pardoned by President James Madison because of his good conduct during the Revolutionary War. Hull returned to Massachusetts, his native state, where he spent the last ten years of his life trying to restore his reputation.

The battle at the River Raisin

The next year was a difficult one for Americans in the Michigan area. William Henry Harrison of Indiana replaced Hull as commander of the western troops, but he was not able to oust the British from Detroit. In the winter of 1813, American troops led by General James Winchester arrived in the area south of Detroit and camped on the snow-covered banks of the River Raisin. Winchester himself settled comfortably in a local farmhouse one half mile from his army. While he slept, troops of British soldiers and their Indian allies crossed the frozen Detroit River. Winchester awoke in the morning to the sound of gunfire and found his troops being defeated in the bloodiest battle ever to take place in Michigan. Winchester and another commander were then taken prisoner.

The embarrassing defeat of Winchester's troops was followed by an incident that caused outrage throughout the frontier. The British left a number of wounded American prisoners at homes near the battlefield under the protection of the citizens and several army doctors. The next day a party of Indians came searching for the prisoners. Angry over the loss of many warriors in the battle, they killed the prisoners and burned the homes where they had been recovering. The episode was especially tragic for the people of Kentucky, for it was mainly their men who had been led by General Winchester into the area. The battle slogan of Kentucky soldiers for the rest of the war was, "Remember the River Raisin."

After the capture of General Winchester, General William Henry Harrison moved his troops to the Maumee River in northwestern Ohio. There he built a fort called Fort Meigs in hopes of attacking Detroit. But the British controlled Lake Erie and were able to keep both Fort Malden and Fort Detroit strong with soldiers, ammunition, and necessary supplies.

Commanding Lake Erie

The first year of the War of 1812 was filled with failure for the young United States. American leaders soon realized that they must seize control of Lake Erie and cut off British supplies. Early in 1813 the United States government had several warships built at Presque Isle, now part of Erie, Pennsylvania. A young naval captain, Oliver Hazard Perry, was in charge of the project.

In September, 1813, Perry led a fleet of nine vessels sailing westward on Lake Erie. Near the western end of the lake, at Put In Bay, he waited for the approach of the British fleet from Fort Malden. Then, early in the morning of September 10, the two navies drifted toward each other. On his command ship, named

Captain Oliver Hazard Perry led American warships to victory on Lake Erie. His success helped Americans reclaim Detroit.

the *Lawrence*, Perry raised a flag with the motto "Don't Give Up The Ship." It was a signal to his other ships that the battle was to begin.

A furious battle followed. Cannons blazed, and from the riggings of the American ships, sharp-shooting Kentucky riflemen fired onto the decks of the British ships. For several hours the battle raged. Perry's *Lawrence* was so damaged it had to be abandoned. Perry ordered the flag of command lowered and a rowboat prepared. He and four men set off amid heavy firing for another American ship called the *Niagara*. There Perry again raised the white and blue banner, "Don't Give Up The Ship." By 3:30 in the afternoon the British decided they could not keep on fighting and raised the white flag of surrender.

The American sailors and riflemen were triumphant. And Captain Perry sent his now famous message of victory to General Harrison, who waited on the Ohio shore. Perry's announcement read, "We have met the enemy, and they are ours: two ships, two brigs, one schooner, and one sloop." The war had reached a turning point.

The defeat of the British fleet meant that the control of supplies to Detroit and Fort Malden was now in the hands of the Americans. The British General Proctor began a march of retreat from Detroit and Fort Malden. Tecumseh, angry with the British for this action, was said to have exchanged his British uniform for Indian buckskins in protest. Meanwhile, General Harrison's troops had been taken across Lake Erie by Captain Perry and were chasing the retreating British. Near the Thames River in Canada the Americans overtook the fleeing army. The Battle of the Thames was the final defeat of the British in the long struggle for control of Detroit and the Michigan Territory. It also resulted in the death of Tecumseh and his dream to unite the Indian people. It is said that his warriors buried him secretly, and his grave has never been found.

Tecumseh's death took place in the Battle of the Thames. It was the Indians' final defeat in their effort to keep Americans out of the Great Lakes region.

Victory and recovery

The Americans joyously reclaimed Detroit after Perry's and Harrison's victories. They renamed the fort Shelby to honor the Kentucky governor who had sent so many soldiers to fight for the Michigan Territory. Harrison and Perry were national heroes, and another outstanding military leader, Lewis Cass, was made governor of the Michigan Territory.

But the spirit of victory at Detroit was dimmed by many serious problems. Before leaving the fort, the British had destroyed most of the supplies. Soldiers, citizens, and Indian families faced a winter with little food, since Lake Erie was frozen and new supplies would have to wait until spring. Some Indians, still angry with the Americans, raided local farms and destroyed what little food had been put away for the winter. A cholera epidemic also swept the community, adding to the misery.

The victory in Detroit caused the British worry at Mackinac Island. The large number of Indians at the island had used up their supplies, and British ships were no longer able to travel across Lake Erie and up the Detroit River. A new route from Georgian Bay on Lake Huron west to the island could still be cut off by Americans who then might try to retake the fort. This was, in fact, exactly what the Americans planned. However, they botched their attempts to carry out the plan, and the British remained in control of Fort Mackinac until the end of the war.

The Americans in the East were more successful in their battles with the British. In September the Americans won two important victories in New York State. American forces at Baltimore withstood a strong attack by the British fleet on Fort McHenry, where Francis Scott Key wrote the famous lines of *The Star Spangled Banner.* Before Christmas, 1814, the British and the Americans signed the Treaty of Ghent in Belgium, declaring that the British would return to their Canadian borders and America would remain free from British rule.

In Detroit the long and bitter struggle had torn families and strained friendships of people along both sides of the river. To help heal the wounds, the citizens of Detroit planned a "Pacification Dinner" for residents of these communities. It was an important step in putting the anger and conflict of the past three years firmly behind them.

M I C H I G A N

I·N T·I·M·E

Date	In Michigan	Outside Michigan
1810	Tiffin makes an unfavorable report on Michigan to Congress (1815) School that becomes the University of Michigan founded in Detroit (1817) Walk-in-the-Water comes to Detroit (1818) Indians sign large area of Michigan over to U.S. in the Treaty of Saginaw (1819) William Woodbridge becomes Michigan's first delegate to Congress (1819)	Construction begins on the Erie Canal (1817) U.S. & British Canada agree to keep only 8 warships each on the Great Lakes (Russ-Bagot Agreement, 1817) Illinois becomes a state (1818) Spain cedes Florida to the U.S. (1819)
1820	The Cass expedition explores the Michigan Territory (1820) Indians give up Michigan lands in the Treaty of Chicago (1821) Fort Brady built at Sault Ste. Marie (1822) Dr. Beaumont saves voyageur's life at Mackinac Island & begins experiments (1822) Road begun from Detroit to Chicago (1825)	Missouri Compromise balances free & slave states (1820) Monroe Doctrine ends European colonization in Americas (1823) John Quincy Adams becomes U.S. President (1825) Erie Canal opens (1825) Andrew Jackson becomes U.S. President (1829)
1830	John T. Mason is named territorial secretary (1830) Cass takes Washington position; Stevens T. Mason becomes acting governor (1831) Cholera epidemic (1832, 1834) Toledo War (1835) Michigan's first constitution is written and approved (1835) Stevens T. Mason elected governor (1835) Indians give up more Michigan lands in the Treaty of Washington (1836) Michigan lawmakers give up Toledo strip in "Frost-bitten convention" (1836) Michigan becomes a state (1837)	Antislavery newspaper, The Liberator, begins publication (1831) A slave revolt, the Nat Turner Rebellion, takes place in Virginia (1831) Black Hawk War results when federal troops try to remove Indians from Great Lakes area (1832) Jackson warns South Carolina that no state has a right to secede from the Union (1832)

Chapter 7

Come all ye yankee farmers
Who wish to change your lot
Who've spunk enough to travel
Beyond your native spot
And leave behind the village
Where Ma and Pa do stay
Come follow me and settle
In Michigan-i-a
Yea-yea-yea-Michigan-i-a.

from the "Emigrant's Song"
published in a Detroit newspaper, 1831

Michigan Territory: The Move Toward Statehood

Michigan's young governor Lewis Cass faced a serious problem as the War of 1812 came to a close. The territory he was to head had only a small population. In its capital, Detroit, there was not enough food for people to eat, and there was no longer a court or a town government. Many of the soldiers and citizens there had died of cholera. When William Woodbridge of Ohio was appointed secretary of the Michigan Territory, he asked about the region before taking on his duties. An American general at Fort Shelby wrote this to him: "From my observation, the Territory appears to be not worth defending, and merely a den for Indians and traitors. The banks of the Detroit River are handsome, but nine-tenths of the land in the Territory is unfit for cultivation."

To make matters worse, the surveyor general of the United States, Edward Tiffin, made some unfavorable reports about the Michigan Territory. Tiffin had surveyed areas in the southeastern part of the Michigan Territory to help Congress find land to give to war veterans as payment for their services. The lands where the survey was done were normally low and damp, and heavy rains had made the project difficult. In his report to Congress, Tiffin complained about Michigan's vast swamps, infertile sandy soil, and poor land. As a result, Congress decided to give the veterans land in Illinois and Missouri instead of Michigan.

Governor Cass set out to undo the damage to the territory's reputation and encourage people to settle there. He told Tiffin to send a new team of surveyors that would go beyond the low,

Illinois | Indiana | Ohio

**Michigan
Territory
1818**

In 1818 Michigan Territory included all of the present state in addition to Wisconsin and part of Minnesota.

swampy land and take a broader look at the territory. This idea paid off. The second survey showed rich prairies and forest lands across the southern area.

But what type of land and resources lay beyond the survey? Cass felt that the whole territory should be explored to determine what the chances for settlement really were. In 1818 Illinois had become a state, and the borders of the Michigan Territory were changed to include the present state of Wisconsin and a part of Minnesota. Although these areas added little to the population of the territory, they added millions of acres of new land to be governed by Cass. Thus, in 1820 he received permission from the United States War Department to travel along the boundaries of the territory, meet with Indians, and make a general study of the region.

The Cass expedition

In May, 1820, three canoes, each over thirty feet long and fitted with sails, left the shores of the Detroit River. The canoes, masterfully built by the Ojibwa Indians just for this trip, were especially large to hold the forty-two travelers and the necessary equipment. Among the group were Cass, a geographer named David Douglass, and Henry Schoolcraft, a geologist. There were

Lewis Cass was one of the most important men in Michigan's past. He was a territorial governor, explorer, authority on Indians, a treaty-maker, and a U.S. Senator.

also soldiers and voyageurs, as well as Indian guides and interpreters.

Several members of the expedition kept journals, both as scientific studies and personal accounts. Henry Schoolcraft wrote his impressions as the journey began:

> . . . The banks of the river St. Clair are handsomely elevated, and well wooded with maple, beech, oak and elm. Settlements continue for a considerable part of the way on the American shores, and contribute very much to the effect of a district of river scenery, which is generally admired. The lands are rich, and handsomely exposed to the sun. . . . We passed a number of Indian canoes in which were generally one family, with their blankets, guns, fishing aperatus and dogs. On conversing with them, through our interpreter, we found they belonged to the Chippeway and Ottaway tribes, who are on a footing of the most perfect friendship with each other, and with the United States.

After about two weeks' travel, averaging thirty miles a day, the party came to the village and fort at Mackinac Island. Schoolcraft, who was bored by the level Lake Huron shoreline, was excited as they approached Mackinac Island:

After paddling for two weeks on Lake Huron, the fort and settlement on Mackinac Island was a welcome sight to Schoolcraft and others in the Cass expedition.

Nothing can present a more picturesque or refreshing spectacle to the traveler . . . than the first sight of the island of Michilimackinac, which rises from the watery horizon . . . and [is] capped with two fortresses on which the American standard is seen conspicuously displayed. A compact town stretches along the narrow plain between the hills, and a beautiful harbour checquered with American vessels at anchor, and Indian canoes rapidly shooting across the water in every direction.

. . . The expedition was received with a national salute from the garrison, and we landed amid the congratulations of a number of citizens who had assembled there on our arrival.

The Cass expedition stayed on the island for six days, visiting, exploring, resting, and renewing their supply of food.

The next part of the trip took them to Sault Ste. Marie, where Cass was to tell the Indians about the government's plans to build a fort near the rapids. Although America had gained the area in the Treaty of Greenville (see page 95), Cass worried about the Indians' reaction and had taken extra soldiers with him from the fort at Mackinac Island. He also wanted to find out how much the British were still involved in the fur trade there.

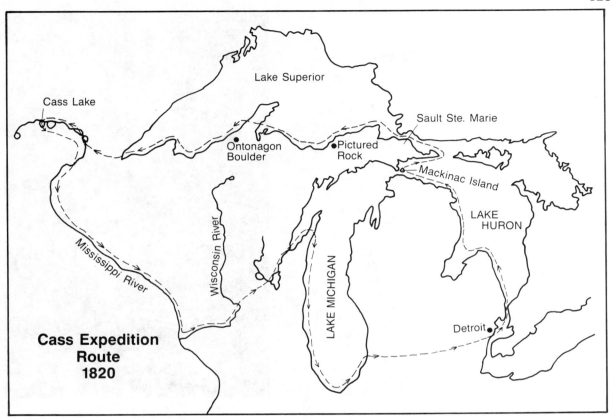

Cass Expedition Route 1820

When the expedition reached the rapids, they set up camp on the shore and visited with the family of John Johnston, a British fur trader who was married to an Indian woman. Johnston was away at the time, but his wife, his son George, and his daughter Jane entertained Cass and made a good impression on the entire party. The young Henry Schoolcraft, in fact, later returned to the Sault as an Indian agent and married Jane Johnston.

Governor Cass's meeting with the Indian leaders of the area was tense. The Ojibwa, or Chippewa, bands were still angry at the Americans, and one of the younger leaders named Sassaba wore a British military jacket. Although the Indians listened carefully to Cass, they were unhappy about the building of a fort in the area. As the meeting came to a close, Sassaba became unruly and threw his hatchet to the ground. Dr. Douglass wrote in his journal: "The Count [Sassaba] behaved with great insolence striking his hatchet to the ground with violence, kicking the tobacco together which was laid on the ground & scarcely offering his hand to the Governor at parting. . . ."

On his journey to explore the vast Michigan Territory, Cass and his companions traveled over 4,000 miles.

Henry Schoolcraft was part of the Cass expedition and was later appointed Indian agent at the Soo. Schoolcraft married Jane Johnston, who was part Indian, and collected Indian legends and materials into a book. His work was the basis of Henry Longfellow's epic poem, "Hiawatha."

Shortly after the meeting a British flag was raised over the Indian camp. Cass was furious. With only an interpreter to accompany him he marched to the camp and tore down the flag. He then told Sassaba that he would not have a foreign flag waving over American territory.

For a time it seemed that a battle would surely break out. Indian women and children ran from the village, and the American soldiers stood ready to fight. But John Johnston's wife, the daughter of a chief, and the Johnstons' son, George, met with the Indian leaders. George later wrote down his words to the leaders:

> One of your young men has misbehaved, and given a gross insult to the Govr. of Mich. a representative of the President of the U.S. by hoisting the British flag on his acknowledged territory. You cannot expect the British government will sustain him in such an act. I understand that he has gone to arm himself and raise warriors. Be wise, be quick, & put a stop to his wild scheme and suppress the rising of your young men. The firing of one gun will bring ruin to your tribe & to the Chippewa nation so that a dog will not be left to howl in your villages. My mother at this time came in & with authority

commanded the assembled chiefs to be quick, quick, and suppress the follies of Sassaba. . . .

The Indian leaders listened to the words of the Johnstons. They soon agreed to the Americans' plan for the land along the rapids. Two years later, Fort Brady was built there.

After matters were settled at the Sault, the Cass expedition went on into Lake Superior. They explored the southern shoreline, looking for the mineral deposits that had been reported by Indians and earlier explorers. Like Radisson and Grosseilliers before them, they were struck by the beauty of the Pictured Rocks. The Indian guides in the party helped Schoolcraft collect samples of copper, jasper, quartz, and agate. They named their geologist friend "Paguabekiega," or "He-who-strikes-the-rock."

From the mouth of the Ontonagon River the exploring party traveled inland to see the Ontonagon boulder, a copper-filled rock whose size and value had been made famous by the stories of voyageurs and Indians. The group was somewhat disappointed in the boulder, however. Schoolcraft wrote, "It has been greatly overrated by former travellers . . . but is nevertheless a remarkable mass of copper, and well worthy a visit. . . ." The famous rock was later moved to Detroit and then on to the Smithsonian Institution in Washington, D.C., where it remains today.

The group traveled for the rest of the summer, going westward to the Mississippi and searching for its beginning. Then

This old engraving shows Indians leading Cass and Schoolcraft to the copper-filled Ontonagon boulder. It is unlikely that the Indian guides wore such headdresses.

they began their return trip by paddling along the Wisconsin and Fox rivers to Green Bay. While some of the group explored Lake Michigan, Cass went south along the western shore of the lake to Fort Dearborn at Chicago. He then went by horseback on the old Sauk Indian trail across southern Michigan to Detroit.

The reports of this 4,000-mile expedition were of great interest to people in Detroit as well as to those in the East. Cass and other party members had many good things to say about the territory and its resources. Without doubt, the trip was an important part of Cass's successful efforts to change the image of the Michigan Territory.

Indian treaties

Cass had to do more than build Michigan's reputation to attract settlers. Most of the land in the territory still lawfully belonged to the Indian people. Treaties had to be made with the Indians and then approved by the United States Senate before settlement could really begin. Along with his role as governor, Cass was appointed Indian Superintendent for the territory. In these positions, he began bargaining with the Indians for control of the Michigan lands.

The treaties made with the Indians were often less than honorable. The goal of the Americans who made the treaties was simply to obtain the land. They gave little or no thought to what would happen to the Indian people.

Lewis Cass, however, was skillful at handling Indian affairs and gave more thought to the Indians' point of view than many other government officials. He believed that the government had a responsibility to the Indian people, and that plans should be made to help them adjust to their changing world. "They have a right," Cass said, "to expect much." In turn, many Indian leaders trusted Cass and liked his way of working with them. They nicknamed him "Big Belly" and thought of him as a friend.

When Cass spoke about Indian cultures or Indian problems, he did so from experience. His expedition and other trips into the territory gave him firsthand experience with Indian customs and ways of thinking. He studied Indian languages and wrote a booklet on the subject. He also interviewed people in Detroit and gathered information about Pontiac and his rebellion. Although he never wrote a book about Pontiac, his materials helped other writers, such as Henry Schoolcraft and Francis Parkman. In the first half of the nineteenth century, Cass was considered one of America's leading authorities on Indians.

Cass was very successful in acquiring the lands of southern Michigan by treaties. In 1817 he led talks at Fort Meigs in Ohio

Medical History At Mackinac

Early one June morning in 1822 a young French voyageur named Alexis St. Martin entered a store of the American Fur Company on Mackinac Island. A trader there was carelessly handling his shotgun when it fired, blowing a hole in St. Martin's stomach. The trader quickly called for an Army doctor, Dr. William Beaumont, from the nearby fort to try and save the badly wounded man.

Dr. Beaumont nursed St. Martin and was able to save his life. But the wound in the voyageur's stomach did not heal and left an opening through which his digestive tract could be seen. It was a disaster for the young man, since he was unable to go back to his job.

Dr. Beaumont saw opportunity in St. Martin's misfortune. Although the doctor had little money, he offered to give the Frenchman food and a place to live if he would allow the doctor to study his digestive system. St. Martin agreed. Over the years Beaumont observed St. Martin and conducted experiments on him. The doctor published a journal on his studies, followed by a book titled *Experiments and Observations on the Gastric Juice and the Physiology of Digestion.*

The voyageur did not fully appreciate the doctor's experiments. Several times he ran away, but Beaumont paid for the return of his living laboratory. Finally Dr. Beaumont died, leaving St. Martin on his own. In spite of his unusual condition, St. Martin married, had many children, and lived to the amazing age of 76.

Beaumont's experiments made an important contribution to the world's medical knowledge. He received no money from his work, but as years went by it became known as a classic study. In 1954 the Michigan Medical Society rebuilt the store where St. Martin was shot and made an exhibit honoring Dr. Beaumont.

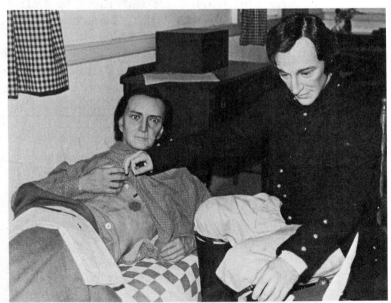

which added a small piece of land along Michigan's southern border to the Territory. In 1819 he secured a large part of the Lower Peninsula through the Treaty of Saginaw. In return for their land, Indians were given reservations so that they would not have to leave their homes. They also received yearly payments of $1,000 plus an additional sum that was determined by the federal government. The government was also to give them farming tools and the services of a blacksmith and a teacher as well. By the end of his career, Cass had obtained millions of acres of land through treaties and purchases, not only in Michigan but throughout the Northwest Territory.

Settlers on the move

On August 27, 1818, a strange craft puffed into the harbor at Detroit. Although it had sails like the rest of the boats there, it also had a giant paddlewheel powered by steam. The boat's arrival created a sensation in the frontier town. It was the first steamboat to cross Lake Erie from Buffalo to Detroit. In the words of America's native people, it was called *Walk-in-the-Water*.

The voyage of *Walk-in-the-Water* was the beginning of a new and improved way of travel to the Michigan territory. It shortened the journey and made it more comfortable for travelers. Although the famous boat sank in a storm only two years after its first trip to Detroit, other steamboats soon began making the journey across Lake Erie and up the Detroit River to Detroit. They brought settlers to the territory that had once been thought of as uninhabitable.

In 1825 something else happened that helped bring settlers to the Michigan area. In New York State, the Erie Canal was completed. This made it possible for settlers to travel by boat across

The Erie Canal provided settlers from the East with a good route to Michigan.

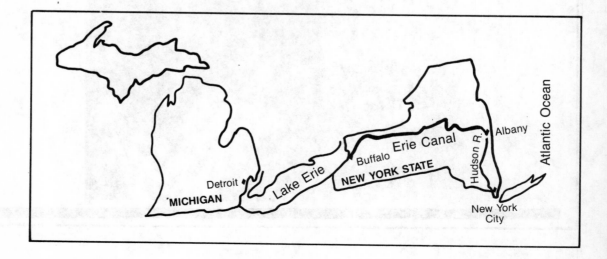

the state from Albany to Buffalo. They could then journey to Michigan by taking a steamer across Lake Erie. This new way to travel was both inexpensive and quite comfortable. And it quickly brought many new settlers to Michigan. In 1820 the population of the Michigan Territory was less than 9,000, not including Indians. By 1830 a census showed a total of 31,639 people. But in the next decade astonishing records were set. By 1840 the population had reached 212,267. This ten-year increase was larger than any other American state or territory had ever experienced!

As water transportation improved and lands became available to settlers, Governor Cass quickly began to work for roads so that farms and towns could be built in the interior. The first completed road ran between Detroit and Fort Meigs on the Maumee River in Ohio. Father Richard, who was a representative in Congress between 1823 and 1827, helped get funds for a road that followed an Indian trail, called the old Sauk trail, between Detroit and Chicago. The survey for this road was begun in 1825, but the project took ten years to complete. Other early roads included one from Detroit to Saginaw, and one branching off the Chicago Road to Ann Arbor, Jackson, Battle Creek, and Kalama-

Canal boats that carried travelers across New York were pulled by mules.

zoo. A road begun in 1832 from Detroit reached Grand Rapids in 1837.

Building a road in the 1820s was a difficult job. With only horses, oxen, and men for power, it took months to clear trees, stumps, and thick underbrush. No attempt was made at this time to cover the roads with any type of surface. Horses and wagons that traveled on the open paths eventually made deep ruts which became impassable with heavy rains.

Michigan's history is full of stories about the discomfort of wagon and carriage travel on the early roads. Some of the mudholes were so deep it was said a team of horses could be drowned in them. A well-known joke in the territory was about a man who found a beaver hat in the middle of a mudhole. When he waded out to it, he was surprised to find a man under it. He immediately called for help, but the man under the hat yelled, "Just leave me alone, stranger. I have a good horse under me and have just found bottom!"

The race for land

By the early 1830s it was clear that the gloomy reports about the Michigan Territory had not stopped settlers from coming there. "Michigan fever," as it was called, was running high. Many of the first Michigan settlers were Easterners who came from New York State and New England across Lake Erie. During 1836, as many as two thousand of these settlers arrived in Detroit daily on steamboats and sailing vessels. Others who had lived in Ohio and Indiana traveled overland into Michigan.

The rush to buy property kept land offices busy. Sometimes, in fact, land offices would close for days to catch up on their bookwork. In 1836, during the height of the rush, one-ninth of all Michigan's land was sold. Prices had been changed several times since the Land Ordinance of 1785. By the 1830s settlers could purchase land for $1.25 an acre with a minimum of eighty acres. Much of the land was sold to speculators. They in turn sold it to settlers at a price of $2.50 an acre. At either price the land was a good buy.

Nearly all of Michigan's first settlers were farmers who quickly bought up the best farmlands. Michigan's natural prairies were especially popular, since the soil was rich and there were few trees to cut down. Plowing the land for the first time was very hard, however. The roots of the tall prairie grass had grown thick and deep, creating a mesh that was nearly impossible to break. As many as twelve oxen were needed to plow land for the first time. Farmers who first plowed these fields were often entered in township and county histories.

Other settlers chose the open, parklike land in the oak forests which were common in the southern areas of Michigan. Crops would be planted in these oak openings, as they were called, with cabins placed in the wooded spots. The farmers' first crop was usually corn, since it could be planted even if the land was not yet plowed. Most farmers soon grew wheat, which was the leading farm crop in Michigan for many years.

The lives of the settlers demanded endless hard work. They had to cut trees by hand for their cabins, living in wagons or tents while they worked. Logs had to be split to make planks for doors and shakes for the roofs. As they built their crude houses they had to continue to provide food. Hunting provided much of their food, and also helped to get rid of the troublesome animals such as bears and wolves which killed their livestock.

Even more troublesome and dangerous than the wild animals were the swarms of mosquitoes that hampered settlers. They were sometimes so thick that work had to be stopped. Some of these mosquitoes carried malaria, or ague, as the settlers called it. Although it was not yet understood what caused ague, most settlers believed it came from living near swampy areas. Because malaria was common in Michigan in the early 1800s, a little jingle was popular in the East:

Don't go to Michigan, that land of ills;
The word means ague, fever, and chills.

Building a home and new way of life in the Michigan wilderness was not an easy task. Settlers often helped each other build their cabins.

These cabins belonged to Titus Bronson, who founded the town of Bronson in the early 1830s. Later the town's name was changed to Kalamazoo.

But the ague, the animals, and the hard work did not discourage settlers. In the 1830s Michigan was the land of opportunity, and they did not want to miss a chance for a better, richer future.

The fur trade's grand finale

While Michigan leaders were promoting their territory and encouraging settlers, the fur trade was reaching its peak in northern Michigan. Under the leadership of Robert Stuart and Ramsay Crooks, the American Fur Company dominated the trade. It employed over two thousand traders and boatmen and more than four hundred clerks in the village of Mackinac. At the end of the winter, when traders and Indians came to trade and barter, Mackinac's population grew by several thousand.

The officials of the American Fur Company were aggressive businessmen. They gave Indian traders better goods than the government stores. They used liquor as a trade item, even though it was against the law. They also worked hard to stamp out the businesses of small, independent traders. All these practices

The First Settler's Story

It ain't the funniest thing a man
  can do—
Existing in a country when it's new;
Nature—who moved in first—a good
  long while—
Has things already somewhat her own
  style,
And she don't want her woodland
  splendors battered,
Her rustic furniture broke up and
  scattered,
Her paintings, which long years ago
  were done
By that old splendid artist-king, the
  Sun,
Torn down and dragged in Civilization's
  gutter,
Or sold to purchase settlers' bread-
  and-butter.
She don't want things exposed, from
  porch to closet—
And so she kind o' nags the man who
  does it.
She carries in her pockets bags of
  seeds,

As general agent of the thriftiest
  weeds;
She sends her blackbirds, in the early
  morn,
To superintend his fields of planted
  corn;
She gives him rain past any duck's
  desire—
Then may be several weeks of quiet
  fire;
She sails mosquitoes—leeches perched
  on wings—
To poison him with blood-devouring
  stings;
She loves her ague-muscle to display,
And shake him up—say every other
  day;
. . .She finds time, 'mongst her other
  family cares,
To keep in stock good wild-cats,
  wolves, and bears;
. . .In short, her toil is every day
  increased,
To scare him out, and hustle him back
  East. . ..

by Will Carleton in *Farm Festivals*, 1881
Carleton was named Michigan's Poet Laureate in 1919.

proved to be successful. They helped to make the company's owner, John Jacob Astor, the nation's richest man.

The great success of the fur-trading business in the Great Lakes area was the major reason for its decline. Companies had pushed so hard for wealth that the fur-bearing animals were nearly gone. In 1836 Ramsay Crooks wrote, "Game has disappeared like snow before the summer's sun." Although the beaver were nearly extinct, John Jacob Astor was safe. He had understood the warnings and sold his company two years earlier, putting much of his money into new investments.

The end of the fur trade marked a turning point in the history of the western Great Lakes area. The region was no longer a wilderness belonging to Indians, trappers, and traders. The farmers, the fishermen, the lumbermen, and the miners were beginning to enter the scene in a new search for natural resources.

A boy takes charge

In 1830 a bright and friendly young man arrived in Detroit to help his father in a new job. Eighteen-year-old Stevens T. Mason was the son of John T. Mason of Virginia. John T. Mason had been appointed secretary of the Michigan Territory by President Andrew Jackson. But the elder Mason did not stay in the job for long. Instead, he resigned and moved to Texas. Before he left, however, he convinced President Jackson that his son, Stevens, was able to take over his job.

The young Mason's responsibilities grew quickly. In 1831 Governor Lewis Cass was appointed Secretary of War in Andrew Jackson's cabinet and had to resign his job as Michigan's territorial governor. The new governor was George Porter of Pennsylvania, who was not able to come to Michigan immediately. Until he arrived, Mason, who was only nineteen years of age, served as acting governor as well as secretary of the territory.

The idea of a boy in a man's job made many Detroiters angry. The local newspaper wrote articles against him and public protest meetings were held. But Stevens was hardworking and convincing. He wrote an essay for the people, promising to serve them well and to ask the advice of older men. He also had the support

Stevens T. Mason, the young and charming leader of Michigan as it became a state, tasted both victory and defeat. He was intelligent and anxious to put new ideas to work.

of Lewis Cass, who swore him into office before leaving for Washington.

Mason's job as acting governor of the territory soon became full time. Porter was often gone, leaving Mason in charge. Then, in 1834, Porter died in a cholera epidemic, and President Jackson did not appoint someone new to take his place. The "Boy Governor" was in charge.

Moving toward statehood

Under the leadership of Stevens T. Mason, Michigan began to take important steps toward becoming a state. By 1834 the

Detroit Epidemics

Tragedy occurred in Detroit and the surrounding area in 1832 when a shipload of soldiers arrived from the East. Several of the soldiers had become ill with cholera, a dreaded disease much like a severe case of intestinal flu. When the soldiers were put ashore for medical care, the illness, which was often fatal, spread throughout the city as quickly as a forest fire. The capitol building was made into a hospital, and workers with carts walked the streets calling, "Bring out your dead!" People who left the city to stay with relatives or friends spread the illness far out into the territory.

It was months before the epidemic was over. One of its victims was the beloved Father Gabriel Richard who had cared for the sick. With his death, which was from exhaustion, the territory lost one of its finest educators and leaders.

Only two years later, a second epidemic of cholera raged through Detroit. Although this epidemic did not last as long, it took the lives of more people. In one month, nearly seven percent of the city's population died. One of the victims was the territorial governor, George Porter, who had replaced Lewis Cass.

The Michigan Territory was not the only place struck by the epidemic. It had spread from Asia, through Europe, to America. Sailors were often carriers of the disease, bringing it to ports throughout the United States during the 1830s. Unsanitary conditions helped the illness to spread. People did not yet know about germs and that washing their hands would help stop the spread of disease. What they did understand was the fear of losing their lives and the lives of their loved ones to a terrible illness.

1837	**Michigan's Ten Largest Towns**		**1837**

Town	Founder(s)	Year	Reasons for location & growth
Detroit	Antoine Cadillac	1701	Grew up around a fort; excellent location on Detroit River
Ann Arbor	John Allen	1824	Along Territorial Road; junction of creek & Huron River; oak opening
Monroe	Francois Navarre	1785	Originally Frenchtown; grew up around land office; port town on River Raisin & Lake Erie
Tecumseh	Austin Wing; Musgrove Evans; Joseph W. Brown	1824	Location of a sawmill, gristmill & tannery; water for power; Quaker settlement
Ypsilanti	Augustus Woodward	1824	Nearby trading post; located Huron River & Territorial Road
Adrian	Addison Comstock	1826	Quaker settlement; river provided power for sawmill & gristmill
Marshall	John Pierce; Sidney Ketchum; Isaac E. Crary	1831	Along the Kalamazoo River & Territorial Road
Pontiac	Pontiac Land Company	1818	Point where the Saginaw Trail crossed the Clinton River
Grand Rapids	Louis Campau	1831	Grew up along rapids in Grand River where travelers had to portage; on Grand River Road
Niles	Isaac McCoy	1829	Area of early fort on St. Joseph River; on the Chicago Road

population of Michigan's Lower Peninsula numbered nearly eighty thousand people, twenty thousand more than needed to become a state. Two thirds of these people lived in the southern part of the territory, many near Detroit. Other large towns in that region included Monroe, Ann Arbor, Ypsilanti, and Flint.

The first step in becoming a state was to have an act passed by the United States Congress. This was needed before a state constitution could be written. In the request to Congress, Mich-

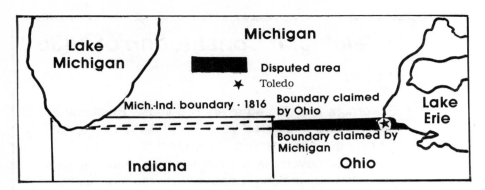

igan leaders outlined the state's territory. It included the present Lower Peninsula and an eastern portion of the Upper Peninsula. The southern border was just as the Northwest Ordinance had defined it earlier: a line east from the "southerly bend or extreme of Lake Michigan" to Lake Erie.

Determining the southern border of Michigan set off a dispute that was not settled for years. The northern border of Ohio, already a state, was different from the boundaries set by the Northwest Ordinance. Now this difference was of great importance. If Michigan's southern border were to agree with the ordinance, the city of Toledo at the mouth of the Maumee River would become part of Michigan! Naturally, the Ohioans were upset at the thought of such a loss.

The fight over a strip of land only five to eight miles wide soon became a national question. Surveys were made to help decide to whom the Toledo Strip really belonged, but the surveys only added to the problem. Soon people began to choose sides. Politicians from Indiana and Illinois, worried about their own boundaries, sided with Ohio. President Jackson also decided it wise to side with citizens of Ohio, Indiana, and Illinois, since he would soon face reelection.

In 1835 the debate threatened to break into actual fighting along the border. Ohio Governor Robert Lucas ordered surveyors to mark the border according to the Ohio constitution, and he put soldiers on standby. Governor Mason, upset because the problem was keeping Michigan from becoming a state, marched to the border with his own troops and arrested the surveyors. But no blood was ever shed. President Jackson took Mason out of office and made the land joint property until a decision could be reached by Congress.

Michigan officials decided to move ahead with plans for statehood even though they did not have an enabling act from Congress. Voters elected ninety-one delegates who began writing the constitution. Years later their work was still being praised for its many outstanding features. It was written clearly and simply and

The debate about who owned the narrow strip of land called the Toledo Strip caused an uproar in the 1830s. Michigan lost the strip to Ohio but gained a large part of the Upper Peninsula.

The Michigan Constitution of 1835

Elections

- Governors are elected every two years. Elections are held on odd numbered years so that voters will not be giving more attention to national elections.
- Lieutenant governors are elected independently from the governor, making it possible for the two leaders to be from separate parties. Lieutenant governors also serve for two years.
- Senators are elected every two years.
- Representatives are elected each year.
- All other state offices are filled through appointment by the governor and the approval of the senate or the legislature. Judges can be removed from their offices by a two-thirds vote of the legislature.

Voters

- Every white male over twenty-one years old who has lived in Michigan for six months is allowed to vote.

Comments

- Historians consider this constitution an excellent one in comparison to others of the time. Michigan's voting rights were about the same as other states.

protected the rights of citizens. Michigan's constitution gave voting rights to more people than many other states did at that time. Any male twenty-one years or older was granted the right to vote in Michigan. The state was also ahead of its time in understanding the importance of education. The constitution stated that Michigan would have a superintendent of education appointed by the governor.

Michigan's new constitution called for an election of state officials to be held in October, 1835. The election restored Stevens T. Mason as governor. It also sent Lucius Lyon and John Norvell to Washington as U.S. senators, and Isaac Crary as a representative. None of them, however, were allowed to take part in the activities of Congress. Still, the Michigan leaders went about their duties as if Michigan had become a state.

Michigan's early lawmakers met in this capitol in Detroit. When the state capital was moved to Lansing, the Detroit building was used for a school until it burned in 1893.

Statehood at last

The border dispute between Michigan and Ohio was not settled until the end of 1836. Congress proposed a compromise that gave Ohio the strip, but gave Michigan the entire Upper Peninsula. But Michiganians did not care for this. It seemed to them that the Upper Peninsula was a barren wilderness. In September, 1836, Michigan's lawmakers voted against this compromise.

Angry as they were, Michigan leaders saw that the compromise would finally have to be accepted. It was a losing battle. But there was another reason to settle the fight. If Michigan were to become a state in 1837, it would receive a large share of money that the federal government was dividing among the states. To meet the deadline for the funds, Michigan lawmakers met a second time and approved the compromise. On January 26, 1837, President Andrew Jackson signed a bill that made Michigan the twenty-sixth state of the United States. And the huge Upper Peninsula, with its forest and mineral resources, soon proved to be a great new asset to the state rather than a drawback.

MICHIGAN

IN TIME

Date	In Michigan	Outside Michigan
1830	First antislavery society in Michigan begins (1832) Detroit has first concert (1833) Kalamazoo College opens (1836) Erie & Kalamazoo railroad begins operations (1836) John Pierce becomes first superintendent of public instruction (1837) Michigan Indians moved westward (1838)	First steam locomotive is built (1830) Indian Removal Bill (1830) Jackson moves against federal banking system (1832) Oberlin College in Ohio is first to admit women and blacks along with men (1833-35) Martin Van Buren becomes U.S. President (1837)
1840	University of Michigan opens in Ann Arbor (1841) Albion College opens (1843) Olivet & Hillsdale colleges open (1844) Michigan sells railroad lines (1846) Michigan becomes first state to abolish capital punishment (1846) Holland is founded (1847) New capitol opens in Lansing (1848)	Mason dies in NYC (1841) William Henry Harrison becomes U.S. President (1841) Bathtubs are introduced (1842) Use of telegraph begins (1844) Cass runs for President & loses to Zachary Taylor (1848)
1850	Michigan rewrites its constitution (1850) First college degree is granted to a woman in Michigan (1851) State normal school opens in Ypsilanti (1853) Republicans hold first convention in Jackson (1854) Abraham Lincoln speaks in Kalamazoo (1856) Michigan Agricultural College opens in Lansing (1857) Adrian College opens (1859)	Underground railroad passes slaves into Canada (1850s) Uncle Tom's Cabin is published (1851) Franklin Pierce becomes U.S. President (1853) Republican party proposed in Ripon, Wisconsin (1854) Kansas-Nebraska bill is passed (1854) James Buchanan becomes U.S. President (1857)
1860	Austin Blair is governor (1861) Michigan sends its first regiment to fight in the Civil War (1861) Voters reject a new constitution (1868)	Abraham Lincoln becomes U.S. President (1861) Civil War is fought (1861-64) Slaves are freed (1863)

Chapter 8

Cling to Michigan but live and act
for your country—your whole country.

Stevens T. Mason in a speech to lawmakers

The
Growing
Years

By today's standards, Michigan was still a wilderness in 1850. Its largest city, Detroit, had only twenty thousand people. Grand Rapids, in the western part of the Lower Peninsula, had just been incorporated as a city. It was described as having fifteen stores, three flour mills, two machine shops, two pail factories, two tanneries, a woolen mill, a sash factory, a salt works, a plaster mill, two hatters, three shoe shops, three tailors, several blacksmith shops, two printing shops, four churches, an academy, and three doctors.

But in 1850 the young state of Michigan was beginning to grow out of its frontier stage and catch up with the rest of the nation. Many people were building frame houses instead of log cabins. Others had houses of brick or stone, and a few showed their wealth with huge houses that looked like Greek temples. Inside the homes there was often carpeting and fine furniture. Stoves were used for heating and cooking. Few houses had bathtubs, since they had just been introduced in America in 1842. Most Americans thought bathing was unhealthy.

In the cities there were other signs that Michigan was catching up with the times. Gas lamps lighted the streets of Detroit, Kalamazoo, and Grand Rapids. Detroit had a water supply, and other cities were working on water-supply plans. Streetcars pulled by horse provided public transportation in Detroit.

Cities within the state were beginning to be linked to each other and to the outside world. Railroads connected some of the towns in southern Michigan. People could send telegraph messages from Detroit to New York and Chicago. There were post offices in the towns and cities, and in 1851 a letter could be sent for three cents by stagecoach or train.

Michigan's harbors were also busy places, and in 1850 more than 2,300 ships entered the port of Detroit. Boats on Michigan's rivers carried passengers and farm products to ports on the Great Lakes. The boats returned with more passengers as well as goods for stores in inland cities, towns, and villages.

This 1850 etching of Grand Rapids shows the importance and activity that took place on many of Michigan's rivers in the state's early history.

Michigan's settlers

In 1850 Michigan was still one of the fastest-growing states in the nation. It had nearly 400,000 people, or about four percent of today's population. For the first time, some of its settlers were people who had been born in foreign countries. People from Ireland had flocked to the United States to escape a horrible famine in their own country. A large number of them came to Michigan, where they settled in the cities. They worked on railroads, were servants, or took other jobs that most people did not want. In a state where most people were Protestant, the Irish were Catholic. Unfortunately they were hated for many years for both their faith and their poverty.

Many of the German immigrants who came to Michigan in the 1800s were also Catholic. But the Germans were not discriminated against like the Irish. The Germans who had come to America years before had already built a reputation for being good farmers or skillful at other occupations. Wherever they settled they supported education and cultural activities. A German singer and chorus gave Detroit its first concert in 1833. The German

immigrants were attracted to Washtenaw, Saginaw, and Clinton counties. Many of them, however, kept traveling across Michigan to the state of Wisconsin.

Other immigrants to Michigan came from England and Holland. The English found it fairly easy to fit into the Michigan way of life, partly because they spoke the same language. The Dutch found life in Michigan more difficult. Led by their pastor, Albertus Van Raalte, a large group of Dutch people traveled to the shores of Lake Michigan. There they founded the town of Holland and several neighboring communities. The earliest settlement at Holland underwent great hardships, since the people did not know how to use axes to clear the land and build houses. They were also troubled by illness shortly after their arrival. In addition, the Dutch found that learning to live with Americans was a challenge. Van Raalte wrote to another Dutch immigrant:

> To live amongst the Americans is hard, because one is one match for them. It is ten times easier to start a business amongst your own people, however, one needs the Americans. . . . I feel that a Dutchman very seldom has a good imagination about the American way of business.

Immigrants who came to Michigan not only had to endure a difficult journey, but adjust to a new way of life.

Black settlers also made their way to Michigan during the early and middle years of the 1800s. They were free blacks, many from the state of New York. Among them were professional people such as lawyers, teachers, and doctors. They settled in Cass county near the southwest border of Michigan and in Ann Arbor. Others went farther north to Charlevoix county.

Whether they had lived in Michigan for many years or had just arrived, the great majority of Michigan's people were farmers in the 1850s. Some worked in lumbering and mining, but these industries were not yet as important as they would be later. Other Michigan people earned a living by fishing or running sawmills, flour mills, and stores. Some also had begun to build furniture and carriages, but these industries were still very young.

The native people

The coming of the settlers and the government treaties gave Michigan's native people smaller and smaller areas in which to

Albertus Van Raalte led a group of Dutch immigrants to western Michigan and founded the city of Holland. With the backing of the Reformed Church of America, Van Raalte also established Hope College in 1866.

live. These Indians lived peaceably with the settlers, and many stories were told about their generous natures. Some lived in log houses and farmed much like the settlers.

Although Michigan's early treaties with the Indians allowed them to remain in their own areas, policies began to change. In 1830 President Andrew Jackson and others in the federal government worked for a law to move all Indians to reservations west of the Mississippi River. Indians throughout the eastern United States suffered when this removal law was passed.

In Michigan the Potawatomi and the Wyandotte were especially affected by the removal act. The Wyandotte gave up their small claim to land in Michigan in 1842. This tribe was the remaining group of Huron peoples that had guided French explorers to Michigan centuries before. Eventually, the Wyandotte band was broken up and scattered. Some of the Potawatomi people were rounded up by soldiers and marched to reservations as far away as Kansas and Oklahoma.

Not all Potawatomi left the state, however. Some moved to reservations in the north. But even the move northward was painful. A chief named Cobmossa talked about the sadness of moving and changing his life. He said: "I am an Indian, and can be nothing else. I know . . . that my people must adopt [your ways] or die. But I cannot change. The young can adopt new ways; the old cannot. I shall soon pass away, living and dying an Indian. You can bend the young tree, but not the old oak."

A Potawatomi chief named Leopold Pokagon managed to keep his band from being moved westward. However, he had to give up the village that was home for him and 250 of his people. As he signed a treaty that turned the village over to the government, tears ran down his cheeks. "I would rather die than do this," he is reported as saying. His son, Simon Pokagon, continued to work and help his people. He became well-known for his writings, which included books, poems, and songs.

Most of the Ottawa and Ojibwa tribes managed to stay in Michigan in spite of the removal act. A treaty made in 1836 gave them land in the northern Lower Peninsula as well as in the Upper Peninsula, where many of their people still live. Others escaped to a new life in Canada.

The Indians who stayed in Michigan soon realized that life would never be the same for them. It was against the law for them to speak their own language or practice their native religion. For many years the federal government did everything possible to make Indian people forget about the past and become more like white Americans. It was indeed a long dark period for the Native Americans.

A government by the people

As they celebrated statehood in 1837, the spirit of Michigan's people was high. They had nothing but praise for young Governor Mason and the greatest confidence in themselves and their new state. Most people in the United States were confident at this time. Andrew Jackson was president, and he was admired as a leader of the common people. Mason shared many of his ideas. They both believed more power should be held by ordinary people, not by a select few.

After President Jackson was elected for a second term in 1832, he moved against a federal banking system that was run by a few wealthy and powerful people. He deposited government funds in a number of state banks, giving them plenty of money to loan to their customers. In a short time people began borrow-

Father Frederic Baraga

Frederic Baraga came to America in 1830 to work among the Indians. Like many other priests, he left behind the comforts of his homeland, which was Slovenia (now part of Yugoslavia). He was wealthy, well-educated, and a master at languages.

For five years Baraga worked among the Ottawa Indians in the western part of the Lower Peninsula. He then moved on to the Lake Superior area, and worked among the Ojibwa people. Eventually he established five major missions with the support of money and priests from his homeland. One of his most famous missions was located at L'Anse near the Keweenaw Peninsula. Here Baraga not only ministered to Indians but to Catholic immigrants who journeyed to the Upper Peninsula during the years of the copper boom. (See Chapter 9.) He also translated the Bible into the Ojibwa language and prepared other religious and educational materials for his Indian followers. Baraga traveled a great deal, often on snowshoes with a dog team, and became known as "the Snowshoe Priest."

ing money. Many of them, in fact, borrowed money and came to Michigan to buy land.

With the federal banking system no longer in control, new banks began to spring up. They were eager to give loans to settlers who wished to buy land. Instead of gold or silver, however, the banks gave people notes which could be used instead of money at the government land offices. Although these notes were supposed to be backed by silver or gold coins known as specie, very often they were not.

In Michigan, Governor Mason was also eager to get banks out of the hands of the rich and powerful. He supported a law to allow any twelve landowners in Michigan to open a bank if they had capital of $50,000. At least $15,000 of that was supposed to be in the form of specie. In a short time about forty banks sprang up in the state. They issued notes to hundreds of people who wished to buy land and then resell it to settlers at a profit.

The banks that sprang up after Michigan's banking law went into effect were called "wildcat banks." Most of them did not have the specie they were supposed to have and issued notes recklessly. When government officials realized that the banking situation was out of hand, they began sending inspectors to review the banks' funds.

But policing the banks was a hopeless task. The inspectors had to make long journeys into wilderness areas. When they arrived at a bank, a barrel of specie would be hauled in for inspection. In some cases the barrel was rushed out the back door as soon as the inspection was over and taken to another bank. One inspector even reported seeing a wagon pass him on the road carrying a familiar-looking barrel!

Some of the wildcat banks that had no specie to back them were not really banks at all. A group of people would create a bank name and have notes printed. They would then go into a town and purchase a large quantity of goods with the notes. At the end of a busy day, shopkeepers would find they had notes from "banks" that did not exist at all. And the "bankers" had, of course, left town with their goods.

Governor Mason was shocked at the corruption that the state's banking laws had created. He ordered the banks that had gone into business after the law had been passed to close. Many of the wildcat bankers were sent to jail. But worst of all, hundreds of settlers and merchants were stuck with bank notes worth nothing. The federal government, too, was unable to collect for land that had been sold.

The years of easy credit and wildcat banks created great money problems all over the nation. In the eastern states many businesses had to shut down, and people were without jobs. This

This bank note was typical of the many notes issued by wildcat banks in the late 1830s.

depression, which did not really reach Michigan until two years later, was called the Panic of 1837.

A program of improvements

While credit was easy and times were still good, Michigan and its leaders had been inspired by an exciting idea. The Erie Canal had opened with great success, and railroads connected many of the nation's cities. Every state, it seemed, had a plan for a grand transportation system. Why not Michigan?

The plan for Michigan's transportation system was called the internal improvements program. It called for a combination of railroads and canals to link the eastern counties in the Lower Peninsula with the western counties. This system would allow travelers to go across the state from Detroit to Lake Michigan, where they could continue to Chicago by boat.

Although it was a grand plan, the internal improvements program was unrealistic and costly. A southern railroad line was to run from Monroe, near Detroit, to New Buffalo on Lake Michigan. A central railroad line was to cross other counties from Detroit to the mouth of the St. Joseph River. A northern line was to link Port Huron with Grand Rapids.

Canals were especially popular at the time, and the Michigan plan called for three to be built. One was to connect the Clinton River in Mount Clemens with the Kalamazoo River near Albion. Another would connect the Saginaw River with the Grand. The third was a canal that was greatly needed. It would route ships around the rapids in the St. Marys River at Sault Ste. Marie, allowing them to pass between Lakes Superior and Huron.

The Michigan legislature passed the bill for the transportation plan and gave Mason the power to secure a loan for five million dollars to get things going. It was a bad idea and also poor timing, since the depression was beginning. Governor Mason traveled to New York City, where he tried to sell bonds, a method used by governments to get loans. But the troubles in Michigan caused by the wildcat banks had given the state a bad name. If investors bought bonds, how could they be sure the young state would be able to repay the money?

Since he was unable to find people who wanted to invest in Michigan, Mason went to a banking company to help him sell the bonds. The company, however, wanted to charge extra to do this. Mason was in trouble. Michigan lawmakers and citizens were expecting him to come home with the loan all arranged. But it was against Michigan law to allow the banking company to take its fee out of the bond sales. Mason did it anyway. The company agreed to sell the bonds and send the money to Michigan in a series of payments.

Although the lawmakers were not too upset by Mason's actions, it was soon clear to him that the grand improvement program was doomed. While one railroad was making progress, the other two were not. The canal projects were bogged down in problems. The five million dollars was only the beginning of the huge sums the state would need to complete the projects. Even if the program had gone perfectly, it needed good times within Michigan and the nation to be a success. But the entire country was struggling in a depression.

Michigan's people blamed Mason for the wildcat banks, the hard times, and the failing program. When election time rolled around in 1839, the Boy Governor did not even try to run for reelection. The new governor was William Woodbridge, a longtime political enemy of Mason's.

Almost immediately after Mason left office, the banking company that was selling Michigan's bonds began to fail. It stopped making payments to the state, and Michigan's internal improvements program was brought to a halt. Contractors could not be paid, and the state found itself in a tangle of problems that took years to solve.

Mason left Michigan, deeply hurt by the attacks against him. Woodbridge tried to hold him legally responsible for Michigan's problems. He also appointed a committee to study Mason's actions and perhaps charge him with fraud. The once-popular young man went to live in New York City where he died two years later from a severe illness. He was not quite thirty-one years old.

Michigan's most successful early railroad was the Erie and Kalamazoo. Completed in 1836, it connected Toledo, Ohio and Adrian, Michigan. Although at first horses pulled the railroad cars, a locomotive was used in 1837.

The people of Michigan forgot and forgave Mason's actions. The *Detroit Free Press* called him a "beloved friend of Michigan, gifted orator, talented statesman, high souled patriot." Although he was buried in New York, his body was brought back to Detroit in 1905 and buried in the heart of the city.

Railroads steam ahead

In spite of the problems of the internal improvements program, there had been some small successes in the railroad part of the project. On a snowy day in 1838, Mason and other officials had boarded the train on the new central line for its first run from Detroit as far as Ypsilanti. The engine for the locomotive had been built in Detroit, and a handsome yellow passenger car was named for Governor Mason.

In spite of the cold weather, crowds gathered in Detroit to see the historic journey begin and also in Ypsilanti where a celebration was planned. The Ypsilanti crowd watched in amazement as the train moved into town. Two men with brooms sat on the front platform of the engine, sweeping snow from the tracks. Bands played in welcome and there was a pig roast and speeches. The celebration ended happily enough, but on the return trip the

Although Stevens T. Mason lost his popularity for awhile, time helped him regain his status as a Michigan patriot.

engine developed a leak in its boiler. Horses had to be brought in to save the day and pull the railroad cars full of weary officials back to Detroit.

The railroad from Detroit to Ypsilanti was not a failure, however. Two trains soon ran daily in each direction between the two cities. By charging $1.50 for a one-way trip, the line was able to earn a healthy profit. It also saved farmers great amounts of time. A trip from Ypsilanti to Detroit with a wagonload of produce took a day or more. Train time was about two and a half hours.

The state was able to continue its successful central line westward all the way to Kalamazoo. But by 1846 Michigan officials and citizens had experienced all the railroad building they wanted. Both the central line and the southern line, which went from Monroe to Adrian, were sold to private companies. Under new management, the lines were completed within a few years.

Although railroad building continued in Michigan in the middle 1800s, it moved at a much slower pace than in other states. Railroad companies were more interested in building lines that connected the nation's large cities than they were in constructing the small local lines needed in Michigan. Construction, too, moved very slowly as crews cleared the land and laid rails across the swamps. At first the rails were made of wood covered with thin strips of iron. By the 1860s, however, most of these rails had been replaced by solid iron ones.

The popularity of plank roads also slowed the growth of railroads in Michigan. Companies that might have built railroads found more profit in building roads of wooden planks. They charged stagecoaches and wagons a toll for using the roads. Many plank roads were built linking towns and villages to railroad lines. The planks, however, soon became warped and uneven, giving travelers unbelievably rough and bumpy rides.

The farmlands

Michigan's people survived the hard times more easily than people in the eastern states because most of them were farmers. There had been several years of good crops, and farmers could supply their own needs and those of their communities. They may have lost money, but they were not going hungry.

Some of Michigan's early roads were built of planks. Over time the planks warped, making travel bumpy. The planks also rotted, causing horses to fall through the weak spots and break their legs.

But farming was a demanding way of life. All family members had to work from dawn to dusk to clear land, plow, plant, weed, and harvest. Michigan weather often created problems, and insects caused trouble at certain times of the year. Families helped their neighbors at harvest time or during illnesses. They knew that at some time or another they themselves would need help.

In the southern part of the Lower Peninsula, farm work paid well. Farmers were able to grow large crops of wheat, corn, and oats in the rich soil. By the end of the 1850s Michigan farms were sending huge amounts of these grains to markets in Chicago, Milwaukee, and Detroit. Until the vast western prairies beyond the Mississippi River were cultivated after the Civil War, Michigan was the nation's major producer of wheat.

Farmers were proud of the hearty crops they raised on their new lands in Michigan. Journals and letters give glowing reports of the farms and their products. One man wrote that seeds could be planted and forgotten until huge crops appeared. Vegetables, he wrote, were beyond compare. Potatoes and tomatoes grew "to perfection," and cabbages to a superior size. One could not discuss the size of pumpkins with people in the East, he decided, for they simply had to be seen to be believed!

High marks in education

Although the new state made bumbling mistakes in some areas, its leaders set up a system of education that was far ahead of the systems in other states. Governor Mason fully believed that education should be shaped and funded by the state. When the constitution was written in 1835, it gave directions for this type of education system in Michigan.

Two well-educated New Englanders who had settled in Marshall were responsible for Michigan's educational direction. Isaac Crary, the state's first member of the United States House of Representatives, had been in charge of the education committee at the 1835 constitutional convention. He urged Governor Mason to choose his friend the Reverend John D. Pierce to be the first superintendent of public instruction.

As soon as Pierce took over his position, he was sent by the governor to travel throughout the East to observe and collect ideas for Michigan's system of education. When he returned, he proposed a plan that was adopted in the form of three laws. The first of these laws stated that there would be elementary schools in every township, to be directed by township officials. The other two laws called for a state university that would have to sponsor intermediate or preparatory schools to help students prepare for university study.

Pierce was an educator far ahead of his time. In the branches of the university he proposed that there be a "female department." Although girls went to elementary school, advanced schooling for women was still not accepted by most people. Pierce also proposed that the branches include an agricultural department. This was a totally new idea that did not become popular until twenty years later. He also believed that university study should prepare people to be teachers.

Although plans for Michigan's university were begun in 1837, classes were not held until 1841. Ann Arbor was chosen as the site, and the college campus was built where there had once been a wheat field, a peach orchard, and a pasture. One of the first buildings was named Mason Hall in honor of the governor. When classes began, there were six students and two professors. Twenty years later the University of Michigan had become one of the most successful state universities in the nation. Preparatory schools that were part of the university system were begun as early as 1837. However, money problems within the state made it difficult for this program to be successful for many years.

Michigan established other important schools in the early years of statehood. In 1853 the Michigan State Normal School

Compared to many other young states, Michigan had a fine system of education. For many years children of all ages attended a one-room school similar to the one shown here.

was opened in Ypsilanti to train teachers. A few years later the Michigan Agricultural College was also opened, the first of its kind in the nation. It was located near the newly established state capital of Lansing. Michigan could also boast of a number of small, private colleges that had been established by 1860. They included Kalamazoo, Albion, Olivet, Adrian, and Hillsdale colleges.

The number of school districts had also grown by 1860. Seventy-five percent of Michigan's children between the ages of five and eighteen were now attending school. In most areas students of all ages gathered in a building with one classroom and one teacher. Older children often taught the younger ones, and the school year was much shorter than today's. In some of Michigan's more populated areas, however, "union schools" were built. In these children were divided into grades, and there was more than one classroom. By the 1860s some of the union schools included what is now high school.

Changes in government

After ten years of statehood, Michigan citizens and lawmakers had begun to see the need for changes. People living on the western side of the state wanted to see the state capital moved from Detroit to a more central location. Several cities were hoping for the honor, and Marshall had even named its chosen site Capitol Hill. To help settle the arguing among cities, a landowner

The University of Michigan opened in Ann Arbor in 1841 with free tuition for all men who lived in the state. In 1870 women were finally allowed to attend. While Michigan was not the first state to allow this, it was an important step in women's struggle for equal rights.

named James Seymour offered to donate twenty acres to the state in an unsettled area of Ingham County.

In 1847 the lawmakers approved the location, and a new capitol was built. Horses and wagons moved the state's records to the new capitol in the woods. It took some time before the lawmakers could decide what the name of the town should be. At first they named it Aloda, which was then changed to Michigan. In 1848 they finally decided on Lansing as the name for the capital city.

More important changes were made in the state's government when the constitution was revised in 1850. Lawmakers wanted to make sure that the mistakes of the internal improvements program did not happen again. For this reason, the new constitution made it unlawful for the state to become involved in any internal improvements. This extreme position later made it difficult for the state to build a good system of roads. The constitution also declared that the state could not take out a loan for more than $50,000.

There were other major changes in the constitution. All state officials, from those on the state board of education to the judges, had to be elected by the people. This lessened the power of the governor, who before could appoint these people. The new constitution set the salaries of the officials very low and stated that any changes would have to be put to a vote of the people. These and other policies would soon prove to be unworkable. The constitution of 1850 was later amended 38 times.

The new constitution did not make any major changes in voting laws. Male immigrants who planned to become citizens were given the right to vote. Voting rights were also given to Indian males who were "civilized." No such privileges were granted to women or blacks, however. Government leaders prepared a proposal that would give blacks the right to vote and put the question before the voters. They were sure, of course, that it would be defeated. It was.

The question of slavery

Although people in the United States had been concerned about slavery for many years, the debate became especially serious in the 1850s. The United States Congress was considering the Kansas-Nebraska bill, which would open the western United States to the possibility of slavery. Before this, slavery had been outlawed there. Now abolitionists, or people strongly opposed to slavery, were furious about the attempted change.

The political parties of the time reflected the different views on slavery. The Democrats, led by the Michigan statesman Lewis

Cass, felt that each territory had a right to choose its own position on slavery. Those Democrats who did not agree left the party and called themselves the Free Soil party, or Free Soilers. The other major party, called the Whigs, was also torn by the slavery question.

In February, 1854, a group of people from the northern states who were unhappy with the mild view of slavery held by both the Whigs and the Democrats, met in Ripon, Wisconsin. They decided to form a new party and agreed to hold a convention in Jackson, Michigan. The crowd that assembled under some large oak trees in Jackson on July 6, 1854, was made up of about 1,500 people. They decided to name themselves Republicans.

The new Republican party was strongly opposed to slavery. Within a few years it became a major political party, and in 1860 ran Abraham Lincoln for president. It also became the most popular party in Michigan. From 1855 to 1882 all of Michigan's governors were Republicans. Michigan also claimed that it was the birthplace of the new party. However, Ripon in Wisconsin made the same claim.

Michigan's people took a stand against slavery in other ways. In 1830 a woman named Elizabeth Chandler, who belonged to a

The first capitol in Lansing was ready for use in 1848. Within thirty years the legislature outgrew it and built the capitol that still stands today. The old capitol burned in 1882.

religious group called Quakers, came from the East and settled on a farm near Adrian. Since the age of eighteen she had been writing poems and articles for abolitionist newspapers. One of her most famous poems, "Slave Ship," told of an African chief who was captured by slave traders and taken from his family. In despair he threw himself overboard rather than be a slave in America.

Miss Chandler worked hard to stir the consciences of white women and remind them of the hardships and sorrows of black slave women. In a poem she wrote, "She is thy sister, woman! shall her cry, uncared for, and unheeded, pass thee by?" Poems such as these were an important force in urging people to take a stand against slavery. Some of them were set to music and sung at antislavery meetings.

Elizabeth Chandler worked for the abolitionist cause in other ways. She urged women not to buy products that were made with slave labor. She also started Michigan's first antislavery society. Unfortunately, she did not live long enough to see the slaves freed, for she died at the early age of 27.

Another woman who worked for the abolitionist cause and later settled in Battle Creek was Sojourner Truth. This outstanding black leader had been a slave in New York State until she was thirty-five years of age. Then a law in that state banning slavery gave her freedom. She spent the next fifty-five years of her long life working for the black cause. She walked westward from Massachusetts and spoke to antislavery groups along the way. She thrilled audiences with her stories and her gospel songs. People who heard these stories and songs described her as having "a sort of magic." She became almost a legend as she worked to change people's ideas about slavery.

Michigan's people who had strong antislavery feelings helped make the state part of the Underground Railroad. This network of people helped slaves run away and find homes in free states or in Canada. Led by the Quakers, this well-organized and secret society united citizens in small Midwestern towns in Indiana, Ohio, and Michigan, as well as states in the East. Members would hide fleeing slaves in their barns or attics by day and at night help them find their way to another member's home.

One of the leaders in Michigan's Underground Railroad was Laura Smith Haviland, who was an early member of the antislavery society started by Elizabeth Chandler. After an epidemic took the lives of Laura Haviland's husband, child, parents, and sister, she devoted herself to antislavery activities. She made speeches and traveled in the South to help blacks who might be unlawfully held as slaves. She also traveled with runaway slaves in their at-

Sojourner Truth

Sojourner Truth was a fearless black woman whose ability to speak the blunt truths about slavery made an impact across the northern states for forty years. Born Isabella Baumfree, a slave child in New York State, her childhood years were filled with experiences common to slave children. Isabella watched her mother's anguish as her older children were sold as slaves.

Isabella herself was sold at an auction when she was eleven years old. She worked for her owner for many years. He bragged that Isabella was "better to me than a man – for she will do a good family's washing in the night and be ready in the morning to go into the field where she will do as much at raking and binding as my best hands."

After the New York legislature freed all slaves in 1827, Isabella began to search for her own son. She hired a lawyer, found the boy, and prosecuted the man who had sold him.

By 1840 Isabella changed her name to Sojourner Truth, meaning a searcher or traveler for truth. She walked countless miles, speaking about the pain and suffering of black people. One Ohio man spoke gruffly to her: "Old woman, do you think that your talk about slavery does any good? Why, I don't care any more for your talk than I do for the bite of a flea." Unruffled, Sojourner replied, "Perhaps not, but Lord willing, I'll keep you scratching."

After the Civil War, Sojourner devoted her energies to helping freed slaves in the northern cities. She also spoke out for women's rights.

During her final years, Sojourner chose Michigan as her home. When she died in Battle Creek in 1884, thousands of Americans mourned her passing. She had touched them with her strength and commitment to human dignity.

FREE LECTURE!

SOJOURNER TRUTH,

Who has been a slave in the State of New York, and who has been a Lecturer for the last twenty-three years, whose characteristics have been so vividly portrayed by Mrs. Harriet Beecher Stowe, as the African Sybil, will deliver a lecture upon the present issues of the day,

At   On

And will give her experience as a Slave mother and religious woman. She comes highly recommended as a public speaker, having the approval of many thousands who have heard her earnest appeals, among whom are Wendell Phillips, Wm. Lloyd Garrison, and other distinguished men of the nation.

☞ At the close of her discourse she will offer for sale her photograph and a few of her choice songs.

tempts to escape. After the Civil War she continued her work by helping freed slaves find a new way of life.

The people of Michigan objected to a federal law passed in 1850 that made it possible to arrest those who protected or helped runaway slaves. Lawmakers in the state even passed "personal liberty laws" to aid citizens who were caught helping runaway slaves. In Marshall a runaway slave was protected by a large group of leading citizens when his owners from Kentucky tried to reclaim him. When the Kentuckians were unable to take the slave back with them, they sued the Marshall citizens, who were eventually fined. Their costs were paid, however, by a wealthy Detroit businessman named Zachariah Chandler who later became a leader of the Republican party.

The Civil War

When the southern states left the Union, there was no question as to where Michigan's people stood. "The Union must be preserved and the laws must be enforced in all parts of it whatever the cost," said the newly elected governor, Austin Blair. And Michigan citizens agreed.

Shortly after the fighting began on April 12, 1861, President Lincoln sent a telegram to Governor Blair asking for a Michigan regiment composed of ten companies. It was a big demand. Michigan's military companies were little more than social organizations that took part in parades. They would have to be trained, housed, clothed, and given weapons.

But Michigan's people responded proudly to the call. In nine days enough men had agreed to serve. Individuals throughout the state gave money to help meet the emergency costs of building an army. Although President Lincoln first asked that soldiers serve for three months, the time was soon changed to three years.

Enthusiasm for the war, of course, could not stay that high. Soon it was clear that predictions made by Governor Blair were coming true. In a speech he had told the people of Michigan this:

> The sudden and splendid outburst of popular enthusiasm . . . will shortly, in a great measure, disappear, and must be replaced by calm determination. . . . There will be calamities and disasters which have not been looked for. He who went forth joyously singing the national anthem will sometime be brought back in a bloody shroud. This is to be no six week's campaign. I do not underestimate the gallantry of Southern men. . . .

Within a year it became difficult for Michigan officials to find men willing to become soldiers. Since that was true in every state of the North, Congress decided that $100 would be paid to each soldier for enlisting. By 1864 that amount was raised to $300. Michigan lawmakers also decided to offer men money to enlist. They proposed that cities, counties, and townships do the same.

Although it was often difficult to enlist soldiers, more than ninety thousand men from Michigan served in the war. But at least one soldier was a woman dressed as a man. Sarah Emma Edmonds, known as Franklin Thompson, fought in several battles. George Custer, the famous officer who was later killed by the Sioux Indians at the Battle of the Little Big Horn, led some of Michigan's troops. Moses Wisner, who had served as governor before Blair, also led a Michigan regiment. Among the Michigan

Public meetings were held to inform people about the Civil War. This one was held in Detroit just after the outbreak of the war.

groups was one made up of more than 1,600 black soldiers. However, unlike Michigan men who stayed with their own local units, the blacks were sent to become part of the United States Colored Infantry Regiment.

Michigan's troops were sent to many different fronts to fight. They were part of major battles at Bull Run, Antietam, Gettysburg, and Vicksburg. They were with General Grant at the siege of Richmond and General Sherman in his march to the sea. Sixty-nine of them received the Medal of Honor for their bravery.

Hundreds of letters and diaries from the Civil War have provided a rich history of the daily lives of the soldiers. They tell of many hardships, from poor food to long marches and long, cold winter nights. Illness was a problem in army camps. Disease spread quickly among the soldiers who were already worn out by lack of food and difficult living conditions.

A young man from Holland, Michigan, wrote home and told about a march southward and how the soldiers helped themselves to Southerners' supplies along the way. "The food was the worst part. We had quarter rations, but we helped ourselves as much as possible. It is very hard on the civilians. There is not much for them."

Michigan soldiers brought honor to the state because they were better trained and disciplined than regiments from other areas.

Michigan and the Civil War 1861-1865

Overview

The questions of slavery and a state's right to allow it created the conflicts that led to the Civil War. The northern states, including Michigan, generally objected to slavery and its spread into western states. The southern states supported these issues. Because of the conflict of ideas, the southern states withdrew from the Union and organized the Confederate States of America. President Abraham Lincoln declared that no state had a right to secede from the Union, and war began. The war waged for four years with great losses to both sides. Northern forces finally won, and the southern states were brought back into the Union.

Hardships

As in all wars, suffering and death were daily facts of life. But there were other hardships for soldiers. Old records show that in January of 1864 many Michigan soldiers were without basic supplies. 210 men of the 17th Michigan infantry were inspected with the following results: 92 had no underclothing; 84 had no shoes; 128 had no overcoats; 40 had no tents; 150 had no socks; 16 had no blanket.

Famous people

General George Custer led a Michigan cavalry unit. A war correspondent at Gettysburg wrote: ". . .Custer's brigade of Michiganders. . . captured more than man for man of an enemy whose force consisted of four times their number. This is cavalry fighting, the superior of which the world never saw."

Michigan's 4th Cavalry unit under the command of Colonel Benjamin Pritchard of Allegan captured Confederate President Jefferson Davis in southern Georgia.

Hurrahs for Michigan soldiers

A New York *Tribune* reporter wrote about Michigan soldiers after battles in Virginia in 1862: "I would covet the honor. . .of adoption into either of the Michigan regiments whom I saw leap through the shot and shell infested wood. . .."

The 16th Michigan infantry was fighting with a Maryland regiment when the Maryland men retreated under fire. The Maryland colonel tried to rally them, but could not. As the Michigan infantry continued the battle, the Maryland colonel approached a Michigan colonel and with tears streaming down his face exclaimed, "Colonel, would to God that I commanded a Michigan regiment!"

In 1863 the 26th Michigan infantry arrived in New York City. The New York *Times* wrote: "We welcome it to the city and we trust our citizens will show appreciation of such a regiment. At the present time the Peninsula State is represented in the three great armies of Grant, Rosecrans, and Meade, and Michigan soldiers have won renown for their bravery and discipline throughout the war and on almost every battlefield."

Although battles were sometimes few and far between, they were hard-fought with many casualties on both sides. Those killed were not always quickly identified. Wounded soldiers were cared for in tents by anyone who was available. The most seriously wounded were taken to an army camp, to a town, or to a hospital if there was one in a nearby city. But even the hospitals had small staffs and were not kept clean. Many soldiers died from infections in their wounds or from disease. If families found that one of their members was in a hospital, they often traveled long distances to care for him or bring him home. About one half of the fourteen thousand Michigan soldiers who lost their lives in the war died from infection and disease.

Since news traveled slowly, it was often a long time before a family knew about a death. In some towns the names of Michigan's dead and wounded from the latest battle were read aloud on the street corners. When a local soldier's name was read, there would be outbursts of tears.

Zachariah Chandler

For twenty-five years, Zachariah Chandler dominated the direction of the newly formed Republican party in Michigan. A successful businessman, Chandler began his political career by becoming mayor of Detroit in 1851. In 1857 he was elected to the United States Senate, replacing the aging Lewis Cass.

During the Civil War, Chandler supported Republican President Abraham Lincoln, although he often condemned the efforts of the northern generals. After the war he led a movement in the Senate to punish the Southern states as they rejoined the Union. Even though his views were extreme, his power as a Republican leader continued to grow.

Chandler's influence shaped the politics of Michigan until his death in 1879. But not all of his work was positive. His intense hatred of Democrats and Southerners slowed the nation's attempt to heal its wounds after the Civil War and build a strong, reunited country.

In Michigan life went on about the same as before, but the war was hard on wives whose husbands were soldiers. A soldier's pay was very low, and townships raised taxes so that they could afford to pay $15 a month to each family whose breadwinner had gone to war. A young woman in Calhoun County left a diary that told of her struggle to care for a farm, a two-year-old son, and a baby daughter while her husband was at war. Caring for the children, making meals, feeding the animals, mending fences, keeping the garden, spinning yarn, and chopping wood were all part of her daily activities.

Women who had fewer chores than the young farm wives with small children helped the war effort in many ways. They made bandages and food to be sent to soldiers. Some went to war as nurses, although nursing was not yet a profession as it is today. Elmina Brainard from Lapeer located wounded Michigan soldiers and worked to make them more comfortable. Julia Wheelock from Ionia also visited hospitals and cared for Michigan soldiers. In 1864 she wrote in her journal about a hospital in Fredericksburg, Virginia: "O what scenes of suffering I have witnessed. . . . In every Hosp. found many Mich. men without blankets, sometimes 50 or 60 in one room. . . . What seems to add greatly to their sufferings is, they have not half enough to eat—not even 'Hardtack.' Many who have just arrived from the front have had nothing to eat for 3 or 4 days—literally starving to death." Later she wrote, "Were it not for the privilege of crying, it seems my heart would break."

Austin Blair was Michigan's governor during most of the war years. After the war he served in the U.S. Congress and was known for his work in helping freed slaves and settling differences between the North and South.

When the war finally ended in 1865, Michigan and the nation faced still another tragedy. Just three days after the surrender of General Lee, President Lincoln was shot and killed. Every Michigan town went into mourning, and churches and public buildings were draped with black cloth. One Michigan man recalled the experience: "Stalwart men wept like children on the streets, which to me, a boy, was exceedingly impressive; women prayed; everybody, young and old, seemed completely crushed."

Back to normal

Far removed from the battlegrounds, life went on as usual in Michigan during the war years and after. The war had a positive influence on farming and manufacturing, since food and other items were in great demand. Michigan crops received top prices and its farmers were able to buy the new machinery that was becoming available. There were new types of reapers, mowing machines, plows, cultivators, and threshing machines.

King James J. Strang

For a brief period in the 1850s, a group of Mormons on Beaver Island in Lake Michigan chose a king, and Michigan became the home of "King James, Vice regent of God on Earth." James J. Strang was a dynamic man who had been converted to the Mormon religion by its leader, Joseph Smith. When Smith was assassinated in Illinois, Strang hoped to lead the group west. But Brigham Young took over the leadership, and Strang led a small group to Wisconsin and then on to Beaver Island.

Strang and his community were disliked on Beaver Island because of their practice of polygamy, or having more than one wife. Irish Catholic fishermen who came to the island also objected to Strang's strict rules concerning the fishing grounds they had used for years.

Although Strang convinced his followers to crown him king in 1850, the residents in the Beaver Island area had him arrested. No charges could be made against the Mormon, however, and Strang returned to the island where his followers elected him to the Michigan legislature. He served there for four years.

Strang's extreme control of his followers eventually caused his downfall. In 1856 he was shot and later died of his wounds. Mainlanders raided the island, and without Strang's leadership, the Mormons fled for safety. The Mormon kingdom of King James disappeared from Michigan with only the town's name of St. James as a reminder of its unusual existence.

With so many men serving in the army, there was a shortage of workers in Michigan. Machinery, however, helped farmers operate with fewer people. Women also went to work in the fields. A number of immigrants came to Michigan during the war years, since jobs were easy to find.

During Lincoln's years in office, a Homestead Act was passed. This act gave government land free to any person who would live and farm on it for five years. The policy helped bring people to the northern areas of Michigan.

But people came to the state for jobs other than farming. Michigan's forests and copper and iron mines had caught the attention of the entire nation. Investors from the East had formed mining and lumbering companies. Michigan had grown beyond its youthful years. And its wealth of natural resources had started a great boom.

Farming underwent many changes in the second half of the 1800s. New machinery and education for farmers were responsible for the changes.

M I C H I G A N

I·N T·I·M·E

Date	In Michigan	Outside Michigan
1840	Douglass Houghton reports on copper deposits in the U.P. (1841)	First large wagon train begins its trip to Oregon (1843)
	William Burt discovers iron ore (1844)	U.S. fights Mexican War (1846-47)
	Cliff Mine opens (1844)	
	Michigan is first in copper production (1847-1887)	Gold is discovered in California (1848)
	Jackson Mining Company begins iron ore operations (1847)	Gold rush pushes California's population to 100,000 (1849)
1850	Circular saws introduced in Michigan sawmills (1850)	U.S. buys southern portions of Arizona & New Mexico (1853)
	The town of Houghton is founded (1852)	
	Soo Ship Canal and Locks open (1855)	Gold rush to Colorado & Nevada (1859)
	Railroad for mining opens between Marquette and Ishpeming (1857)	First oil well drilled in Pennsylvania (1859)
	Hancock is founded (1859)	
1860	Calumet Mine Company is formed (1861)	First transcontinental railroad completed (1869)
	Hecla Mine opens (1866)	
1870	Forest fires sweep state (1871)	Standard Oil Company organized (1870)
	Calumet & Hecla Mines combined (1871)	Huge Chicago fire (1871)
	Ship canal opens across Keweenaw Peninsula (1872)	Forest fire destroys Peshtigo, Wisconsin (1871)
	Fish Commission established to aid commercial and game fishing (1873)	Huge grasshopper plague destroys wheat crops in Great Plains (1874)
	Lumbermen begin using narrow gauge railroads (1877)	Gold rush to Black Hills (1875)
	Iron mines open on the Menominee Range (1877)	Violent coal miners union is broken in Pennsylvania (1875)
	Last great nesting of passenger pigeons in Michigan (1878)	
1880	Forest fires hit eastern Michigan (1881)	Western cattle boom begins (1880)
	Mines open on Gogebic iron range (1884)	Red Cross is organized (1881)
	Michigan School of Mines opens (1886)	Ten year cycle of drought begins in Great Plains (1887)
	Michigan reaches peak of lumber production (1888)	

Chapter 9

The music of our burnished ax shall make the woods resound,
And many a lofty ancient pine will tumble to the ground;
At night round our shanty fire we'll sing while rude winds blow
O! we'll range the wild woods o'er while a lumbering we go.

from *The Shanty Boy*
by John W. Fitzmaurice
Used with permission of Hardsrabble Books

A Wealth of Resources

Robert Dollar came to Michigan from Canada. Jobs were plentiful in the lumber camps that were popping up around the state. Robert signed on as a lumberjack, or shanty boy, as the job was called then. The pay was the same as his name—a dollar for every day he worked. Shanty boys collected their wages in the spring after a long winter of lumbering in the forests. Everyone knew what happened then. At least half their wages were spent in celebration in the nearest town.

But not Robert. Other shanty boys were disgusted with him. Instead of having a good time, Robert went out and bought a few acres of pine trees for himself. He did that for several seasons. He also moved up from shanty boy to camp boss. That meant better wages and more pines.

As years went by Robert Dollar had his own lumber camps. He also owned sawmills. He even started a town called Dollarville in the eastern part of Michigan's Upper Peninsula. When the pines eventually ran out, he went to the West coast and started a shipping company, with the same success.

Michigan's forests

Until the 1840s, most of the people in Michigan thought of the state's many trees as a problem. What the settlers wanted was farmland, and the trees were in the way. Cutting them down was a great chore.

It was said that Michigan's forests were so thick a squirrel could travel five hundred miles without touching ground. And they were especially dense in the northern parts of the state. There pines were most common, with some hardwoods. The white pines were the trees that attracted the lumbermen. These great trees grew to towering heights. They had few branches, and their trunks were three or four feet across. The wood of the white pine was not only beautiful, but soft and easy to work with.

Around the 1840s Michigan's people began to think of the thick forests as a valuable resource. Many of the forests in the East had been cut down, and there was a ready market for lumber. Although there were no railroads and only a few poor roads, Michigan's river system was perfect for shipping logs. Some of the rivers flowed toward Lake Huron, while others flowed to Lake Michigan. Businessmen, former fur traders, and sawmill operators began to understand the possibilities of a new industry.

Sawmills that had once met only the needs of the local settlers began producing lumber to sell in other parts of the country. This idea first caught on in the Saginaw area. The story was repeated on the western side of the state at the places where the Grand and Muskegon rivers meet Lake Michigan.

The race for white pine

Once the value of Michigan's huge pines was understood, a race was on to harvest these giants of the forest. Investors hired men called timber cruisers to search the forests looking for the best stands of trees. A timber cruiser would survey an area and then return to a land office and purchase the property for his company. The races between timber cruisers of rival companies became well-known.

One of the races for land was between David Ward and Addison Brewer. Both had discovered an especially good stand of pine near the Au Sable River in the northeastern part of the Lower Peninsula. The claim for the land, however, had to be filed at an office in Ionia in the central part of the state.

Ward knew he had no time to lose. He walked eighty miles to a river that would take him south and then canoed another eighty miles to Saginaw. At Saginaw he took a stagecoach to a train station and boarded a train to Detroit. There he picked up the money needed for the purchase. He then rented a horse and carriage and drove eighteen hours to Lansing. At Lansing he caught a stage for Ionia. Exhausted, he filed the claim. It was none too soon. In came Brewer.

The logging camps

Once the land was purchased, companies built logging camps in the heart of the area. These camps were crude, since they were abandoned once the lumber was cut. The main building in the camp was the mess hall. It was full of wooden tables and benches. The place was lighted by kerosene lanterns and heated by a huge iron stove.

Mealtime was the highlight of the day, and the cook was an important person in camp. The size of the meal was valued more than variety in menu. Pork and beans, hot biscuits, pancakes with gravy or syrup, and gallons of hot coffee were the most common items served.

A bunkhouse, barn, and toolshed were also part of a lumber camp. Bunks lined the walls of the bunkhouse like shelves in a cupboard and were very small. Branches, hay, or straw served as mattresses, and bedbugs were a common problem. Wet clothes were hung over the stove to dry, and the bunkhouses were usually known for their unpleasant odors.

Lumbermen had to make their own fun in the remote logging camps. They told stories, wrote letters, and sang and danced.

Not only did loggers have to fell the giant pines, they had to cut them into 16-foot logs. Many, such as this one, were over 150 feet long which meant it had to be cut by hand 8 more times!

The loggers were usually rugged, hearty men who left their families behind to spend months in the forests. The hard work was divided into different tasks. Loggers called choppers and saw-yers felled the trees with axes and crosscut saws. When a tree was down, they cut it into logs that were sixteen feet long. Men called swampers cut off the branches and cleared them away.

When it was time for the logs to be moved, workers called skidders joined the swampers to haul the logs to a nearby logging road. They put chains around the log and used horses or oxen to skid it along. Another crew of men called teamsters came along and piled the logs on giant sleds pulled by horses. They were then taken to a riverbank where they were stacked until spring.

Hauling the logs was an important and difficult task. Loggers had to keep the outside of the roads icy for sled runners, and the inside bare so that horses would not slip. The horses also had to have special shoes to help keep them from slipping. There was always the chance that the load would tip, get stuck, or rush out of control on a hill. Occasionally accidents did happen.

At the riverbanks workers called scalers measured each log in the huge piles and recorded its size in terms of the board feet

of lumber that could be cut from it. Stampers put the logging company's mark on the end of each log so that it could be identified at the sawmill. The logs were then ready to be pushed down the banks or rollways into the river and floated to sawmills.

The river drives

When the rivers were free from ice and their waters high from spring rains, skilled crews called river drivers began to float the logs downstream. Their job was to keep the logs moving and free from jams. It was a more exciting job than working in the woods, but very often dangerous.

A raft with a shed built on it moved along with the logs. This was called a wanigan, and it carried the cook, the food, and other supplies needed for the drive. Hot food and coffee were important to the river drivers, who were often cold and wet from wading after stray logs.

Log jams happened often and were usually dangerous. Sometimes river drivers worked weeks to break up a jam. When a jam finally broke, the logs pushed forward with such force that crews

Moving the logs down the rivers could often be a cold, wet, and dangerous job. Wanigans carrying supplies followed the drive.

had to rush to safety to avoid being killed. A giant log jam on the Grand River smashed three iron railroad bridges at Grand Rapids when it broke loose. A reporter from the Grand Rapids *Daily Democrat* wrote this:

> Following the broken spans of the bridge came the great mass of logs like a monster demon mad and bent on destruction. The logs groaned and pitched and tumbled in every conceivable shape in the mad chase through the breach. Wherever the water was visible, . . . it seethed and boiled and foamed like the whirlpool at Niagara. Logs were time and again thrown clear out of the water as they got out of the jam.

Log jams created problems for river drivers. This one occurred on the Grand River in 1883 and destroyed three railroad bridges.

When the logs finally reached the river's mouth, they were directed into booms, or floating dividers, that separated the river channel into sections. Crews of workers called sorters pushed the logs with their company's mark on them into the correct booms. The logs would then be tied together into rafts and towed by tugboats to the sawmill. When lumbering was at its peak in the state, the river drives of many companies created confusion. Separate boom companies were established to handle the traffic in the crowded rivers.

New methods and improvements

As lumbering became big business, companies found new and betters ways to do things. The invention of machines called big wheels made it possible for logs to be carried on something other than sleds. Invented by Silas Overpack of Manistee, these machines had two large wheels. Logs could be hooked by chains and dragged along between the wheels. The weight of the logs was not on the horse or horses that pulled the load, but on the axle between the wheels. And once the wheels began turning, they kept rolling along even with the heaviest loads. Big wheels made it possible for lumbering to continue even when there was no snow.

Another invention that made it possible to carry on lumbering throughout the year was devised by a young lumberman named Scott Gerrish, who worked in lumber camps along the Muskegon River. This was a small railroad train that would travel on tracks laid much closer together than those for regular trains. The ease of laying tracks for this narrow-gauge railroad made it

The big wheel allowed lumbermen to haul logs from the woods when sleds could not be used. They were used in the early 1870s.

possible to reach areas far from the rivers. At first, lines ran from these more distant forests to the rivers. Later, however, tracks were laid directly to the sawmills.

In the sawmills there were also changes. The first lumber sawed was rough and crooked. As the lumbering business grew, however, better saws were invented. Gang saws were used that cut several logs at one time. Large circular saws were also invented that cut boards smoothly and quickly.

The improvements and changes in the industry made it possible for companies to produce more lumber than ever before. Companies in the Saginaw valley were the state's leading producers. When timber ran out in this part of Michigan, the sawmills had logs brought in from the Canadian forests across Lake Huron. The region also became well-known for its timber-related industry of shipbuilding. Other mill cities on the eastern side of the state included Tawas City, Alpena, and Cheboygan.

But the Saginaw region was not the only one that prospered from the lumbering boom. Western Michigan's mill cities of Grand Rapids and Grand Haven were thriving. Muskegon, Ludington,

The narrow gauge railroad was the greatest boost to the lumber industry. The model shown here with a caterpillar type of engine was only used for a few years.

and Manistee were also busy with lumbering activity. On the Lake Michigan shore of the Upper Peninsula, the cities of Menominee, Escanaba, and Manistique developed a successful lumber trade. Munising and Grand Marais on Lake Superior and Sault Ste. Marie on the St. Marys River processed and exported lumber from Upper Peninsula forests.

Fortunes, failures, and fires

Besides Robert Dollar from Ontario, a number of businessmen became wealthy during Michigan's lumber boom. Some of them used their wealth to help their communities. Charles Hackley of Muskegon donated money for a library, an art gallery, and a hospital, and helped the community in other ways. He was only one millionaire, however, in a city that was reported to have forty lumber barons, as they were called. Other wealthy businessmen gained leadership roles in their communities in the state. Russell Alger, a governor and United States senator from Michigan, had

Charles W. Hackley, Lumber Baron

During Michigan's lumber boom, thousands came to the state seeking their fortunes. Many succeeded. Muskegon, which led the state in lumber production along with Saginaw, produced forty millionaires. One of these lumber barons was Charles W. Hackley.

Hackley came to Michigan to find a job in the lumber industry when he was nineteen years old. Since he was both pleasant and eager to work, he was quickly hired by Durkee, Truesdell and Company. When a depression upset the industry, Hackley's boss encouraged him to return to his home in Wisconsin and learn some accounting and bookkeeping skills.

When the lumbering business improved, Hackley returned to Muskegon. Eventually he and other partners purchased several mills. By 1880 he and his partners owned a logging railroad, ships to transport lumber, and timber lands in other states and Canada.

Unlike many lumber barons who took their fortunes and left the state, Hackley devoted both time and money to the community. He served in both the city and county government and was president of the board of education. His generous gifts to Muskegon included an art gallery, a public library, and a hospital. He also established other funds so that there would be money to help run them for many years.

David Jerome was one of several Michigan governors who made a fortune in the lumber industry. Before his success selling supplies to lumbering firms, he had an exciting life as a river driver, a steamboat captain, and a soldier.

made a fortune in lumbering. Other Michigan governors who had made their fortunes from the lumber boom were Henry Crapo, David Jerome, Aaron Bliss, and Josiah Begole.

The race for the green gold had its bad side. Entire forests were cut, and no effort was made to plant new trees. The Michigan countryside was dotted with stumps and strewn with brush. Wildlife left the area in search of new homes. Lumbermen seemed to give no thought to the wastelands they left behind. They had made their money.

Because lumbermen tended to think there was no end to the trees, they were also wasteful and careless. Thousands of logs were left to rot, since companies wanted to use only the finest wood. Every tree was cut instead of allowing the smaller ones to remain standing.

The scarred and ugly land the lumbermen left behind was very apt to catch fire. Not much of anything was left green, and even a small spark could lead to disaster. In the fall of 1871, after an extremely dry summer, huge fires broke out thoughout the Great Lakes area. The same day as the famous Chicago fire, a town named Peshtigo in northeastern Wisconsin also caught fire killing nearly 1,200 people. The fire moved into the towns and forest lands of Michigan's Upper Peninsula.

On the same day, fires also broke out in the Lower Peninsula. The town of Holland was destroyed in less than two hours. Farther north, the town of Manistee also burned. The fires continued

Dr. Douglass Houghton, state geologist, was a leading figure in starting the copper rush to the Upper Peninsula. Houghton was also a chemist and a doctor and had served as mayor of Detroit. He drowned in Lake Superior in 1845 at the age of 36.

to burn their way across the state to Saginaw Bay and the Thumb region.

Ten years later another huge fire struck the eastern part of the state, again after a very dry summer. About three hundred people lost their lives in the blaze, which was whipped out of control by a sudden gale. Again Michigan's land was scarred by an industry that had grown too quickly and without regard to the future.

Mining the copper

At the same time that Michigan was discovering its valuable timber resources in the 1840s, it was also beginning to use its copper resources in the western part of the Upper Peninsula. No mining had been done there since the Indian people had worked the deposits of copper centuries before. However, a few people knew that this resource existed. In the 1830s Dr. Douglass Houghton, a physician and scientist, explored the area with Henry Schoolcraft. When Houghton was appointed state geologist by Governor Mason in 1837, he immediately set out to find the real value of the copper deposits.

In 1841 Houghton presented a report to the Michigan legislature about the copper deposits in the Keweenaw Peninsula and in the Ontonagon River area of the Upper Peninsula. He pointed out that there were indeed rich deposits of the pure metal, called native copper. But he also stressed the problems of mining in the region. The area was undeveloped and far from any towns. The winters were long and bitter. Also, there was no easy way to move the copper to the Lower Peninsula, since a canal around the rapids on the St. Marys River had not yet been built.

But people rushed to the western part of the Upper Peninsula anyway. They expected to find masses of copper and become rich. They found that Houghton was right. It was a wilderness with swamps and thick forests. It was difficult to get food and other supplies, and what they did obtain was costly. In the summer the mosquitoes were a constant problem, and the winters were freezing cold. In addition, copper mining was hard work!

It was soon obvious that copper mining would take a large amount of work and money to be done successfully. Several companies began operations in the 1840s with investors from the East. Among the most successful was the Cliff Mine near Eagle River which was opened by the Boston and Pittsburgh Company. The Minesota Mine operated in the Ontonagon region, and the Quincy mine was located on the Keweenaw Peninsula.

To reach the copper deposits, miners had to dig a shaft, or opening, into the ground near the copper. From the shaft, tunnels were dug at different levels into the deposits. Miners used drills and sometimes explosives to break up the rock that contained the copper. Then they hauled the rock to the shaft in a wheelbarrow. It was lifted to the surface by a hoist that was driven by a large wheel and a horse. Later, steam engines were used to run the hoists.

The copper mines had brought many people to the western Upper Peninsula, and new towns were created. Houghton and Hancock were begun in the 1850s, and by 1860 the small village of Central had grown to a community of several hundred. Many of the area's new inhabitants came from Cornwall in England. Their experience working in tin mines in Cornwall was very valuable to the copper companies. Some of their methods, such as their way of hoisting rock to the surface, came to be used regularly in the Upper Peninsula mines. Their foods were also quickly adopted. Pasties, a mixture of meat, potatoes, and vegetables in a pie crust, are still famous in the Upper Peninsula today. These would stay warm for a long period of time, and miners took them into the mines in their back pockets.

The Cliff Mine operated in the Keweenaw Peninsula from the 1840s to 1870. Its owners earned over 2.5 million dollars.

The peak years

The Civil War brought new demands and higher prices for metals, including copper. Although some of the Michigan mines were beginning to run out of copper, others were opened. One was started after a discovery was made by a mining engineer named Edwin Hulbert. While exploring in a region north of Portage Lake in the Upper Peninsula, Hulbert found some interesting pieces of copper on the ground. Searching further, he came upon a pit. At the bottom of the pit he found stone hammers, copper ornaments, and ancient birchbark baskets used by Indians centuries before. Hulbert's discovery led to the establishment of the largest, most successful mine in the Upper Peninsula, the Calumet-Hecla.

Just as in lumbering, improved methods and machinery helped the copper industry grow. Steam hoists were used to bring rock from the shaft, and miners had new types of air drills instead of the hand-operated ones they had been using. Better explosives were also invented, and the process of stamping, or removing the metal from the rock, was improved.

Life in the copper country also changed drastically. The Calumet and Hecla Mining Company, for example, invested large amounts of money in the nearby communities. A library, hospital, and several parks made life more comfortable. Elegant theaters and opera houses were also built. The company also took care of everyday things for the miners' families. It produced electricity for their homes, supplied coal for heat, and even collected garbage.

Importance was also placed on education in mining towns. Many Easterners came to direct the mining companies, and they helped organize good schools in the area. Michigan lawmakers also established the Michigan College of Mines at Houghton. By 1891 the college was producing more mining engineers than any other college in the country.

Even with its schools and theaters, life in the copper country had its problems. Julia Hubbard Adams spent part of her childhood in Houghton and later described those years. She told about taking a hot-water bottle to bed during the long cold winters and wading in snow up to her waist as she made her way to school. In the summer, dust from the unpaved roads settled into the houses. She wrote:

> It seemed to me that my mother spent half her life brushing, brushing, brushing. . . . And then, of course, when the rains came there was MUD! Shelden Street had board walks for sidewalks and planks were laid across it at intervals to make a crossing possible. If you lost your balance and stepped off

Easterners who came to Copper Country wanted to live in a civilized way. They built schools and theaters and enjoyed a variety of social functions.

the board you could easily sink over your ankle in thick mud.
. . . For people who have never experienced it, I do not think
it is quite possible to gauge the impact of unpaved roads on
life.

Until 1887 Michigan was the nation's biggest copper producer. When mining began in the western states, Michigan lost
its leadership role. However, its mines continued to produce high-
grade copper.

As in other industries, there were also problems. By the late
1800s and early 1900s workers began to form labor unions. The
companies, which felt they had taken care of their workers as a
father would take care of his children, were angry and fired miners who tried to work for change. For many years there were a
number of strikes and riots.

The longest and most bitter strike began in 1913 at the Calumet and Hecla Mining Company. Michigan's governor had to
send troops to stop the violence. While the strike was in progress,
a tragedy occurred. Four hundred miners and their families were
holding a Christmas party when a cry of "fire" rang through the
hall. Frantically the people tried to rush out the only door and

*The Calumet and
Hecla Mining Com-
pany became the
giant in the copper
mining business.
It began its opera-
tions after the Civil
War.*

down a staircase. There was panic. People shoved and women and children fell forward down the stairs. The mob rushed over them, and seventy-three people died, most of them children.

There had been no fire. It was a senseless tragedy. Labor union leaders blamed the company managers, but no wrongdoing could be proved. Gradually, the strike came to an end. But the event had left a bloody stain on the copper industry.

Iron mining begins

At the same time Douglass Houghton was making surveys in the copper country, one of his surveyors named William Burt was measuring some territory near the present-day city of Marquette. Burt noticed his compass needle acting in a strange way. Looking around, he discovered some large pieces of iron ore that were causing the disturbance.

When a prospector named Philo M. Everett heard about Burt's discovery, he journeyed to the region looking for iron ore. Unable to locate any, he went to an Indian settlement and asked for help. An Ojibwa chief, named Marji-Gesiek, took him to a huge felled tree and showed him large chunks of ore in the roots and soil. He also pointed to a ridge of rock nearby, which Everett described as a 150-foot mountain of solid ore. The excited Everett then traveled to the town of Copper Harbor on the Keweenaw Peninsula to lease the land. By 1847 the Jackson Mining Company, which was owned by Everett, had begun to mine the iron ore. Marji-Gesiek was given stock in the company for helping locate the ore.

William Burt discovered iron ore deposits while doing a geological survey in the Upper Peninsula. He found the iron ore because of the unusual actions of his solar compass, which Burt himself had invented.

Since much of the ore was on the surface, it was quite easily mined. Miners could break the ore into manageable chunks with sledge hammers and other tools. But moving it was a problem. The harbor at Marquette, on the shore of Lake Superior, was only about twelve miles away. But there was no road or railroad, and the route was hilly and forested. At first the ore was hauled by sled in the winter. Later a plank road was built, and horses pulled wagons filled with ore. A railroad was started, but a number of years passed before it was completed.

The Jackson company and other early companies built small blast furnaces to smelt the iron before it was transported. Some of these blast furnaces, or forges, as they were called, operated for many years. Most producers of iron ore made more money, however, by shipping the ore to larger blast furnaces in other parts of the country.

The problems of transporting the iron ore did not end when the heavy mineral reached the harbor at Marquette. Loading the ore onto the ships was a major task until late in the 1850s. At that time the Cleveland Iron Mining Company built a high sturdy

The Jackson Mine at Negaunee was the state's first iron mine and led others in iron ore production for seventy-five years. The first mines were open pits like the one shown. After 1870 companies began undergound mining.

In the mid-1800s the Jackson Mining Company used this shipping dock in Marquette. Railroad tracks were built out over the water so that ore could be dumped into the waiting ships.

dock far out into the harbor. On top were railroad tracks that allowed trains to push their loads out over the water. Beneath the docks were ships, ready to be filled with ore. The mineral was then sent down chutes from the railroad cars into the ships' cargo areas.

The Soo locks

When the ore carriers left Marquette, they faced another problem. At the rapids in the St. Marys River at Sault Ste. Marie their cargoes had to be unloaded and moved to another carrier below the rapids. The process took a great deal of time and labor. There were also few ships built along Lake Superior, and ore carriers for that part of the journey were in short supply.

Governor Mason's program to build a canal at Sault Ste. Marie had never really gotten off the ground. (See page 149.) One of the problems was the permission needed from the United States Congress. Three times a bill was defeated that would give Michigan the federal land needed for the project. Senator Henry Clay

Building the Soo Locks and Canal was a huge task without modern machinery. Still, the job which was supervised by Charles Harvey, took only two years.

was outspoken in his views on a canal in that area. It would be, in his words, "a work quite beyond the remotest settlement of the United States if not in the moon."

The growing copper and iron industries along Lake Superior proved that Clay was wrong. A canal was desperately needed, and in 1852 plans were finally approved by Congress. The project had to be completed in ten years, however, or the land would be lost.

A young man named Charles Harvey was hired to head the canal-and-lock project, which was known as the St. Marys Falls Ship Canal Company. The task was a huge one. Workers had to be brought in from the East, since many of the men who had worked transporting loads around the rapids refused to work on the project. During the long winter months no progress could be made. An epidemic of cholera also slowed the work. Then, when the project was nearly done, it was discovered that the canal had to be a foot deeper. Correcting this error caused additional loss of time and money.

On June 18, 1855, the steamer *Illinois* passed through the locks, the first to do so. In spite of the difficulties, the project had been completed in just two years. Although its cost was nearly twice as much as planned, the company made large sums of money. In terms of time, money, and need, it was perhaps the best project the state had yet undertaken.

The growth of iron mining

The Soo Canal and Locks ("Soo" is the short name commonly used for Sault Ste. Marie) gave a giant boost to the iron-ore industry. So did the Civil War. And demands for iron after the war continued as industry grew rapidly in Michigan and the rest of the nation.

Part of the iron industry's growth was due to new methods and machines, just as it was in the copper industry. Steam-powered machinery was used in the mines, and by 1895 the mines were lighted by electric power. Miners also had more safety equipment, such as hard hats, boots, and glasses that would not shatter.

New and better ships were built to transport the ore on the Great Lakes. In the 1880s iron ships began to replace wooden sailing ships and steamboats. A new design called the whaleback, resembling the submarine of later years, became a common ore

Iron whalebacks often passed through the Soo Locks around the turn of the century. They were thought to be very safe ships, but they did not hold very large cargoes of iron ore and were hard to unload.

carrier. The size, construction, and design of the carriers continued to improve as years went by.

In the Marquette range, the first area of iron mining in the Upper Peninsula, mining companies continued to prosper. When the surface ore was gone, companies sank shafts to reach the rich deposits beneath the earth. A railroad was built to transport the ore to Escanaba, a port on Lake Michigan. Railroads continued to be built and were important not only for hauling ore to ports on the Great Lakes, but also in bringing supplies to remote mining towns.

In the last part of the 1800s, mining began in two other ranges in the Upper Peninsula. Iron mines were opened in the Menominee Range near the Wisconsin border in 1877. Iron Mountain, Iron River, and Crystal Falls became important mining towns in that area. Farther west the Gogebic Range was discovered, although much of the ore was on the Wisconsin side of the border. Most of the iron ore there was carried to Ashland, Wisconsin, a port on Lake Superior.

During the 1890s Michigan was the nation's leading producer of iron ore. But by 1900 the Mesabi Range in Minnesota

Today the Soo Canal and Locks are still a vital part of the Great Lakes waterway. Many changes have been made since the 1850s. Four locks, one which can accommodate extra-large freighters, allows ships to travel through the area without long delays.

A Lost Resource

In the late 1800s Michigan was one of the favorite homes of huge flocks of passenger pigeons. These beautiful and graceful birds had sleek feathers of deep purple and shades of red and blue. They came in the early spring and built nests while feeding on acorns and beechnuts. Flocks were so big that the weight of the many birds and their nests would break branches from trees.

For many years the pigeons were ignored by everyone but the Indians and the settlers who killed a few for food. But young pigeons, or squabs, became a popular food at fine restaurants. Hunters came from distant states to trap the birds and sell them to restaurants. Squabs were knocked from their nests and pigeons of all sizes were lured by grain into net traps. Hunters twisted off the heads of most birds and packed them for shipment to large cities. Some birds were kept alive and sold to sportsmen for target practice.

In 1878 the last large flock of passenger pigeons came to Michigan. The mass of birds was so large that it was said to have formed a dark cloud about forty miles long and five miles wide as it moved across the sky! But hundreds of hunters were waiting. It is believed that well over three million of these birds were killed and shipped from Michigan's forests.

By the early 1890s, people in Michigan still reported seeing small flocks of passenger pigeons in the spring. But most had been killed by hunters. The few that remained had trouble finding food or trees to nest in, since most of Michigan's forests had been destroyed by lumbermen and forest fires. Within a few years, the passenger pigeon was a bird of the past.

It was many years before Michigan's people began to value their resources. Too many times these resources were destroyed by people's greed. And some, like the passenger pigeon, could never be regained.

1911

Fishing was an important industry in many harbor towns along the Great Lakes. This 1911 photo shows commercial fishermen in Grand Haven in the state's western Lower Peninsula.

took over the lead. Michigan mines continued to produce important quantities of the mineral, however. In both World War I and World War II, this Michigan resource was vital to the entire nation.

The fishing industry

Another resource that provided Michigan's people with a way to earn a living was fishing. In 1860 fishing was listed as Michigan's most important industry after farming and lumbering. Most of the commercial fishing was done in the Great Lakes, off the coasts of the Upper Peninsula and the northern half of the Lower Peninsula. The most common fish taken were whitefish, lake trout, and perch. They were packed in salt and shipped in barrels, since there was no refrigeration. By the turn of the century, fishing had begun to decline. It is still, however, a minor industry in the state.

MICHIGAN

IN TIME

Date	In Michigan	Outside Michigan
1890	Michigan is first in iron ore production (1890-1900) Dow Chemical Company is organized (1890) Railroad car building is Detroit's leading industry (1890) Durant-Dort Carriage Company is incorporated (1895) C. W. Post begins manufacturing health foods (1895) The first autos are driven in Michigan by Charles King & Henry Ford (1896) Olds Motor Works begins (1899)	Thomas Edison patents his moving-picture camera (1891) Grover Cleveland is U.S. President (1893) Duryea brothers successfully test an auto in Massachusetts (1893) Sears & Roebuck opens mail order business (1895) William McKinley becomes U.S. President (1897) Spanish-American War (1898-1899)
1900	25% of Michigan's people work in factory jobs (1900) Ford Motor Company begins (1903) Buick Motors Company begins making cars (1903) Reo Motor Car Company is formed by Ransom Olds (1904) W. K. Kellogg starts the Toasted Corn Flake Company (1906) General Motors Company is organized by William Durant (1908) Ford begins the production of Model Ts, or Tin Lizzies (1908)	United States Steel Corporation is formed, the largest in the world (1901) McKinley is shot; Theodore Roosevelt takes over (1901) Packard auto travels across the U.S. in 52 days (1903) Wright brothers make first airplane flights (1903) The first motion picture with a plot is produced (1903) San Francisco earthquake (1906) First radio broadcast (1906) William H. Taft becomes U.S. President (1909)
1910	Chevrolet Motor Company is organized (1911) Dodge Brothers begin auto production (1914) Ford offers workers $5 per day (1914) Ford Motor Company leads the auto industry (1915)	Titanic sinks (1912) Woodrow Wilson becomes U.S. President (1913) Panama Canal opens (1914) World War I (1914-1918) First phone call across the nation (1914)

Chapter 10

[Henry Ford was] driving his mechanical buggy, sitting there at the lever jauntily dressed in a tightbuttoned jacket and a high collar and a derby hat, back and forth over the level illpaved streets of Detroit,

*   scaring the big brewery horses and the skinny trotting horses and the sleekrumped pacers with the motor's loud explosions,*

*   looking for men scatterbrained enough to invest money in a factory for building automobiles.*

from "Tin Lizzie" in *U.S.A.* by John Dos Passos
Copyright 1937 by John Dos Passos.
Reprinted by permission of Mrs. John
Dos Passos.

Leader in a Changing World

At Chicago's 1893 Columbian Exposition, a huge exhibit of industrial products, crowds were drawn to the booth of the Michigan Stove Company. A fifteen-ton, twenty-five-foot-high stove towered over the display of normal-size stoves produced by this Detroit company. The giant stove was built especially for the Exposition to advertise the "Garland" cookstoves, which the company called the "greatest invention of the age." The chief engineer, William Keep, had discovered a combination of cast iron and aluminum that had made the company's 700 styles of stoves so popular that about 75,000 were sold each year.

Although the Garland cookstoves, with the exception of one model, were still fueled by wood and coal in the 1890s (gas stoves were considered a novelty), the Michigan Stove Company was an industrial leader in many ways. Its headquarters was located in Detroit, but there were branches in Buffalo, New York City, and Chicago as well as in foreign countries. When the Detroit factory burned in 1907, the company quickly built a new plant which was extremely modern and efficient. Each employee worked on only one aspect of the manufacturing process, becoming a specialist in that area. The company had modern showrooms and took advantage of the latest advertising trends to sell its products.

The Michigan Stove Company was not the only firm to make Michigan a leader in stove production. Its president, Jeremiah Dwyer, had a brother James who was also in the business. James

After the 1893 Columbian Exposition, the Michigan Stove Company displayed their giant stove model at their plant in Detroit.

Dwyer founded the Peninsular Stove Company, also in Detroit. Nineteen additional stove factories were located in Lansing, Dowagiac, and other Michigan cities. In Kalamazoo a stove company organized in 1900 sold stoves through mail orders. Its slogan became famous: "Kalamazoo Direct to You."

At the turn of the century, stove manufacturing was one of many industries pushing Michigan and the rest of the nation into an era of great industrial growth. Their products were bringing changes to the lives of every American. And to a nation that had been built by the sweat and toil of long, hard physical labor, these inventions and changes were almost unbelievable!

The growth of manufacturing

A large part of the story of industry in Michigan lies, of course, with the development and manufacture of the automobile, which began early in the twentieth century. But for many years Michigan's industrial growth had nothing to do with automaking. Instead, many different industries began to develop in the last half

MORTON HOUSE LIVERY.

of the 1800s. Some, such as the production of furniture and cereal, laid the groundwork for companies that are still in operation today. Others were short-lived. But the rise of these industries and the jobs they offered Michigan's people was the beginning of the state's change from an economy based on agriculture to one based on manufacturing. In 1850 about one percent of Michigan's workers had what could be called factory jobs. By 1900 that figure had risen to twenty-five percent.

Most of Michigan's early manufacturing companies were small ones, each employing only a handful of workers. It was not until the turn of the century that companies such as Michigan Stove were employing large numbers of workers. Also, many of the industries, such as bakeries and flour mills, served local needs. There were not yet factories like those in the New England states, for example, that produced huge amounts of textiles to be sold all across the nation. Until the 1870s most business activity in Michigan revolved around the exporting of raw materials such as copper and iron ore and the buying and selling of everyday items. Although these beginnings were modest ones, drastic changes were on the way.

Wagons and carriages were built in Michigan before automobiles made them out-of-date. Flint, Jackson, and Pontiac all claimed to be the leader in wagon production.

Industry and resources

The stove industry began in Michigan largely because of the difficulty of getting stove parts from the East. This was not the case with most of Michigan's other industries in the late 1800s. They began as a natural outgrowth of resources available in the state: furniture-making from wood, food-processing from farming, and ship-building from lumbering and the abundant water resources. These industries provided a launching pad for Michigan's industrial growth, which began to make important progress after the Civil War. In 1860, for example, there were only 1,363 manufacturing jobs in Detroit. By 1870 that number had risen to 10,612.

Farming, the main occupation of the early settlers, quickly led to the development of a number of industries. For many years wheat was the main farm crop. Grist mills that turned the grain into flour were early factories that sprang up particularly in the southern part of the state. By 1890 various grains were used to make cereal. The center of that production was in Battle Creek, where W. K. Kellogg and C. W. Post were both interested in de-

The Ferry Seed Company of Detroit sold seeds to people all over the country through stores and catalogs.

veloping health foods. Post's Grape-Nuts (they were first called Elija's Manna) and Kellogg's Corn Flakes were early products that are still popular today.

Several other industries developed because of the many farms in the state. D. M. Ferry & Company of Detroit produced seeds and sold them through stores and catalogs. By the end of the 1800s Ferry employed hundreds of people, both in his warehouse and on the farm where the seeds were grown. Some companies also began to produce farm machinery. The Gale Manufacturing Company of Albion was famous for its plows and cultivators, and the Advance Thresher Company of Battle Creek claimed to make more threshing machinery than any other city in the nation.

Lumbering had also had its impact on the growth of several major industries in Michigan. Furniture made from Michigan's hardwood forests became a major industry in the city of Grand Rapids. The first furniture factories began in that city in the mid-1800s. By the end of the century they had grown in number and reputation. Today, over a century later, Grand Rapids and neighboring cities are well-known for office furniture, even though wood is no longer the main raw material.

Post Toasties was only one of several cereals that made the Michigan city of Battle Creek famous for cereal production.

The Morning Chorus: **Post Toasties** –"The Memory Lingers" 'Most as much fun as a Christmas tree!

Michigan's lumber supply as well as its location along the Great Lakes helped create a shipbuilding industry in the state in the 1800s. The first ships produced were sailing vessels, which were often built by the individual owners in many different locations along the Great Lakes. Gradually, however, the building of boats became an industry. In 1827 the first steamboat was built in Detroit and in fifty years over 175 steamboats had been produced in that area. Other factories sprang up to supply the shipbuilding business with engines, varnishes, and other boat needs. The change from wood to steel as the most important material for ships shook the industry as the 1800s came to a close. However, the production of ships continued in Michigan well into the 1900s.

Another industry that relied on wood was the manufacture of wagons and carriages. For many years the wagon industry in Michigan was made up of many small companies throughout the southern part of the state. Cities such as Jackson and Pontiac both claimed to lead the others, while Flint called itself the "Vehicle City." In the 1880s larger wagon and carriage companies began to appear. The Flint Wagon Works produced about 50,000 vehicles a year at the peak of its business. In 1895 the Durant-Dort Carriage Company was incorporated and was producing

Elijah McCoy

One of the people who stands out in Michigan's history is Elijah McCoy, a black inventor. McCoy's parents were slaves who escaped to Canada. Elijah was born there in 1844. After receiving an elementary education he studied mechanical engineering at the University of Edinburgh in Scotland.

McCoy came to Ypsilanti, Michigan, hoping to become a mechanical engineer. Companies refused to hire him for this job, however, because he was black. As a result, he took a job as a fireman on the Michigan Central Railroad.

McCoy's genius could not be ignored. In 1872 he patented his first major invention, a cup designed to lubricate machinery. McCoy went on to invent many more lubricating devices, now as an employee at a Detroit firm. In his career he produced seventy-eight inventions, and later in life also had his own company.

about 100,000 vehicles at the beginning of the 1900s. By this time, however, most of Michigan's timber resources had been used, and it was necessary for carriage companies to import lumber from the southern states.

Paper was another early product made in Michigan. The first paper mills did not use wood in their manufacturing processes, however, but made paper from rags and straw from the wheat fields. It was not until nearly 1900 that wood pulp began to be used for paper in Michigan mills. Most of these paper mills were located in cities along rivers such as the Raisin, the Huron, the St. Joseph, and the Kalamazoo, since a plentiful supply of water was necessary for papermaking.

Shipbuilding was done in many places along the Great Lakes. This stern wheeler, "the Grand," was built in 1905 in Grand Rapids.

Industries at the turn of the century

As the 1800s came to a close, Michigan's industries began to grow more diverse. Although many of them still relied on the available resources, others did not. The manufacture of chewing tobacco and other tobacco products, for instance, was one of De-

The Interurban

In 1891 a railway was completed between Ypsilanti and Ann Arbor, seven and a half miles away. The railway, which became known as the interurban, was the first of its kind in Michigan. Halfway between a streetcar and a regular railroad train, the interurban could be built more cheaply than a regular railroad. Although the first ones were powered by steam engines, later interurbans were run with electric motors.

The interurban line between Ann Arbor and Ypsilanti was an instant success. Fare was ten cents, while the railroad charged a quarter for the same distance. The University of Michigan students, most of whom were males at that time, were some of the interurban's most important customers. They traveled back and forth to Michigan State Normal (now Eastern Michigan University) where most of the students were females.

Within ten years a large network of interurban lines was built in Michigan. A large number went from Detroit to outlying cities such as Royal Oak and Pontiac, but there were also interurbans in other parts of the state. In Jackson, lines ran to Lansing, Marshall and other cities. An interurban system linked the communities of Muskegon, Holland, Grand Haven, and Saugatuck to Grand Rapids. In the Upper Peninsula interurbans ran between Ironwood and Bessemer, Negaunee and Ispeming, and several other towns.

The increased production of automobiles and the development of good roads brought interurban transportation to an end in the 1920s. Many of its customers bought cars and drove them to work or the beach or to do their shopping. With cars it was easy to come and go without having to meet the interurban schedule. Besides, it was great fun to take the Tin Lizzie or the "Merry Oldsmobile"!

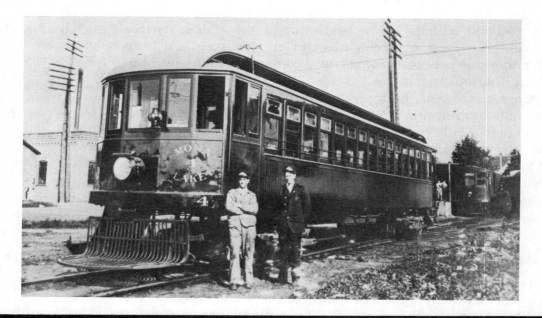

troit's leading industries in the late 1800s. The tobacco was not grown in Michigan, but was imported from farms in Canada.

One of the booming businesses in Detroit during the 1890s was the railroad car industry. A number of companies in the "car" business, as it was then called, joined forces to become the Michigan-Peninsular Car Company. This company made Detroit the nation's leader in the production of railroad cars, employing about 9,000 men at the turn of the century. The success of that industry in Michigan was short-lived, however. By 1910 it had already begun its decline.

Although salt had been mined in Michigan since the 1860s, new uses for it were developed toward the turn of the century. A chemist from Ohio named Herbert Dow came to Michigan to experiment with a salt brine well near Midland in 1890. His experiments and discoveries resulted in the establishment of the Dow Chemical Company. Other chemical companies were begun in the state because of the salt resources. Captain John B. Ford, a leader in the paint industry in the East, started a chemical company in Detroit with his son and grandsons. Another large chemical company in the Detroit area called the Solvay Process Company also

Between 1880 and 1890 Michigan produced half of the nation's salt. At this salt plant in Manistee, wells pumped salt brine to the surface. After the water evaporated, the salt was shipped out in barrels.

made a business of creating baking soda, soda ash, and other by-products of Michigan's salt mines.

The Ford family of the salt and chemical business also helped to start another of Michigan's important industries. They began to produce cement from Michigan's marl deposits. (Marl is a mixture of clay and limestone.) Although cement is still made in Michigan today, it is now produced with limestone in a process that is less costly than the original cement-making process that used marl.

The birth of the automobile

The story of the automobile did not begin in Michigan, nor did it begin with that famous Michigan automobile manufacturer Henry Ford. The gasoline-powered, internal combustion engine that became the standard source of power for automobiles was first successfully developed in Germany in the late 1800s. Europeans such as Gottlieb Daimler and Carl Benz began manufacturing cars somewhat earlier than developers in the United States.

Inventors living in the eastern part of the United States began experimenting with the gasoline engine in the 1870s. It was not until 1893, however, that an engine in the United States was successfully adapted to an automobile. This feat was accomplished in Springfield, Massachusetts, by Charles and Frank Duryea. They then put their experimental automobile into production, founding the Duryea Motor Wagon Company in 1895.

At the same time that the Duryeas began producing automobiles, or horseless carriages, as they were then called, many other people were working on ideas for a motor vehicle. The most famous of these was, of course, Henry Ford. Ford was born in Dearborn, Michigan, the son of a prosperous farmer. Young Ford was not interested in farming, however, because he believed it required too much physical labor. He had a love of machinery that was to lead him to wealth and fame.

In the mid 1890s Henry Ford was chief engineer for the Edison Illuminating Company. But in his small backyard workshop, Henry was building a gas-operated vehicle that he called a quadricycle. When the time came for Henry to make his test run, he found he had overlooked something. The small cart-like machine, which was steered with a tiller, was too large to move out the door. According to stories, he quickly knocked out part of a brick wall to get his experimental vehicle under way.

The quadricycle that Henry Ford drove up and down the streets of Dearborn was not entirely his own creation. Giving him advice along the way was Charles B. King, a man who had already invented a vehicle of his own. But King had many other interests, including art and music, and he was not interested in automobile manufacturing. Henry was. But it was not until 1903 that Ford was really on the way to producing horseless carriages.

The beginning of the Oldsmobile

While Henry Ford was developing his car and a company to manufacture it, another automobile pioneer was also hard at work. Ransom E. Olds belonged to a family who owned an engine company in Lansing. A bright and energetic young man, Olds developed a successful steam engine and then an engine powered by gasoline. Once he had completed the gasoline engine, he went to work adapting it to a carriage.

Although the sales of Olds's engine alone made him a financial success, he was anxious to move ahead into new and risky

Henry Ford was only one of several men who were first to experiment with automobiles. But he made an impact on the industry and the nation quite unlike any of the other automotive leaders.

ventures. With a number of financial supporters, Ransom Olds formed the Olds Motor Works in 1899. He based his auto company in Detroit, where his partners were located, and became the first auto manufacturer in that city. Within a few years, however, he moved the company to Lansing.

The first few years of Ransom Olds's business were uncertain ones. Although he had first planned to build a small, easy-to-operate vehicle that would please the average buyer, Olds began experimenting with many types of cars. When none of these were particularly successful, he went back to his original plan, producing what was called an Oldsmobile. This small runabout, which looked something like a wagon, had a one-cylinder engine and sold for $600. By the end of 1901 the company had produced 450 Oldsmobiles, an incredible number at that time. By 1905 the company was manufacturing 6,500 of these popular vehicles a year.

In 1904 Ransom Olds sold his stock in the company that bore his name. With new associates, he started the Reo Motor Car Company in Lansing. The Reo cars and trucks made by this company remained on the market until the 1930s. Even though the Reo Motor Car Company did not survive, Olds was a great leader in the industry. He had proven without a doubt that automobile manufacturing was an up-and-coming industry that promised its investors unbelievable profits.

The development of the Tin Lizzie

While Ransom Olds was producing cars that sold, Henry Ford was having a difficult time getting a manufacturing company under way. Although he was able to find financial backers, he was uncertain that he had developed a car that was good enough to sell. Many of those who supported him withdrew in disgust.

The Reo was manufactured by Ramson Olds and his Reo Motor Car Company. Olds advertised that his car had been tested in a trip from New York to San Francisco in 10 days, 15 hours, and 13 minutes. Its price: $1,300.

For a time Ford concentrated on racing cars, which he was able to build satisfactorily. But racing cars were hardly what the country needed at the turn of the century. The real market continued to be for a small, inexpensive car like the Oldsmobile.

Finally, in 1903, Henry Ford signed with a group of investors and began the Ford Motor Company. The company built a runabout called the Model A, but again Ford did not want the cars to be shipped out. There were defects, he declared, and the cars should undergo more work before the company offered them for sale. This time, however, one of the firm's investors, James Couzens, insisted the cars be sold. In spite of Ford's protests, the cars went on the market. The Model A was a success, and within a year the Ford Motor Company was already free of financial worry.

Over the next few years the Ford Motor Company produced several new models. But in 1908 the historic Tin Lizzie made its debut. Unlike most automobiles, the Tin Lizzie, or Model T, had the steering wheel on the left side and an engine that was made of one cast iron piece instead of several. It was easy to repair, and stories were told that this car could be driven forever. It earned its nickname, however, because it seemed to develop rattles easily, and jokes about it were abundant. It was typical to hear comments like this: "After all, the Ford is the best family car. It has a tank for Father, a hood for Mother, and a rattle for Baby."

This 1910 Ford Model T, or Tin Lizzie, had a bucket seat in the rear and a tank on the running board with headlight fuel. Ford said the Tin Lizzie could be ordered in any color as long as it was black.

Mass production was the key to making automobiles affordable. Each group of workers had a special task as the automobiles were assembled.

No matter how much it rattled, the Tin Lizzie was an all-time bestseller. Its price was affordable to everyone except the very poor. Starting at $850 in 1908, Ford found ways to bring the price down drastically. By 1916 the Model T sold for $360! Even more amazing was the fact that the Model T was produced by Ford for nearly nineteen years. For most of that time it was the only model produced by the Ford Motor Company.

The key to making the Model T affordable was mass production. The idea was not a new one at the turn of the century, but it had not been applied to so complicated a product. Ford and his staff divided the task of building a car into 84 operations. Special groups were assigned to each operation. The car passed along an assembly line to each of the groups. The experts in one operation quickly did their job and allowed the auto to move along to another operation. In this way a vehicle could be produced at least three times as fast as it could with the same workers assembling the entire car. The cost of each car, then, was greatly reduced, allowing the company to sell its product at a lower price.

Becoming the leader

The huge success of the Model T spurred the growth of the Ford Motor Company. But there were other reasons for the company's growing popularity. One was a huge lawsuit against the Ford company, as well as several other automobile companies, by a man named George Selden. Selden had patented a gasoline engine in the 1890s, and he and his associates believed that automobile manufacturers should buy licenses from them before producing cars. Ford was one of the automobile companies that had not done so.

The trial, which went on for a long time, created a great deal of publicity. Then, quite unexpectedly, the judge sided with Selden. Other automobile companies gave up the fight, purchasing licenses from Selden no matter what the cost. But Henry Ford did not. Instead he appealed the case in a higher court and won. The incident made Ford something of a hero. Selden and his associates had made up a powerful trust that people believed could not be broken. But the maker of Tin Lizzies had won the fight!

Thousands flocked to the Ford Motor company in 1914 when Ford announced he would pay workers an amazing $5.00 a day! Of course, there were strings attached to the offer.

After winning his court case, Henry Ford went on to create another sensation. In 1914 he advertised that he would pay his employees a minimum of $5.00 a day, double the amount paid by other automobile companies. Thousands of workers flocked to the Ford company, creating such a disturbance that fire hoses had to be used to control the crowd. In the fine print Henry Ford had qualified his offer. The men had to work for six months before that rate of pay could begin. They also had to be men who met his moral standards—that is, men who didn't smoke, drink, or cheat on their wives. Still, the public did not seem to mind. Henry Ford was a hero of the people. By 1915 the Ford Motor Company had become the leader in the automotive world.

The birth of General Motors

In the early 1900s many different cars were being built, not only in Michigan, but in other states as well. One of them was the Buick, built by David Buick of Detroit. But Buick was a better inventor than a businessman and was unable to make the Buick company a success. In 1903 it was purchased by the Flint Wagon

Ford was not the only one to use mass production methods. This photo shows an early General Motors assembly line.

Works. A year later the Buick company was still struggling. Its owners decided to hire a successful carriage maker by the name of William C. Durant to save the failing auto company.

Durant began his spectacular career in the automobile industry with a program to promote the Buick. He took it to all types of races and contests. Within four years the Buick was competing with Ford for the best-known car on the market. But Durant had ideas that were different from Ford's. He did not believe that one car could give lasting success and set about to buy up automobile companies. To carry out his plan for acquiring these companies he formed the General Motors Company in 1908, years before most investors would take a chance that the automobile industry would last.

Within a few years Durant had achieved remarkable success. He had purchased the Olds Motor Works, followed by the Cadillac and Oakland Motor Car Company, which became the Pontiac line. He also bought several truck and car companies that did not survive. At one point Durant came close to purchasing the Ford Motor Company. Henry Ford, who was ill at the time, agreed to sell his company to Durant for $8,000,000. Durant, however, was

William Durant formed the General Motors Company and the Chevrolet Motor Car Company. In this photo his son is driving the Chevrolet. Durant himself is in the front row of men on the right.

unable to raise the money and complete this business deal that would have drastically changed automotive history.

A recession in 1910 led to other history-setting changes. Short on money, Durant was forced to borrow from bankers in the East. They insisted, however, that Durant step out of the company's leadership role for five years. During that time Durant directed his efforts to a new company, the Chevrolet Motor Car Company. By the end of the five years, Durant had made enough money to buy back General Motors stock and become company president once again. This time the company became the present General Motors Corporation.

Durant did not spend the remainder of his career as head of General Motors, however. Another recession in 1921 again forced Durant from leadership, and once again he formed a new automobile company, Durant Motors. Although his company was successful for a time, Durant was unable to repeat his earlier spectacular performance. He later lost his fortune in the Depression and died a poor man.

Probably more than any other invention, the automobile changed the life of people throughout the nation.

Michigan takes the lead

Although the first automobile had been built in Massachusetts and automobile factories sprang up in dozens of cities, Detroit had firmly taken the national lead by the early 1900s. Other cities were as well suited as Detroit to become automobile manufacturing centers, with good transportation, a ready supply of labor, and access to raw materials. But Detroit seemed to have something that the others did not—an assortment of talented people who had the imagination and daring to take risks. Henry Ford and William Durant and David Buick and Ransom Olds happened to be Michigan people who might have been successful anywhere. But together they gave the industry the spark it needed and helped to make Michigan a new industrial leader.

The automobile did more than create one giant new industry, however. It spurred dozens of other businesses. Suddenly the nation needed new and better road systems, gas stations, and parking lots. It needed more factories to produce gasoline and rubber tires and automobile parts. Travelers needed restaurants and motels.

The automobile also changed American life in so many ways that an entire book could be devoted to it. It affected almost every part of life, from the world of fashion, where designers made long coats and goggles for automobile operators, to farming, where the introduction of trucks and tractors made revolutionary changes. When two sociologists named Robert and Helen Lynd wrote a book in the 1920s about life in America, one of the people they interviewed said it this way: "Why on earth do you need to study what's changing this country? I can tell you what's happening in just four letters: A-U-T-O."

MICHIGAN

IN TIME

Date	In Michigan	Outside Michigan
1880	Ferris Institute opens (1884) Child labor law passed (1885) 10-hour workday law is passed (1885) Grand Hotel opens on Mackinac Island (1887) Jo Labadie becomes first president of Michigan Federation of Labor (1889) Hazen Pingree is Detroit's mayor (1889)	Chester Arthur becomes President after shooting of Pres. James Garfield (1881) Haymarket Square Massacre between police & strikers (1885) American Federation of Labor founded (1886) Jane Addams opens Hull House in Chicago (1889)
1890	A railroad ferry line begins operating between Frankfort, Mich. & Kewaunee, Wis. (1892) Central Michigan College of Education opens in Mt. Pleasant (1895) Pingree becomes governor (1897) Northern Michigan College of Education opens in Marquette (1899)	Massacre at Wounded Knee kills over 200 Indians (1890) Four-year depression begins (Panic of 1893) Supreme Court says segregation of blacks is legal (1895) Boston has first subway (1897)
1900	Fred Warner is governor (1905) State highway department organized (1905) Western Michigan School of Education opens (1905) Third Michigan constitution is approved (1908) Citizens can choose candidates for governor & other offices (1909) First concrete road in Detroit (1909)	Department of Commerce and Labor established (1903) "Wobblies" union formed in Chicago (1905) Pure Food & Drug Act passed (1906) Child labor law passed (1908) Jack Johnson first black boxing champion (1908) NAACP founded (1909)
1910	Chase Osborn is governor (1911) Workmen's compensation act passed (1912) Copper miners strike (1913) Woodbridge Ferris is governor (1913) Prohibition amendment passed (1916) Camp Custer founded (1917) Women's suffrage amendment adopted (1918)	Boy Scouts organized (1910) Campfire Girls founded (1910) La Follette leads progressive reforms (1911) Supreme Court breaks Standard Oil monopoly (1911) U.S. enters W.W. I (1917)

Chapter 11

Living In A Changing World

Long ago it was said that "one half of the world does not know how the other half lives." That was true then. The half that was on top cared little for the struggles, and less for the fate of those who were underneath, so long as it was able to hold them there and keep its own seat. There came a time when the discomfort and crowding below were so great, and the consequent upheavals so violent, that it was no longer an easy thing to do, and then the upper half fell to inquiring what was the matter. . . . The whole world has had its hands full answering for its old ignorance.

from *How the Other Half Lives* by Jacob A. Riis

Sitting in a Confederate prisoner-of-war camp in Georgia, a Union soldier from Maine listened to the stories of other prisoners who happened to be from Michigan. It seemed to him that his fellow prisoners might be right. Perhaps Michigan was a good place to live and work. He had left his home state of Maine when he was fourteen because there were not enough jobs. He had worked in Massachusetts and learned the trade of shoemaking. But there was no real reason to go back to Massachusetts, especially if he could make more money somewhere else. When the war was over, he decided, he would go to Detroit.

And that was exactly what Hazen Pingree did. During the next few years Pingree's life became a perfect example of an American success story. He worked hard, became wealthy, and was an important citizen of Detroit. Within twenty years after the Civil War, he and a partner named Charles H. Smith owned the largest shoe company west of New York City. Pingree was known for treating his seven hundred employees well.

In 1889 Hazen Pingree seemed to Republican leaders in Detroit to be a perfect candidate for mayor. He was wealthy, just as they were. Surely he would understand that it was important for wealthy people to be in charge of government. It did not seem that he would be a powerful leader. That was a good sign. He would no doubt do as they wished and take their orders easily.

But the party bosses were dead wrong about Hazen Pingree. Beneath his mild exterior was a determined man who could be very emotional. Unlike many others who had risen to great wealth, Pingree had a concern for people who were less fortunate. And he was shocked at the corruption in the city's government. Actually, Detroit was not so very different from other American cities in the late 1800s. Before the nation as a whole had entered into what is now called the reform movement, Hazen Pingree was taking giant reform steps.

Leader of the people

After only a short time in office, Pingree was upsetting the people who had elected him. Instead of supporting their business interests, Pingree began exposing the injustices that had helped make his backers rich. One of the mayor's first targets was the streets. Earlier, lumbermen had convinced residents that the old cobblestones should be torn up and replaced by cedar blocks, which, of course, they would happily sell to them. The cedar blocks, however, were not practical for street use. Although they were set into a gravel and asphalt base, they tended to rise and

Detroit's mayor Hazen Pingree inspects gardens planted on city property. Pingree was one of the first political leaders to propose reform bills and try to improve life for the common people.

float during heavy rains. In the dryness of summer they would catch on fire.

The problem of the streets was corrected by another group eager to make money from the city's taxpayers. This time the streets were paved with asphalt, but the pavers knew little about the material. Also, they tried to thin it so that they could use as little as possible. Detroit's street surfaces then stuck to wheels and shoes, and children even chewed on the sticky substance.

Pingree set about quickly to solve the street problems. He laid out a program to pave the streets with a better asphalt coating, giving Detroit some of the best streets in any of the nation's cities. He spread the payment of taxes for the street repairs over the whole city, instead of just the people who lived along the streets. He also forced the powerful railroads to stop blocking crossings for long periods of time and creating huge traffic jams. Supporting Pingree in these projects were the bicyclists who were working hard in Michigan to secure better streets for their sport.

Pingree went on from the streets to attack more sensitive issues. He found that the gas company was charging far more in Detroit than in other cities. Two electric companies were fighting

Michigan's bicycle clubs worked hard to get government leaders to raise funds to build better roads in Michigan. This photo shows cyclists in Calumet in 1886.

Fannie Richards

In 1869 the Fourteenth Amendment was ratified, promising black people the same rights as white citizens. A black school teacher named Fannie Richards was one of a group of Detroit citizens who were anxious for the new amendment to be put to work. With several others Richards supported a lawsuit against the Detroit school system. The suit argued that the Detroit schools could not segregate white and black pupils. The lawsuit's success was a great boost for Richards and her pupils.

Fannie Richards came to Detroit with her family in the 1850s. After the first years of her education, she went to Canada to study. She then returned to Detroit and attended a teachers training school. In 1865 she began teaching at Detroit's Colored School No. 2.

Fannie Richards became the first black teacher in Detroit's schools as they became integrated. She taught for forty-four years and was assigned the job of bringing new kindergarten teaching methods into the system. She also helped start a home for poor and elderly black people in Detroit. Fannie Richards did not become a famous person. But she worked tirelessly for her people, and her pleasure, she later stated, came in their progress.

for Detroit's business and bribing city officials to help them gain control. The streetcar company was charging high rates and not paying the city for the right to do business there. Taxes were unequal, and tax assessors were not charging factory owners and wealthy landowners the full amounts.

Within a short time the businessmen who had supported Pingree found they had greatly misjudged him. Banks refused to do business with him and even the newspapers turned against him. To get his messages to the people, Pingree posted his news outside City Hall. When a depression called the Panic of 1893 closed factories and left people without work, money, and food, the mayor made city land available for gardens. Those who were living comfortably at the time laughed and nicknamed him "Potato Pingree." But the people who were hungry and without jobs

Jo Labadie was one of Michigan's early labor leaders who wanted drastic changes in government. But he was also a journalist, a poet, and a very gentle man who hoped to make the world a better place to live.

didn't laugh. To them Pingree, who even sold his own horse to purchase seeds and tools, was a hero.

In a very real way, Pingree taught the working class to value their right to vote. Since he had lost his original backers, it was up to these people to keep Pingree in office. And that was exactly what they did. Pingree served for three terms as mayor and was also sent to Lansing to serve as Michigan's governor at the turn of the century.

The problems of the poor

The problems in America at the time of Pingree's service as mayor and governor were overwhelming. The rapid growth of industry had made many people rich. But most of the rest were very poor. Cities did not have enough housing, and people lived in crowded conditions. They had poor water supplies and sewer systems. There was little or no protection from criminals. When people became sick, there were few if any hospitals, and doctors had little training. People who were mentally ill were often chained and kept like animals.

Although there were many jobs available during prosperous years, the pay was usually poor. Workers were expected to work long hours. Sometimes their jobs were dangerous to their health and even to their lives. When business slowed and factories had to close, as happened during the Panic of 1893, workers and their families went without adequate food, clothing, and shelter.

By the 1890s labor unions had begun to make life a little better for workers. In 1878 the Knights of Labor, a national labor organization that existed for about ten years, opened a branch in Detroit. Headed by Charles "Jo" Labadie, the Knights became active in politics and helped to pass important laws. Among them was a child labor law that made it illegal for children under ten to work in factories. This law also stated that young people under eighteen could not work more than ten hours a day!

The poor and overworked often released their anger in violent ways. There were sometimes strikes, and workers had to be controlled by police. There was also fighting among the many immigrant groups that settled in Michigan's large cities. Instead of mixing, immigrant families grouped with others who had come from the same country and spoke the same language. Various

The meat industry was one of many areas that needed changing at the turn of the century.

Michigan's People – 1890

Country of birth	Number	Country of birth	Number
Canada	181,416	Denmark	6,335
Mexico	89	Russia	11,889
Central & South America	89	Hungary	637
Cuba, West Indies	138	Bohemia	2,311
England	55,388	Poland	15,669
Scotland	12,068	France	5,182
Wales	769	Italy	3,088
Ireland	39,065	Spain	61
Germany	135,509	Portugal	26
Austria	3,639	Greece	10
Holland	29,410	China	140
Belgium & Luxembourg	2,286	Japan	39
Switzerland	2,562	India	143
Norway	7,795	All others	761
Sweden	27,366		

parts of a city became associated with its immigrant group, whether it was Polish, German, or Irish. Jealousies over jobs and other matters led to unrest among the groups. Many employers added to the problems by refusing to hire workers from certain groups, such as the Italians or the Irish.

Toward the turn of the century, the problems of the poor and the selfishness of the wealthy gradually forced Americans into action. People who were angered by the social injustices set to work to make life better by passing new laws and making changes. These reformers worked in many areas and took on many projects. They improved hospitals and passed laws that made it necessary for all children to attend school. They also forced employers to create better working conditions in their shops and factories.

The years dominated by these many social changes are known as the Progressive era. The United States was no longer a young nation where most of the people were farmers. There were now crowded cities with thousands of people who did not have jobs, and many who did not speak the English language. There were railroads and factories and new inventions such as the telephone and the electric light. Life was no longer simple. If America was to survive these changes, the government had to begin to step in with laws that would help bring order to the confusion.

Caroline Barlett Crane

In the 1890s, Caroline Barlett began her career in Michigan as a minister of a Unitarian church in Kalamazoo. Known as the People's Church, it had daily programs that included a kindergarten, an orchestra, and a literary club for blacks. It also held classes on practical skills, such as homemaking.

After marriage to Dr. Augustus Crane, a pioneer in x-ray research, Caroline Barlett Crane left her job as minister and began to work on health and sanitation problems. Visits to dirty slaughterhouses where animals were butchered for meat shocked her into action. By herself she convinced the Michigan legislature to make it legal for a city government to inspect local slaughterhouses. She then convinced the city of Kalamazoo to set a model for other cities to follow.

Caroline Crane continued her work on health and sanitation problems for over fifteen years. During this part of her career she visited sixty-two cities in fourteen states. Nationally she was known as "America's public housekeeper." More than a critic, however, Crane was known for finding solutions to difficult problems. She was an intelligent and respected reformer who helped make life better for Michigan's people.

Changes in government

The Progressive movement that was taking place throughout the nation was also felt in Michigan's government. Hazen Pingree was the forerunner of several governors who worked for reform. One of them was Fred Warner, who had a successful cheese and dairy business. First elected in 1905, Warner was the first governor to serve the state for three consecutive terms.

During Warner's terms as governor a number of important reform measures were passed. One was an updating of the state constitution that would help lawmakers better meet the problems of an industrial state. In the new constitution, cities had a right to own and operate public utilities, such as gas and electric services. This idea had first been introduced in the state by Pingree. Legislators were given the right to make laws concerning child labor, juvenile criminals, and similar issues. Although women throughout the nation had been working for the right to vote, the

Chase Osborn was Michigan's first governor from the Upper Peninsula. He supported wildlife conservation and worked to pass laws to preserve wild game.

Michigan constitution of 1906 still did not give women the same rights as men. However, it took a very small step in that direction by allowing women who were taxpayers to vote on issues that involved the spending of certain public funds.

An area that was in need of reform at the turn of the century was government itself. Party bosses controlled the candidates for government offices, and there was widespread corruption. In many states, groups were working to introduce laws to give people the right to vote and choose candidates in primaries. In 1909 a law pushed by Warner gave Michigan citizens the right to choose candidates for governor and many other offices.

The governor who followed Warner also worked for reform. Chase Osborn was the first person from the Upper Peninsula to lead the state. Osborn was an unusual man with many interests. He was a journalist, a noted speaker, and a successful businessman. As governor, Osborn helped pass a workmen's compensation law that became a model for other states. Under that law, employers had to pay the expenses of employees who were injured while working. Osborn also worked for more restrictions on some of the large companies, such as the railroads, which often misused their power and wealth. One of his goals was not achieved, however. Although he believed women should have the right to vote, women's suffrage was once again defeated in Michigan in 1913. It was finally passed in the state in 1918.

As governor of Michigan, Woodbridge Ferris supported the Seventeenth Amendment to the U.S. Constitution which stated that the people, not the state legislators, should elect U.S. Senators.

Woodbridge Ferris was the last Michigan governor to hold office during the years of the Progressive movement. Ferris had been a teacher and a founder of business schools. In Michigan too he founded a business school—the forerunner of Muskegon Business College. Then in 1884 he moved to Big Rapids and established an unusual school with no entrance requirements. It offered high school subjects, teachers' education, and courses in business and pharmacy. Today it is known as Ferris State College.

Ferris described himself as a "natural born fighter" and was happy to work for reform measures. As governor Ferris helped pass an amendment to the constitution that made it possible for people, not just legislators, to propose laws. It also provided them with a process to remove elected officials from office.

Ferris was also governor when Michigan voters adopted a prohibition amendment to the state constitution. This stopped the sale of liquor in Michigan. The struggle to achieve prohibition had been a long one in the state. In 1855 a law had been passed outlawing the manufacture or sale of alcoholic beverages in the state. Officials soon found that this law was nearly impossible to enforce, however, and it was repealed in 1875. The prohibition amendment passed in Ferris' term, however, was soon matched by a similar amendment to the United States Constitution.

Ferris, who did not drink, was a strong believer in prohibition as were many other Michigan citizens. And the use of alcohol had been an issue in the state since the early days of the fur trade. The use of rum, brandy, and other such beverages had a disastrous effect on the Indian people. Supporters of prohibition claimed that the "demon rum," as it was then called, had destroyed families. Saloon keepers and manufacturers of alcoholic beverages were often lawless people who were willing to do anything to make money. These factors, along with the enthusiasm for reform, caused Michigan's people to take an extreme stand against the use of any alcoholic drink. The prohibition amendment they adopted remained in effect for a number of years.

Near the end of the 1800s and the beginning of the 1900s many reforms had taken place in Michigan, and several new organizations had begun to help people have a better life. New prison systems were created, and many hospitals were built. People began to understand that mentally ill people had to be treated as sick people, not animals. The state established institutions to help children and adults who were blind, deaf, insane, or handicapped in some other way. Organizations were formed to care for orphans. Boy Scouts, Girl Scouts, and boys' and girls' camps were founded to provide healthy activities for young people. Of course, much remained to be done. But giant steps had been made, and many ordinary people were finding that their efforts could make the state a better place to live.

Gradually, however, World War I and other events helped to bring the age of reform to a close. But it had been an important stage in both Michigan's and the nation's history. People had taken time to think about the needs of others. Best of all, they had taken action to relieve some of the suffering.

The great war

The entry of the United States into World War I in 1917 affected the lives of Michigan's people. The nation had been slow to enter the war, and hundreds of Michigan men had already gone to Canada and enlisted as soldiers. But when Congress declared war against Germany and its allies, thousands of Michigan men left their homes, jobs, and families to join the armed forces. Camp Custer near Battle Creek was built to train soldiers from Michigan and Wisconsin. Selfridge Field near Mount Pleasant was also built to train pilots and other specialists.

Men and women who were civilians were left with the important task of working in mines and factories. In the Upper Peninsula the copper and iron mines were producing more minerals than ever before. Shipyards in the eastern part of the state built steel ships for the United States and its allies, Automobile factories cut down on the number of automobiles they normally produced in order to build war vehicles such as trucks and tanks. The Packard Motor Car Company developed an important airplane engine called the Liberty engine which was then manufactured by a number of companies.

The jobs available in the busy mines and factories encouraged people from other states to come to Michigan. Many of them were blacks from the South. Some factories even brought trainloads of Negroes, as they were called then, to work in Detroit and other areas. Although some Negroes had come to Michigan earlier, the great increase in their numbers at this time angered many of the white residents who feared and disliked people of other races.

Michigan's farms were as important as its factories during the war years. People in Europe were suffering from a shortage of food, and Americans were encouraged to cut down on the food they ate. Government officials set aside certain days when no meat was to be eaten or no wheat used. The Michigan government gave farmers extra seeds, and people in cities were given seeds for gardens. Harvest time created problems, since there were not enough people to do the work. In some areas schools were closed and children helped with the harvest.

In 1917 Camp Custer opened near Battle Creek to train soldiers for World War I. Here they are taught trench warfare by an experienced British officer.

Michigan
and World War I

Overview

Europe was torn by strife in the early 1900s, and in 1914 war broke out. France, Russia, and Great Britain fought against Germany and Austria-Hungary. Although the United States tried to remain isolated from the war, German submarines attacked American ships. The United States finally declared war on Germany in 1917. Germany surrendered in November of 1918.

Michigan soldiers

Nearly 110,000 Michigan men served in the armed forces during the war. 96,480 were in the Army, 11,463 were in the Navy, and 2,051 were Marines.

Troops from Michigan and Wisconsin made up the 32nd Division and were the first to land on German soil. The French people admired this division and named them "Les Terribles."

Volunteers at home

Those who did not go to war took on other jobs to help the war cause. Before the war was over, over a million Michigan people joined the Red Cross. They made bandages, hospital gowns, and other supplies. Red Cross workers helped families where fathers or sons had gone off to war. They also set up canteens near training camps. There they offered soldiers refreshments as well as paper, pen, ink, and stamps so that they could write letters home.

Some troops, called Michigan state troops, stayed at home. They guarded factories where war supplies were made and kept workers on the job in Upper Peninsula iron mines when strikes threatened. After the war, the group continued their work as the Michigan State Police.

Great amounts of food were needed for the American troops as well as for America's allies in Europe. Everyone was encouraged to have gardens. Even schools had gardens and held contests to see which school could raise the most food. Many boys were part of the Boys' Working Reserve and were placed on farms to work during the summer.

Building patriotism

President Woodrow Wilson said, "It is not an army we must shape and train for war; it is a nation." At the war's beginning nearly one quarter of Michigan's people had been born in another country. Communities held sings, pageants, and parades to help make people more patriotic. There were great drives to sell Liberty Bonds, and those who refused to buy them were considered unpatriotic and suspicious.

Shipbuilding

Ships were built in Saginaw, Port Huron, Marine City, Ecorse, Wyandotte, and Benton Harbor. Most of the warships built were too big to go through the Great Lakes locks and canal system. They were cut in two and put together again on the St. Lawrence River.

There was also a serious fuel shortage during the war years. Many homes and buildings were heated with coal, and industries used coal for manufacturing. With the great demand for war products and the shortage of labor, coal could not be mined fast enough to keep up with the demands. The winter of 1917-18 also added to the problem. It was one of the coldest in years.

In January, 1918, the fuel shortage was so serious that both the state and national governments took drastic steps. Only selected businesses important to the war could operate on a normal schedule. The rest were closed for a week and the following Mondays for nine weeks. Public buildings, including theaters and churches, could only be heated on certain days. People who lived in northern Michigan turned to wood to supply their heat. But many who lived in large cities found themselves with no fuel at all.

This parade was held in Detroit in 1918 to help sell Liberty Bonds and support the war effort.

Although people were willing to cooperate in the war effort, their patriotism was sometimes too intense. Thousands of people of German descent had come to live in Michigan. These people, who had already contributed to the life and culture of Michigan's towns and cities, were treated as enemies. Rumors started that one German family or another was working secretly to support Germany in the war effort. Not only were German people suspect, but it was even unpopular to use words such as hamburger or frankfurter, since these came from names of German cities. Schools and colleges stopped teaching the German language, and people thought it was un-American to listen to German music.

When victory was finally proclaimed on November 11, 1918, Michigan was in the process of changing into a state that was quite different from the Michigan of the past. It was no longer a frontier, where most people were farmers and cities and towns were struggling to set up new industries and governments. The state was now in the mainstream of American life, producing goods such as war equipment, food, and automobiles. Most of Michigan's people lived in cities in the southern half of the state, and its population was growing as people came to find jobs in its factories. After eighty years of statehood, Michigan was coming of age.

M I C H I G A N

I·N T·I·M·E

Date	In Michigan	Outside Michigan
1920	Michigan's first radio station begins broadcasting (1920)	The Prohibition Amendment is in effect (1919-1933)
	First woman elected to Michigan Senate (1920)	The 19th Amendment giving women the right to vote is ratified (1920)
	Alexander Groesbeck is governor (1921-26)	Calvin Coolidge becomes President when Warren Harding dies (1923)
	Ford adopts a 40-hour work week (1922)	
	First woman elected to Michigan's House of Representatives (1924)	Charles Lindbergh flies across the Atlantic (1927)
	Car-ferry service begins between the Lower & Upper peninsulas (1924)	The first movie with a sound track, or "talkie," is produced (1927)
	Chrysler Motor Company formed (1925)	
	Ford ends production of the Model T (1927)	Herbert Hoover becomes President (1929)
	Airline passenger service begins in Detroit (1927)	The stock market crashes & the Depression begins (1929)
	Ford introduces the Model A (1928)	
1930	Tunnel opens between Detroit & Windsor, Canada (1930)	Several thousand banks close (1930-31)
	Michigan citizens vote to end Prohibition (1933)	Amelia Earhart is the first woman to fly solo across the Atlantic (1932)
	Height of the Depression in the state (1933)	40% of people in large cities have no jobs (1932)
	CCC camps open (1933)	
	Wayne University is organized (1934)	Franklin D. Roosevelt becomes President & starts New Deal programs (1932)
	United Auto Workers is formed (1935)	Drought makes Great Plains a dust bowl (1932)
	Tigers, Lions, and Red Wings all win national championships (1935)	
	WPA program begins (1935)	Banks begin reopening (1933)
	Joe Louis becomes heavyweight champion of the world (1937)	Farms get electricity under a Rural Electrification Act (1935)
	Sit-down strike at General Motors plant in Flint (1937)	World War II begins (1939)

Chapter 12

Drum on your drums, batter on your banjoes,
Sob on the long cool winding saxophones.
Go to it, O jazzmen.

from "Jazz Fantasia" by Carl Sandburg
Copyright 1920 by Harcourt Brace
Jovanovich, Inc.; renewed 1948 by
Carl Sandburg. Reprinted by
permission of the publisher.

Good Times and Bad

"Go to it, O jazzmen." The decade of the 1920s had much in common with the jazz that was so popular at the time. Life had a new freedom. Just as the jazz musicians played without following the notes of the music in front of them, America's people were no longer following the traditions of the past. Just as the jazz musicians explored many new melodies as the spirit moved them, men and women explored all the new possibilities that a changing world had brought them. "Go to it, O jazzmen." They did not listen or look for warnings. They wanted only to enjoy the new wonders of a changing world.

And there were wonders. By the beginning of World War I, silent movies had become part of American life. In the 1920s the movies were improved by adding sound, and people loved to go to "the talkies." The radio was invented and brought both entertainment and the latest news into American homes. More families than ever had automobiles, and although only a few people were traveling by airplane, the airplane was becoming an important part of the nation's transportation system.

But what the American people were enjoying most of all was their money. Although there were some serious problems after World War I, by 1923 the nation's factories and businesses were booming. There were many new things for people to buy, from electric irons to vacuum cleaners. Advertising became big business as it urged people to buy this product or that.

Women's new rights

In 1920 an amendment to the United States Constitution was approved by enough states to make it law. That amendment gave women the right to vote. It was an end to a struggle that had been carried on for over fifty years.

While the Nineteenth Amendment was a great victory for women, voting was only one of many battles that women had been fighting. Women had always been second-class citizens, unable to own property or even to keep their children if their husbands died. Gradually, some of these laws were changed. In the 1890s, for example, the Michigan legislature did away with the law that ordered a woman to turn over her earnings to her husband.

Besides the old laws, however, there was also the feeling that women were not as smart as men and were best suited for jobs within their households. But the rapidly changing world was also helping change people's ideas about women. With inventions such as telephones and typewriters, new jobs were created that men felt were suitable for women to fill. World War I took thousands of women out of their homes and into factory jobs left by the men who became soldiers. And women themselves had been proving for many years that they were as capable as men. Many women graduated from Michigan's high schools and some from college.

The passing of the Nineteenth Amendment and the spirit of the 1920s had a great impact on women in America. They began wearing both short hair and short skirts. Many of them took up smoking, and the subject of sex, which simply was not talked about before, was now open for discussion. For the older gener-

Women students march at Michigan State. Only after long hard struggles did women in Michigan and other states find a place in the classrooms and other educational organizations once restricted to men.

ation, the 1920s was indeed a shocking time, both in Michigan's and in America's history.

The bootleggers

Another amendment to the United States Constitution that greatly affected life in the 1920s was the Eighteenth Amendment. This law stopped the manufacture and use of liquor throughout the nation. Although it was designed to put an end to the problems of alcohol, it created many new ones. Both men and women drank openly, defying the new law. Families made their own home brews, and illegal selling, or "bootlegging," of liquor became big business.

Detroit was a center for the bootleggers. The Canadian government did not have a prohibition law. Canadian officials did not mind if their manufacturers shipped liquor across the border as long as they paid the normal Canadian taxes on their sales. Therefore bootleggers only had to worry about transporting the liquor across the United States border. In Detroit that was rather a simple matter. Many authorities were themselves part of the

Private academies provided the only type of high school education in Michigan's early years. The first public high schools began about 1860. This photo shows a study hall in a Grand Rapids area high school in the early 1900s.

In 1929 a Detroit newsman hid in a nearby building and took this photo of bootleggers carrying suitcases full of liquor from a boat to their car. The liquor probably came from Canada.

bootlegging business and allowed shipping to be carried on, sometimes in broad daylight.

After the liquor made it safely across the border, it was sold to businesses which seemed to be meat markets or flower shops. Their real source of income, however, was illegal liquor. By the late 1920s, bootlegging was one of Michigan's largest industries. Competition was so great that there were killings and bombings among the bootleggers. The police, many of whom were also involved in the bootlegging, killed 70 people in 1927 and 1928, and wounded twice as many. Within a few years the Eighteenth Amendment had created more violent crime than the legal use of liquor ever had. A new amendment to the U.S. Constitution was proposed to end prohibition, and in 1933, Michigan's people, along with the rest of the nation, voted overwhelmingly in its favor.

The booming industry

Growth and change marked the auto industry in the 1920s. Difficult years after the end of World War I led to the collapse of several of the smaller companies. Two of these failing companies, which made cars called the Maxwell and the Chalmers, were purchased by Walter P. Chrysler. Within a few years Chrysler stopped manufacturing these cars and began a new line that included the Plymouth and the De Soto. At this time he also changed his company's name to the Chrysler Corporation. In 1928 he bought the Dodge Company and added that popular car to his line of automobiles.

Moving to first place among the automobile manufacturers was General Motors, headed by Alfred P. Sloan, Jr. The General Motors management was the first to understand that the industry was changing. Now that so many people owned cars, they needed urging to buy newer and better models. While Ford was producing only Tin Lizzies, General Motors was offering several cars at different prices. The company also began to make changes each year in the cars' appearances. This encouraged customers to buy new,

In the 1920s Walter P. Chrysler started the Chrysler Corporation. In 1925 the company produced this sporty Chrysler roadster.

James Couzens

When the Ford Motor Company was formed in 1903, one of its investors was a business man named James Couzens. Not a wealthy man, Couzens scraped up his savings and mortgaged his house to come up with the $2,000 he needed to be part of the new company. When Henry Ford delayed the shipment of his first cars and declared they were not yet perfect, Couzens protested. As treasurer, he realized that the company would go bankrupt if they did not begin to sell the automobiles.

The Ford cars were sold and, of course, were a big success. For a number of years Couzens remained with the company and played an important part in its growth. In 1919 Henry Ford bought the shares of the company owned by his partners so that he could have complete control. By that time Couzens' shares amounted to well over 29 million dollars!

For three years after leaving the Ford Motor Company, Couzens served as mayor of Detroit. Like Hazen Pingree, Couzens believed in reform. A government which did not serve the needs of people, he felt, needed changing. One of his accomplishments was setting up city-owned and operated streetcar and bus lines. These served the people much more completely and cheaply than private lines had done.

While serving as mayor, Couzens was appointed by Governor Alexander Groesbeck to fill the position left vacant by one of Michigan's senators in Washington, D.C. Couzens was then elected to this position which he held until his death in 1936. Couzens continued his battle for reform in the federal government. One of his famous fights was with Andrew Mellon,

U.S. Secretary of the Treasury. Mellon, one on the richest men in the country, worked to make income taxes lower for wealthy people. He also used loopholes in the system so that his own family would not have to pay high taxes.

When Couzens led an attack against Mellon, the Secretary tried to get even by suing Couzens and claiming that the Senator himself owed ten million dollars in taxes. After a famous trial, Couzens' name was cleared and it was found that he had actually overpaid his taxes! But Couzens did not breathe a sigh of relief and store away the ten million in question. Delighted with his victory, he gave the ten million to charity, setting up a fund "to promote the health, welfare, happiness and development of the children of Michigan primarily, and elsewhere in the world."

more attractive models even though their old cars were still in good condition.

It was not until 1927 that Henry Ford admitted that changes had taken place in the industry and that he was behind the times. He ended production of the Model T and in the following year introduced the Model A. Although the Model A was a popular low-priced automobile, Ford had clearly lost his lead to General Motors. This was hardly a death blow to the company, however. Ford, along with General Motors and Chrysler, were making about seventy-five percent of all cars in the nation by the end of the 1920s. They had become the "Big Three" of the auto world.

Although some automobile plants were located outside Michigan, there was no question that Michigan was the home of this ballooning industry. Although the center of the industry was in Detroit, other Michigan cities grew rapidly as their industries began supplying auto parts such as spark plugs and tires. Just as Michigan's thick forests had once been responsible for the lumber boom, its factories were now creating wealth that would have made the great lumber barons green with envy.

A growing state

The blossoming automobile industry was, of course, an attraction for people in other states or countries who were looking for jobs. In the early 1900s they rushed to Michigan much in the way they had come looking for land in the 1830s. Detroit, bulging at the seams, made its boundaries larger and struggled to supply city services to its new people. Once known as a beautiful city with small-town features, Detroit began to have a new image. Its slogan, "Dynamic Detroit," showed the excitement of industry and big business.

Most of the people who came to Michigan in the first part of the 20th century were European immigrants. These were not Michigan's first people from European countries. Many had come in the late 1800s from the British Isles and northwest European countries including Germany and the Netherlands. A large number also came from Canada. But the immigration of the 1900s included more people from eastern and southern Europe. They had few skills and took simple jobs in the assembly lines of the automobile factories.

One of the eastern European groups to come in large numbers was the Poles. Many of them found jobs at the Dodge plant located at Hamtramck in the Detroit area. The city of Hamtramck became well-known for its Polish celebrations, markets, and even newspapers written in the Polish language. Other Polish people settled in Lansing, Saginaw, and Grand Rapids.

By the end of the 1920s Michigan's large cities could boast of many other national groups. There were large numbers of Italians and Russians. Immigrants also came from countries such as Hungary, Yugoslavia, and Czechoslovakia. A number of Arabs settled in Dearborn to work at the Ford Motor Company.

The growth of the cities and the rush of immigration worried the people of Michigan and the rest of the nation. The problems of poverty and crime were blamed on immigrants, even though in most cases they were not at fault. There was a feeling that people from northwest European countries such as England had built this nation, and that foreigners from many different lands

It hasn't a single belt, fan or drain pipe....

It always works perfectly and never needs oiling . . . .

In the 1920s many of Michigan's people were enjoying spending their money on all the new inventions of the age. The good life, however, did not last. In 1929 the country went into the Great Depression.

were now taking it over. The belief that immigration should be closely controlled was a growing one.

In the 1920s new laws were made to limit immigration. These laws made it clear that America was no longer living by the words printed on the Statue of Liberty in New York City, where most immigrants entered the country. "Give me your tired, your poor" was a noble idea, many Americans thought, but not a practical policy that could go on forever.

The laws limiting immigration encouraged blacks from the southern states to move northward and get the jobs once filled by immigrants. Many of these blacks came to Michigan. White workers tended to resent the black workers, believing they were taking away jobs. Even many of the newest European immigrants seemed to share this intolerance for black workers and their families. As a result, blacks were only able to get the worst jobs and the worst houses in the worst parts of the cities. It was the beginning of a problem that would grow to an immense size in later years.

The beginning of good roads

With cities growing and the automobile industry booming, it was natural that great improvements slowly began to be made in Michigan's road system. Although the state had established a good railroad system by the 1900s, it took years of hard work by many individuals and groups to get a road program under way. Bicycle clubs were joined by automobile clubs in urging the state to replace its poor system of "wagon roads."

Michigan's best wagon roads were built with gravel surfaces. While this kind of surface worked fairly well for wagons, the rubber tires of the speedier cars flung the gravel in all directions. There had been some experimenting with asphalt, but Michigan's road builders felt the best idea for roads was concrete. In 1909 a portion of Woodward Avenue in Detroit became the nation's first mile of concrete road. Other road builders were impressed, and within a few years concrete roads were being constructed in Michigan as well as in other parts of the nation.

Alexander Groesbeck, who served as Michigan's governor from 1921 through 1925, played an important part in the state's road development. Groesbeck used federal money that was available and combined it with state funds to build excellent new highways. Many modern ideas were also used as the highways were built. Some divided highways were constructed in the Detroit area, and all new roads were made wider than ever before. Roadbuilders in Michigan were among the first to create bypasses that routed cars around the busy centers of cities. Under Groesbeck's guidance, a car-ferry service was established between Michigan's Upper and Lower peninsulas, greatly improving the transportation link between the two parts of the state.

Life on Michigan farms

Although Michigan's industries were enjoying good years during the 1920s, farmers were having a difficult time. After the great demand for farm products during World War I, farmers' income had taken a disappointing drop. At the same time, the prices of the goods farm families needed had gone up. It simply was more difficult to earn a living from the land.

The low incomes from farming and the demand for workers in Michigan's growing industries caused many farmers to leave the land in the 1920s. But there were other reasons why many families left their farms. In northern Michigan farmers were finding that the thin soil there was no longer producing good crops. Also, farmers were learning that to be successful they needed

With the auto industry booming, new roads were needed in the state. In the early 1920s many new roads were built.

education both in modern methods of farming and in running a business. Some left to find easier ways of earning a living.

The farmers who stayed in agriculture found their life changing quickly. By the 1920s nearly half owned automobiles. Trucks and tractors were beginning to replace horses and mules. The use of tractors helped farmers grow larger crops, and the size of Michigan's farms began to grow. Automobiles and trucks also made it easier for farmers to move their products to towns and cities.

The life of farm families was also changing. Phone companies began to move into rural areas, and by 1920 about half of Michigan's farmers had telephones. In a few areas farms had electricity, and families were able to enjoy labor-saving appliances. These changes helped make farmers more aware of the world around them. It helped to break down old ways of thinking and brought some progress into the lives of rural people.

As farmers gained more education, they began to see the advantages of putting their efforts into one main type of farming. Instead of raising livestock and several types of crops, they began to specialize in products that grew best in their area. Along Lake

New farm equipment helped Michigan farmers produce larger crops. The machinery also meant that fewer farm workers were needed.

Michigan many became fruit farmers, while those in eastern Michigan grew sugar beets or beans. Farmers in northern Michigan found that crops such as potatoes and hay grew best. Although some still raised grain, they no longer tried to grow large quantities of wheat in competition with the huge wheat farms of the prairie states.

The presence of the Michigan Agricultural College, which became Michigan State College in 1925, provided important information to farmers in the state. Training and information sessions were held in different parts of the state to teach farmers new methods or help their wives learn new household skills such as canning food. In 1917, 4-H club programs began teaching skills to farm children. By the end of the 1920s, Michigan farms were no longer places where families met all their own needs and lived a life far removed from the rest of society.

Too much, too fast

The high times of the 1920s did not last. By the end of the decade there were problems arising in Michigan, as well as throughout the nation. Prices had gone higher and higher. In many families both husband and wife had to work to make ends meet. They bought many items on credit, a new idea of the 1920s. Since it was not uncommon for workers to lose their jobs, families often could not finish paying for their goods and had them reclaimed.

Mass production was helping American industries manufacture more goods than ever before. But there were not enough people who were able to buy these products. Many Americans were very poor. The number of rich people was too small to buy all the goods produced. What was needed was a larger middle class—people who earned enough in their jobs to buy the things factories produced.

In October, 1929, a money crisis took place in America. Prices on the stock market, where people bought shares of large corporations, fell so low it was called a crash. Thousands of people lost huge amounts of money, and for many it was their life savings. This financial crash was the beginning of one of the worst periods in American history—the Great Depression. Many industries came to a standstill, leaving millions of people without jobs or money. At the height of the Depression, about one half of Michigan's workers, not including farmers, were without jobs. About one fourth of Michigan's banks had closed. Cities, towns, and even some state governments were close to becoming bankrupt as they used their money to help people who had lost their homes and had no clothes or food.

For several years Michigan's people, along with others throughout the nation, struggled to survive. More and more industries went out of business. The smaller automobile companies closed their doors, and the Big Three cut their production of cars. In the Upper Peninsula many copper and iron mines closed, and people tried to earn a living by farming. Many farmers, unable to make payments on their farms, pay taxes, or even buy seeds, lost their land. It was an age of despair.

A new deal

When the Depression began in 1929, President Herbert Hoover believed that businesses should be left to work out problems for themselves. Americans were a rugged lot, he believed, who would survive the bad times. And he was convinced that things would get better if the government kept out of it.

For a time, Americans believed Hoover was right. But things became worse instead of better. In the past most Americans had looked down on the poor. They considered people without jobs to be lazy. But now many of these people who had never been poor and thought of themselves as hardworking and independent were unable to get jobs. They were poor too, and so were their friends. When the time came for the election of a president in 1932, most

There were hard times for nearly all of Michigan's people during the years of the Depression.

of them voted for a change. Democrat Franklin D. Roosevelt was elected. It was the first time a Democrat candidate for president had received a majority of votes in Michigan since 1852.

As soon as Roosevelt became president, he began to change the mood of the country. "The only thing we have to fear is fear itself," he told the American people as he immediately began government programs for those without jobs. Under his "New Deal," as it was called, Roosevelt gave relief funds to the poor and hungry. But the programs that followed did not provide money without work.

One of the most famous programs of Roosevelt's New Deal was the Civilian Conservation Corps, or CCC. This put young men to work who were between the ages of 17 and 28. They worked on many projects, from planting trees and fighting forest fires to building picnic areas and campgrounds. They lived in camps near their work and earned $30 each month, $25 of which was sent home to their families. The CCC work in Michigan helped reforest many acres that had been left useless by the lumbering business of earlier years.

Root, Root, Root
For The Home Team

In the midst of the hardships of the 1930s there was a brighter side to life. Sports were at their peak in Michigan, and fans enjoyed baseball, football, hockey, and boxing. What was even better, Michigan athletes were winning!

Baseball began in Michigan in the 1800s. The first team was called the Detroits, but was changed to the Tigers when the players began wearing orange and black socks. In 1900 the Detroit Tigers became part of the American League. Within a few years they acquired Ty Cobb, a player who became one of the greatest baseball stars of all time. Other early stars included Charlie Gehringer, Harry Heilman, and Mickey Cochrane.

Football and hockey also drew crowds in the 1920s and 1930s. The University of Michigan built a large stadium for its popular football team in the 1920s. In 1934 the Detroit Lions became part of the National Football League, winning a championship the following year! In 1926 the Detroit Hockey Club was organized and purchased a team from Canada that became the Detroit Red Wings.

In the 1930s Detroit was called the City of Champions. The Tigers won the American League pennant in 1934 and the following year won the World Series. Along with the Lions' football victory in 1935, the Detroit Red Wings won the Stanley Cup. Detroit's boxing star Joe Louis was also working his way to the top. In 1937 he became the world's heavyweight champion, a title he held for twelve years.

The Works Progress Administration, or WPA, was another important program of the New Deal. It gave jobs to white collar workers such as teachers, writers, artists, and actors. Some WPA workers built public buildings such as hospitals and libraries. Others worked on special projects, including making clothes for the needy or serving lunches to schoolchildren. Eventually, over 200,000 people in Michigan had jobs through the WPA program.

By 1934 the New Deal was beginning to improve conditions throughout the nation. Slowly people began to have money to buy the things they needed. Industries began to produce more goods and provide more jobs. Although hard times had not disappeared, life was becoming brighter for Michigan and the rest of the nation.

The growth of labor unions

The Depression changed many workers' ways of thinking about their jobs. As factories slowly began to produce again, the owners demanded more and more work at the lowest wages possible. In these hard times, workers saw the need to organize and demand higher wages.

The Works Progress Administration gave jobs to many people. Here WPA workers are repairing a Detroit street. Often more workers were put on a job than would usually be used.

About the same time, the federal government saw the need for workers to organize and bargain for better wages. Several laws were passed allowing the formation of unions. From this point on, unions began to grow in Michigan. In 1935 the United Automobile Workers of America, or the U.A.W., was formed and began to work for better wages and other improvements at General Motors. But the leaders at General Motors would not work with the new U.A.W. There was a rumor that the company was going to move some of its work from a Flint plant to a city where the union was not so strong. As a result, workers in Flint held a sit-down strike.

The strike soon was out of control. A local judge ordered police to remove the workers from the Flint plant. Nearly thirty men had been injured when General Motors leaders asked Michigan Governor Frank Murphy to send National Guard troops to complete the job the police had begun. But Murphy believed the workers had a right to protest. Although he sent National Guard troops to Flint, he allowed the workers to stay in the plants. He then worked to reach an agreement between General Motors and the labor union officials. Finally General Motors leaders agreed to

When Walter Reuther (third from left) and other labor union leaders tried to hand out information to Ford workers, they were met and beaten by strongmen hired by Ford.

recognize the union as the bargaining agent of its workers and allowed its employees to become members.

The success of the U.A.W. at General Motors led the union to begin organizing at other automobile companies. Although Chrysler immediately recognized the union, the Ford Motor Company refused to do so. As union leaders approached the plant at River Rouge to talk to workers and hand out flyers, they were beaten by strongmen hired by Ford. One of the injured was Walter Reuther, who was to become one of the greatest leaders in the union movement.

Ford's attempt to stop the union did not work. In 1941 a Supreme Court ruling forced the company to recognize the union. With unions in all the Big Three companies, Michigan lost its reputation as an "open shop" state where workers were not organized. It now had one of the most powerful unions in the nation and was setting the trend for relations between management and workers throughout the country.

M I C H I G A N

I·N T·I·M·E

Date	In Michigan	Outside Michigan
1940	Automobile factories begin producing war supplies (1941)	Japan attacks Pearl Harbor & U.S. enters W.W. II (1941)
	Race riots take place in Detroit (1943)	Race riots take place in several U.S. cities (1943)
	Michigan people celebrate V-E Day & V-J Day as war ends (1945)	Franklin Roosevelt dies & Harry Truman becomes President (1945)
	Automobile factories return to the production of cars (1945)	United Nations charter is approved (1945)
	Michigan's U.S. Senator Arthur Vandenberg helps write the United Nations charter (1945)	U.S. drops atomic bombs on Japan (1945)
	The Kaiser-Fraser Corporation begins producing cars (1945)	W.W. II ends (1945)
	U.A.W. begins a long strike at General Motors (1945)	Hundreds of unions strike for higher wages (1946)
	Walter Reuther becomes U.A.W. president (1946)	Atomic Energy Commission formed to control nuclear development (1946)
	Michigan's first television station begins broadcasting (1947)	Jackie Robinson becomes the first black baseball player in major leagues (1947)
	G. Mennen Williams begins his six terms as governor (1949)	
1950	American Motors Corporation is formed (1954)	Senator Joseph McCarthy creates Communist scare & puts many Americans on trial (1950-54)
	The Mackinac Bridge is built (1954-57)	U.S. enters Korean War (1950-53)
	Interstate highway program marks road improvements in state (1957)	Dwight Eisenhower becomes President (1953)
	Money crisis ends William's years as governor (1959)	Boycott of buses in Alabama marks beginning of nonviolent protests by blacks (1955)
		Soviet Union puts first satellite into orbit (1957)
		St. Lawrence Seaway opens (1957)
		Alaska & Hawaii become states (1959)

Chapter 13

"In company with our brave Allies and brothers-in-arms on other Fronts, you will bring about the destruction of the German war machine, the elimination of Nazi tyranny over the oppressed peoples of Europe, and security for ourselves in a free world."

General Dwight D. Eisenhower in a message to Allied forces,
June 5, 1944

Wars and Uneasy Peace

Giant searchlights scanned the dark skies over the locks at Sault Ste. Marie. Radar beacons stretched farther than the lights could beam, and machine guns sat silent but ready, pointed upward into the night. On nearby airfields fighter planes stood guard, waiting to take to the sky.

Meanwhile giant freighters made their way through the locks. Some, traveling southward, were loaded with iron ore and copper. Others were empty, making their way to Michigan's harbors along Lake Superior. There they would reload and carry the valuable resources southward to bustling factories and steel mills in cities such as Detroit, Gary, Cleveland, and Buffalo. The movement of raw materials to the factories was vital. The United States was at war!

At Willow Run, a farming town near Ypsilanti, thousands of workers bent over their work on giant assembly lines. They were building bombers, B-24s, in a huge building that was one mile long and one quarter mile wide. When the planes were completed, pilots flew them from the runway next to the factory to U.S. air bases in many parts of the world.

Many of the workers at Willow Run were women. Others were men who were too old to be in the armed forces or did not qualify for some other reason. A great number of the workers were new to Michigan. They had come for just one reason—to get a job. They lived wherever they could, in nearby rooming houses, in housing built especially for the workers, or in the neighboring cities of Ypsilanti and Detroit.

It was much the same in many Michigan communities. In Iron Mountain workers were making gliders. In Kalamazoo they were building tanks that could be driven in water and on land. The Hudson Motor Company was manufacturing guns that could shoot down planes. At the Packard Motor Company in Detroit airplane engines were being built. Michigan was called the "Arsenal of Democracy." Its workers were not risking their lives in battle, but they were helping to win the war. As a factory worker said to her pilot boyfriend in a Hollywood movie scene, "While you're flying them, honey, I'll be building them."

The state at war

World War II had an effect on all of Michigan's people. Over 600,000 men and women left their homes to serve in the armed forces. Even so, the state's population grew as other men and women came to work in the factories. Life for Michigan's farmers had never been better. They could easily sell as much as they could produce.

Michigan's colleges and universities were also busy places during the war. The United States Government sent thousands of men and women to school in war-training programs. Officers were sent to take engineering courses, and scientists became part of research teams to produce new weapons.

People's life styles changed in drastic ways. No passenger cars were built after 1942, and there were shortages of many goods, including gasoline, sugar, meat, and cigarettes. People could not purchase these items without ration stamps, which were handed out by the federal government. People of all ages worked to help the war effort through Boy Scouts, Girl Scouts, churches, and other organizations. These groups collected scrap metal, waste paper, and even milkweed pods whose floss was used to stuff life jackets.

The factory at Willow Run manufactured over 8,500 B-24s during the years of World War II.

Michigan leaders

Just as Michigan's industries, soldiers, and workers were important in the war years, so were its leaders. One of these was William Knudsen, president of General Motors. Knudsen was in

charge of the nation's production of war materials. In this very important post Knudsen could overrule all but the highest generals. Harold D. Smith of Michigan also held an important job in the federal government. He directed the nation's budget and acted as business manager for President Franklin D. Roosevelt. The Secretary of the Navy, Frank Knox, had also lived in Michigan and owned a newspaper in Sault Ste. Marie. Knox built the greatest Navy the nation had ever had.

Frank Murphy, a former Michigan governor, also played an important part in the national government. In 1939 President Roosevelt appointed Murphy Attorney General. Shortly afterward, Murphy became an associate justice of the Supreme Court. By the time of his death in 1949 he had held more high offices in the state and federal government than any Michigan citizen. Although he had made enemies during the union trouble in Flint in 1937, he was highly thought of as a defender of human rights.

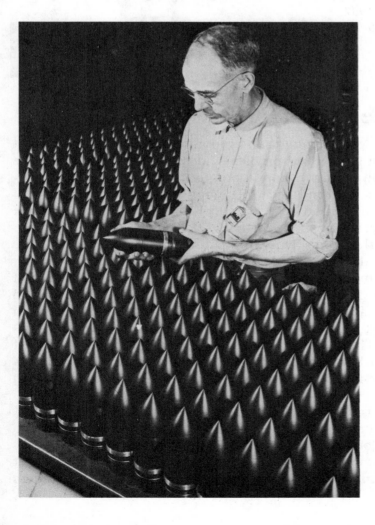

Michigan's factories played an extremely important role in providing the nation with war equipment in World War II. Many of the factory workers were women. Others were men who were too old to serve in the armed forces.

Frank Murphy served as Michigan's governor from 1937 to 1939. During the 1940s he held many positions in the federal government.

Violence in Detroit

The war years brought an economic boom to Michigan, but they also brought serious problems. Most of these problems came from the crowded living conditions in its cities, particularly Detroit. Houses that had been left empty years before because of their terrible condition were rented for high prices. Families were crowded together in single rooms without water or toilets.

Most of the people living in the worst sections of Detroit were black. It was difficult if not impossible for them to live elsewhere, even if they made enough money to pay the rent. The hatred of many whites kept them locked into the slums. A riot occurred even when blacks tried to move into apartments built for them by the federal government and called the Sojourner Truth Housing Project. The project angered thousands of whites because it was built in what they considered to be a white area. When blacks finally moved in, they had to be protected by army troops as well as police.

Racial problems had grown in Detroit for a number of reasons. In addition to the large number of blacks that had come to the city for jobs were many poor white people from the South. They brought with them an unthinking hatred toward blacks that had been handed down from generation to generation. Leaders

such as Father Charles Coughlin, a popular priest who had been giving radio shows for a number of years, added to the problem. Coughlin was a dramatic speaker and considered himself a leader of the common people. As time went by his views became more outspoken and extreme. He had many followers, and large amounts of money were given him as he stirred people's hatred against Communists, Jews, blacks, or anyone who was "different." After the riot at the Sojourner Truth Housing Project, Father Coughlin's church ordered him to stop his hate messages.

Others involved in stirring people's hatred were the Reverend Gerald L. K. Smith and the Ku Klux Klan. Smith was a preacher who inspired hate in his Protestant followers just as Father Coughlin had done with the Catholics. Smith, too, spoke against Jews and blacks as he led an organization he hoped would someday be able to overthrow the American government. The Ku Klux Klan, or KKK as it was called, had long been strong in the South. Beginning in the 1920s, it also had a large following in Michigan. Its membership in Michigan grew to over 800,000 people, more than in any other state. The KKK also preached hatred of Jews and blacks and often carried out violent acts against them.

Father Charles Coughlin combined his radio messages with a newspaper called "Father Couglin's Weekly." It had extreme views and was barred from the mails during W.W. II.

Michigan
and World War II

Overview

War broke out in Europe when Germany invaded Poland in 1939. Under Adolph Hitler, German troops continued to invade the countries of Europe while Benito Mussolini of Italy led his forces into Africa. In Japan military forces controlled the government and in 1941 attacked a U.S. naval base at Pearl Harbor in Hawaii. At that time the United States declared war on Japan and soon after on Germany. For over three and a half years American forces, along with those of Great Britain, France, Russia, and other Allied powers, fought against German, Italian, and Japanese troops. The Allies were victorious in 1945.

Michigan soldiers

In 1940 the United States began to draft young men to become soldiers. Most of the people on the draft boards were volunteers who had to decide what men would go to war. Some were excused since they were needed on farms or had some important job making war equipment. Others were allowed to remain in college since the nation needed scientists, engineers, and doctors. But most went to war. Michigan supplied 613,542 men during World War II. Michigan women also joined the WACS, WAVES, and other female divisions.

Michigan's war industries

Michigan was a leading state in the production of war materials. Much of the manufacturing was done at automobile plants in the southeastern part of the state. Auto manufacturers made machine guns, airplane engines, diesel engines, shells, and torpedoes for submarines. Chrysler Corporation operated a tank factory and made over 25,000 tanks during the war. Ford ran the liberator bomber plant at Willow Run. General Motors factories made tanks and tank parts, while Hudson Motor Company made anti-aircraft guns.

Factories in other parts of Michigan also made war equipment. Bay City factories produced different types of war boats. Helicopter parts were made in Grand Rapids, and gliders were made in Iron Mountain. The Army and Navy gave special flags to companies who were important producers of war machinery. Workers at these plants were also awarded with special buttons.

Guarding the home front

Because Michigan was such an important producer of war equipment, people feared a possible raid by enemy planes. There were special drills in the state to practice for air attacks. Sometimes night blackouts were also held.

The Japanese sent balloons carrying bombs which they planned would explode in the United States. Some of these balloons crossed the Pacific Ocean and landed in the U.S. One was found near Detroit and another near Grand Rapids. both had burned themselves out and caused no damage. Several forest fires at the time were later blamed on the balloon bombs.

By 1943 tension in Detroit was reaching its peak. Fights between black and white youths broke out at Belle Isle, a city park. News of the fights spread. Soon whites were overturning cars in a black neighborhood, and white motorists were attacked by blacks. Before the police restored order, thirty-four people had been killed and hundreds injured.

The riot upset many Detroiters who had not realized the situation had become so serious. Community leaders quickly made plans to help solve their city's problems. A plan formed by R. J. Thomas, a union leader from the U.A.W., was the one finally used by the city. He called for new laws that would make it necessary for employers to treat black and other minority workers more fairly. Plans were made for more housing and parks. City leaders also set up a committee of both blacks and whites to deal with racial problems before they became too serious and burst into violence. For a number of years the problems were kept under control, and until the 1960s Detroit was considered a model city for race relations.

The Detroit riot of 1943 caused senseless destruction, injury, and even death. The riot was caused largely because of the hatred of the city's white citizens for the blacks that had moved in from the South.

New views of the world

World War II came to an end on August 14, 1945, with the surrender of Japan. Throughout Michigan and the rest of the nation people gathered in towns and cities, shouting and cheering. After six years of heavy fighting and a huge loss of lives, the war was finally over! (See page 252.)

But victory did not come without worry. Somehow, after World War II, the world did not seem as safe as it once had. When the United States dropped an atomic bomb on Japan near the end of the war, it made people aware that those same new and powerful weapons might someday be used to destroy them. As never before, the people of the United States saw the importance of working with other nations to find a lasting peace.

A Michigan man in Washington who stood for these new ideas about the world was Arthur H. Vandenberg. Vandenberg, who had been a Grand Rapids newspaper editor, was first elected senator from the state in 1928. For much of his career, Vandenberg was against this nation's involvement in world affairs.

As chairman of the nation's Foreign Policy Committee, Senator Vandenberg began to change his mind. In 1945 he made a brave speech calling for the United States to cooperate with other nations. From that time on, Vandenberg became a highly respected leader. He helped write the charter for the United Nations and was part of every important foreign policy decision. Although he was a Republican, Democratic presidents Franklin D. Roosevelt and Harry S. Truman consulted him and respected his advice. By the time of his death in 1951 Vandenberg had earned his place as one of the most important senators in Michigan's history.

Even with the establishment of the United Nations, a lasting peace did not seem to be something that could really be achieved. The Soviet Union was encouraging the growth of Communism in eastern European countries as well as in China and other Asian countries. A "cold war" of words and other forms of propaganda began between the Soviet Union and the United States and its allies as Communism spread, especially in the poor and war-torn countries of the world.

In 1950 the cold war turned into a war of guns and bombs. American troops were sent to Korea, where they helped protect South Korea against the Communist soldiers of North Korea. By the time the war was over, about 250,000 men and women from Michigan had been involved in the struggle through their service in the armed forces.

The truce in Korea, like the end of World War II, still did not seem to bring real peace. There had been great changes in the

Arthur H. Vandenberg was a U.S. Senator from Michigan that played a leading role in the nation's foreign policy in the 1940s.

world in the 1900s. Michigan's people, like residents in other states, could no longer live isolated lives on farms or in small northern communities. Cars and telephones and planes and bombs all had a way of making the world smaller. What happened in Korea now made a difference in even the smallest Michigan village. Like it or not, Michigan citizens were beginning to realize that they were also citizens of the world. The whole idea was frightening.

Back to automobiles!

At the end of World War II, Michigan's automobile industry had once again begun producing cars. It was no problem to sell them, since many people needed to replace their worn-out models. The great demand for new cars made it possible for small automobile companies to survive. One new company was the Kaiser-Frazer Company which began manufacturing in the bomber factory at Willow Run. It produced several different cars until 1955, when it began building Jeeps.

Cars made by the Hudson, Packard, and Studebaker companies were also popular after World War II and competed with cars made by the Big Three. In 1954 the Hudson company joined with the Nash company of Wisconsin and became American Motors. Although American Motors had its headquarters in Michigan, the cars were assembled in Wisconsin.

After World War II, the only major changes in the Big Three automobile companies took place at Ford. Henry Ford's grandson, Henry Ford II, took over the company and began to manage it in new and better ways. He hired a group of men who had been Air Force officers, and within five years the Whiz Kids, as they were called, brought success that the company had not enjoyed for years.

During the war years, workers in the auto factories had agreed not to strike or slow down the production of war equipment in any way. Now that the war was over, they were anxious for pay raises and other benefits. To help them reach these goals, they elected Walter P. Reuther as president of the U.A.W. in 1946.

At a time when some of the union leaders were Communists, Walter Reuther was a Socialist. His views were not as extreme as those of his rivals. Still, Reuther was a fighter and outspoken about his ideas. He had been to Europe and studied labor unions there. His strong feelings had lost him a job at Ford during the Depression, and he had also been beaten in an effort to start a union at that company. (See page 245).

At the end of the war and into the 1950s, Reuther led a number of strikes against the Big Three companies. Gradually he was able to win large increases in pay for auto workers. He also helped win other benefits for them, including payments after they retired. At the same time, he pushed Communist leaders from their places of control in the union. In 1948 he was badly wounded by a gunshot into his home. Although no one was ever caught, it was believed to be the work of his Communist enemies. Reuther recovered, however, and continued to lead the U.A.W. until his death in 1970.

Even with strikes and higher wages paid to workers, the auto industry prospered until 1955. Business then began to drop off rapidly. A major reason for this was a general slowdown of business in the United States. Although it was not as serious a situation as the Depression, many people again found themselves without jobs and money. During this recession, as it was called, many people worried about having enough money for everyday needs and did not even think about buying new cars.

Another reason for a drop in the automobile business in Michigan was the growing popularity of foreign-made cars. These cars were smaller, cheaper to buy, and used less gas. American Motors was the first American company to take this interest in small cars seriously. It began building small, compact cars. By 1960 the Big Three companies followed this example.

The slowdown in automobile production meant that there were more people in Michigan without jobs. But it was not just fewer sales that made for higher unemployment in the state's automobile factories. After World War II the industry began using machinery that needed fewer people to operate it. In addition, the auto companies began building plants in other parts of the country to save money in transporting the finished vehicles. This also meant that Michigan needed fewer auto workers.

Michigan leaders began to realize that the state depended too heavily on the automobile industry. When people did not buy cars at a steady rate, thousands of auto workers were left without jobs. Other industries also had to let workers go, since they made parts for automobiles. What Michigan needed was a greater variety of industries that did not have as many ups and downs as the automobile business.

Williams leads the state

For many years after World War II, Michigan was led by a popular governor named G. Mennen Williams. Called "Soapy" be-

Walter Reuther

Walter Reuther was born into a West Virginia family which was always involved in labor and social issues. And so when Reuther began work as a tool and die maker, he soon tried to organize workers in a protest against working on Sundays. His rebellion cost him the job, but Reuther went to Detroit where he held several jobs and took high school and college classes in the evenings.

In the middle 1930s, Reuther spent several years with his brother touring Europe, Russia, India, and Japan. On his return to America he began his career as a labor union leader. He had a major role in settling disputes between workers and management of the General Motors Corporation in the late 1930s.

During World War II Reuther made a plan to adapt the auto industry to war production. Although it was not accepted in its whole form, many of its ideas were used as the war went on. He and other labor leaders passed a "no-strike" agreement so that war work would not be interrupted.

After World War II Reuther became president of the U.A.W., a position he held until his death in a plane crash in 1970. He helped auto workers gain wage increases and other benefits. Strikes and negotiations were more orderly with fewer outbreaks of violence than there had been in the past.

Through the years Reuther changed his political beliefs. Once a member of the Socialist party, he let his membership expire and voted for Democratic candidates. His life efforts were spent in helping workers grow from scattered minority groups that were often abused, to one powerful voice that helped shape the auto industry.

cause he was part of a family that had become wealthy by making shaving cream, Williams was first elected governor in 1948 at the age of 36. He and his wife made a handsome couple, and although they had come from wealthy backgrounds, they were popular with the working people. Williams drove an old car during his campaign for governor, since he knew many people were still unable to get new ones after the war. For years he was famous for wearing a green polka dot bow tie.

Although he was a popular governor, Williams had problems getting his programs through the Michigan legislature. He was a Democrat, while the majority of the lawmakers were Republicans. His programs, which included money for education and welfare for the unemployed, were always reduced as they passed through the state senate and house of representatives. However, his concern for ordinary people and his continual efforts to help make life better for them, helped him win six consecutive elections. This was more than any governor in the nation had ever won.

One of the greatest achievements of Williams' career as governor was the building of the Mackinac Bridge, linking Michi-

G. Mennen Williams was Michigan's governor for twelve years. One of his favorite pasttimes was calling a square dance or being part of a polka party.

gan's Upper and Lower peninsulas. After much study and planning to determine if the massive project could even be done, the actual construction began in 1954. By the end of 1957 the first cars and trucks made their way across the four-lane, five-mile bridge suspended five hundred feet above the Straits of Mackinac. Williams called it the "Michigan Dream." But it is more than one of the state's finest accomplishments. It is the fourth longest suspension bridge in the world.

One of Michigan's most serious problems during Williams' terms was finding new ways to raise more money. The state's three percent sales tax did not bring in enough money to take care of the increased services needed by a growing population. Governor Williams worked to place a tax on people's incomes as well as a tax on large industries. But Michigan's lawmakers disagreed. Instead, they placed nuisance taxes on liquor, beer, cigarettes, and other things they felt people could live without.

In 1959 the money problems in Michigan came to a crisis. Word went out that the state would not be able to pay its employees because it was bankrupt. This was not true. However, the legislature held off passing bills to help solve the immediate money

Before the construction of the Mackinac Bridge, ferries carried cars between the two peninsulas. During the heavy traffic seasons, such as deer hunting season, the wait for a ferry could be a long one.

The building of the Mackinac Bridge was one of the grand accomplishments in Michigan's history.

problems for such a long time that Governor Williams' reputation was injured. Still, the lawmakers had not dealt with the real issue, the need for major tax reform in the state.

Steps to reform

Although the group of Republicans that had so strongly opposed Williams succeeded in ending his career as governor, they also damaged their own reputations. Many Michigan citizens were angry to find that this group had let their own political battles endanger the state and its reputation. They did not elect a Republican to replace Williams, but instead another Democrat, John B. Swainson.

Many of Michigan's money problems could not be easily solved because of guidelines set in the state's constitution. Since lawmakers seemed to be ignoring the problems of the constitution, some of Michigan's concerned citizens began working for changes.

The League of Women Voters and the Junior Chamber of Commerce led a campaign that finally brought about a constitutional convention. Members of this convention created a new state constitution which was approved in April, 1963. The new document was better suited to meet the needs of a state that was now an industrial one. Among the changes was one making the governor's term four years instead of two.

The long-term solutions to Michigan's money problems were not reached until later in the 1960s. Although the new constitution allowed an income tax, it was not until 1967 that such a tax was passed by the lawmakers. Under Republican Governor George Romney the income tax law that Republicans had fought against so long finally went into effect.

A better way of life

By the time Michigan's people approved their new constitution, they could look back in amazement at the many changes in their lives. Within the short time since World War II, life in Michigan and the rest of the United States had been greatly improved.

The Michigan Constitution of 1963

Elections

- The governor is elected to a four-year term.

- The governor and the lieutenant governor run as a team. They are no longer elected separately.

- Elections for governor are not held on the same year as presidential elections.

- Senators are elected by the people instead of being appointed. They run on a nonpartisan ballot, or not part of a political party.

Comments

- Experts consider this a better constitution than the one revised in 1908. It was better suited to meet the needs and problems of a modern industrial state.

Workers were receiving better pay and more benefits than people even dreamed about in the 1920s. Many people moved from the cities into the suburbs, where each family owned its own home and at least one car. More and more families were buying television sets, an invention that was first introduced in Michigan in 1947.

Cities and smaller communities became better places to live. Now that people's money was not being spent on war or their energy on surviving the hard times of the Depression, their efforts could go into creating more schools, churches, hospitals, and various public projects. Between 1940 and 1960 Michigan had one of the fastest-growing populations in the nation. The state responded quickly by building more schools and training more teachers. Colleges also expanded during this time. Michigan State College in Lansing became a university. More areas of study were added to teacher training schools, or normal schools. The normal schools at Kalamazoo, Ypsilanti, and Mount Pleasant became Western Michigan, Eastern Michigan, and Central Michigan universities.

Interstate highways built in the 1960s helped give Michigan an excellent transportation network.

Great strides were also made in transportation in the years following World War II. A highway program begun in 1957 gave the state miles of nonstop driving free of tolls. These interstate highways, paid for largely by the federal government, link Michigan with other states. They also link cities and towns in the Lower Peninsula. The new highways, along with the construction of the Mackinac Bridge, helped encourage tourists to visit Michigan. They also helped the growth of businesses based on recreation, from fishing camps to ski resorts.

Highway improvement was not the only change in Michigan's transportation system. Air travel became much more important, and airports were built in the state's large cities. The ageless Great Lakes water route to Michigan was also improved by the opening of the St. Lawrence Seaway in the spring of 1959. In spite of its inland position, Michigan could now be reached by oceangoing vessels. By land, by air, and by sea, Michigan and its future were closely linked to the rest of the world.

How a Bill Becomes a Law

1. A bill is introduced in either the Senate or House. It is sent to an appropriate committee.

2. The committee discusses and debates the bill and makes a report.

3. If a bill is reported favorably, it is returned to the Senate or House. Amendments to the bill may be adopted.

4. The entire bill is considered once again. It then can be passed, defeated, sent back to the committee, or postponed. If the bill is defeated, a legislator may move to have the bill reconsidered.

5. If a bill passes in either the House or Senate, it goes on to the other for consideration.

6. If the bill is passed by the second house, it is sent to the governor. If it fails in the second house, a conference committee tries to resolve the problems so that both houses agree on the bill.

7. The governor has fourteen days to consider the bill. If the governor signs it, it becomes a law. If the governor vetoes it, the legislators may still make it a law if two-thirds of their members vote to do so.

Government Leaders

Governor	The head of the government who enforces laws, appoints many state officials, and has much to do with making state laws.
Lieutenant governor	Fills the office of governor in case the governor dies, becomes sick, or is absent from the state. The person in this office is the leader of the senate but votes only in case of ties.
Secretary of state	Heads the department of state which keeps all state records, from laws to licenses for automobiles.
Attorney general	The state lawyer who answers legal questions and takes part in any legal matter which involves the state.
Senators	Those who serve in the Senate, or upper house of the legislature, and make, change, or do away with laws.
Representatives	Lawmakers who serve in the House of Representatives, or lower house.
Speaker of the House	The leader of the House of Representatives who is chosen by the other lawmakers.

Three Branches of Michigan's Government

Executive

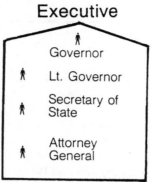

Governor

Lt. Governor

Secretary of State

Attorney General

Runs the government

Legislative

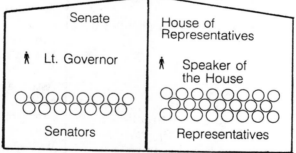

Senate

Lt. Governor

Senators

House of Representatives

Speaker of the House

Representatives

Makes the laws

Judicial

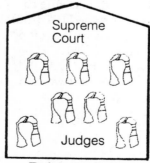

Supreme Court

Judges

Enforces laws

M I C H I G A N

I·N T·I·M·E

Date	In Michigan	Outside Michigan
1960	George Romney is governor (1963) State approves a new constitution (1963) Martin Luther King, Jr. marches with others in Detroit to protest racial injustices (1963) James McDivitt is Michigan's first man in space (1965) State begins successful experiments to adapt salmon to the Great Lakes (1966) Race riots take place in Detroit & other Michigan cities (1967) State passes income tax amendment (1967) Voters take steps to curb water pollution (1968) William Milliken is governor (1969-82)	President John Kennedy creates Peace Corps (1961) John Glenn, Jr. orbits around earth in space capsule (1962) Martin Luther King, Jr. leads peaceful demonstrations and gives "I Have a Dream" speech (1963) U.S. involved in Vietnam War (1963-1973) Lyndon Johnson becomes President when Kennedy is assassinated (1963) Race riot breaks out in Los Angeles ghetto, Watts (1965) Anti-war parades begin (1967) King is assassinated (1968) Robert Kennedy is assassinated (1968) Astronauts walk on moon (1969)
1970	State establishes a lottery to raise money for education (1972) Michigan's Gerald Ford becomes President of the U.S. (1974) Coleman Young is first black mayor of Detroit (1974) Auto industry suffers setbacks due to recessions & energy shortage (1973-83) Renaissance Center opens in Detroit & marks new city development (1977)	Anti-pollution programs begin (1970) Watergate break-in (1972) Richard Nixon resigns as President and Gerald Ford takes his place (1974) The nation celebrates its 200th birthday (1976) Jimmy Carter becomes President (1977)
1980	James Blanchard is governor (1983) Martha Griffiths is state's first woman lieutenant governor (1983) Michiganians celebrate 150 years of statehood (1987)	Ronald Reagan becomes President (1981) Space shuttle explodes (1986) Celebrations mark Statue of Liberty's 100th birthday (1986)

Chapter 14

Let the word go forth from this time and place, to friend and foe alike, that the torch has been passed to a new generation of Americans—born in this century, tempered by war, disciplined by a hard and bitter peace, proud of our ancient heritage—and unwilling to witness or permit the slow undoing of those human rights to which this Nation has always been committed today at home and around the world.

Inaugural speech, 1961
John F. Kennedy

Michigan's Recent History

The 1960s and early 1970s were confusing years. There seemed to be, as President Kennedy said, a new generation of Americans. Many of the people shaping the nation were young, like Kennedy himself. The fifties had seemed to give American families all the good things in life, such as television, luxury cars, and homes in the suburbs.

But the new generation of the sixties and seventies looked at all the things that had not been done. Black people still had to ride at the back of the bus. Women who had run America's factories in World War II had to give their jobs to men. Others were expected to limit their occupations to nursing, teaching, secretarial work, or running a household. Automobiles were polluting the air with their exhausts. And the world outside the United States seemed to hold the constant threat of war.

Michigan, like the rest of the country, was full of protest and restless energy. A black leader who had lived in Lansing and changed his name from Malcolm Little to Malcolm X had become nationally famous. Unlike Martin Luther King, who called for blacks to solve problems in peaceful ways, Malcolm X felt that violence was bound to come. He urged his people to be proud of their race and warned the country about the seriousness of its racial problems. "You should not feel that I am inciting someone to violence," he told a group of labor leaders in 1964. "I am only warning of a powder keg situation. . . . The day of nonviolent resistance is over." Unfortunately his life ended in violence the

Malcolm Little, or Malcom X, lived in Lansing as a boy and became famous as a leader in the Black Muslim movement in the 1960s.

following year when he was shot, probably by one of the Black Muslim group to which he had once belonged.

On the college and university campuses throughout Michigan many students wore long hair and dressed in "hippie" fashion to show their disapproval of the Vietnam War and various social conditions. At the University of Michigan students formed a group called Students for a Democratic Society (SDS) to work for social change. One of its leaders, Tom Hayden, wrote down the political ideas of the group and called it the "Port Huron Statement." The SDS soon became well-known for its protests and spread to many universities. It later moved its base to California.

Not all of life was so serious. In Detroit some high school girls formed a singing group called the Primettes and tried to get a job at a young record company begun by Berry Gordy. He told the girls to come back when they were older, and they did. By the mid sixties the record company and the group were among the hottest names in show business. The group, renamed the Su-

A group from Detroit called the Supremes hit the top of the charts with their music in the mid-1960s. They sang for Motown Records, which was based in Detroit.

premes, and its lead singer, Diana Ross, had such hits as "Stop! In the Name of Love" and "I Hear a Symphony." Berry Gordy and his Motown record company had created a musical empire in Detroit. Motown promoted black singers such as Stevie Wonder and Marvin Gaye and groups like the Temptations and Gladys Knight and the Pips. In the 1970s, however, he moved his company to California.

The problems of race

In a very real way Michigan, as always, reflected the mood of the nation and was a center for many of the activities of the era. This was again the case in the hot summer of 1967. For six days gunfire echoed and buildings burned in a race riot that shocked the state and the nation. The scene was Detroit's black district, but the other Michigan cities of Pontiac, Grand Rapids, Saginaw, Albion, and Kalamazoo also had outbursts of violence.

Martin Luther King, Jr., right of the policeman, came to Detroit to join the "Walk to Freedom March" in 1963. The march marked the twentieth anniversary of Detroit's 1943 race riot.

To many it seemed strange that Detroit should be the scene of this large-scale riot. It was not a time of high unemployment. The city could boast that pay for workers with few skills was the second highest in the country. Detroit's mayor, Jerome Cavanaugh, had the support of many black people and had been working on the problems that concerned them. Only a few years earlier, Cavanaugh had invited Governor Swainson, Walter Reuther, and Martin Luther King, Jr., to join a huge march in the city. Over 125,000 people had shown their support for the rights of blacks. King had also made one of his famous speeches about working for rights in a peaceful way.

But beneath this surface were the unpleasant facts of everyday life for black people in Detroit and in many other parts of the nation. Although laws passed in the 1950s had made it possible for blacks to go into any restaurant or hotel, it was nearly impossible for even wealthy blacks to move out of the slums. White people who sold homes and white bankers who arranged loans

for houses worked quietly to keep blacks out of white areas. When new automobile plants opened in the suburbs, very few blacks were transferred or hired to work there. Other plants kept blacks in the lowest paid jobs.

Moving beyond the position of an unskilled worker was also more difficult for blacks than for other groups. The programs within the auto companies that trained workers and moved them up into higher positions had almost no blacks. Out of nearly 7,500 workers in a job skills program at General Motors, for example, only ten were black. Lacking the skills needed to move up, blacks were, of course, the first to lose their jobs as machines took the place of unskilled workers. And while the city was boasting of low unemployment, most people had overlooked the fact that nearly eighty percent of the unemployed were blacks.

On that hot July night in 1967 police entered a bar after hours and began arresting customers who should not have been there and loading them into police vans. People in the neighborhood, which was black, gathered and watched. For a time nothing unusual happened. But slowly the crowd began to ask themselves if police did these things in white neighborhoods. After the police drove away someone threw a bottle into a store window. Then

Race riots broke out again in Detroit in 1967. They also occurred in other Michigan cities, but on a much smaller scale.

there was another. Within a short time the crowd's anger was out of control. Stores were looted and buildings set on fire.

As rioting continued into the next day, Mayor Cavanaugh and Michigan's Governor Romney sent the state police and the Michigan National Guard to help the Detroit police restore order. But it was not enough. Declaring a state of emergency, the Michigan leaders sent for federal troops. But confusion, mistakes, and other details slowed the soldiers' arrival for 24 hours. After the troops came, it took days to stop the violence. When the riot was over, forty-three people had died. Nearly three thousand stores and buildings had been looted or burned. About fifty million dollars' worth of property had been destroyed.

As after the riots of 1943, Detroit and other Michigan cities set to work to solve race problems. Efforts were made to try to bring an end to discrimination in labor unions, in housing, and in government. Some of the cities as well as the state made laws to help blacks move into new neighborhoods. Cities began to hire blacks to work in police and fire departments. Ypsilanti and Flint chose blacks for mayors.

After the Detroit riot ended, sections of the city looked as if a war had taken place. Forty-three lives were lost and fifty million dollars worth of property was destroyed.

Many of Detroit's white residents began to move out of the city. By 1970 nearly half of the people remaining in the city were black. In ten years that figure jumped to two-thirds. In 1974 Detroit's citizens elected their first black mayor, Coleman A. Young. But the problems of the city, including poverty and crime, remained.

A leader from the auto industry

In 1963 a Republican candidate became Michigan's governor. George Romney had come to Michigan during World War II to take a job in the automobile industry. He went on to become an executive at Nash and then president of American Motors Corporation. Unlike other auto leaders, Romney felt that small cars should be built to compete with the foreign cars that had become popular in America. Calling the Big Three models "gas-guzzling dinosaurs," he helped American Motors introduce the Rambler. The sales of the Rambler proved that small American cars could be profitable.

But Romney's interests did not lie only in the automobile business. In the late 1950s he organized Citizens for Michigan, a group that had finally convinced the people of Michigan that the state's constitution needed changing. He then was elected a member of the constitutional convention. With this background he ran successfully for governor.

In his position as governor, Romney quickly won the respect of Michigan's citizens. He was good at saving money, and in a short time the state could boast of a surplus. But the good times did not last. Government costs were rising. Romney was able to convince lawmakers that the only long-term answer to Michigan's money problems was an income tax, which Governor Williams had suggested years earlier. A bill for a tax on people's personal income, as well as on the income of corporations, was passed in 1967.

Romney's success in working with people made him a possible candidate for president in 1968. He was a sincere and honest man, the type voters admired. But Romney made a fatal mistake. On a television program he was asked his opinion about the war in Vietnam. Although Romney had once supported the war effort, he admitted he had since changed his mind. Military leaders, he said, had "brainwashed" him into thinking that the war was right.

The press, as well as Republican leaders, were upset by Romney's statements. Within a short time he was forced to withdraw from the race for president. Although public opinion was turning against the war, it had been too soon for a political leader to take this strong stand.

Romney left his position as governor of Michigan to take a job in the federal government. He headed the Department of Housing and Urban Development under President Richard Nixon. William Milliken, who was Romney's lieutenant governor, took over the governorship and then was elected to three terms of his own.

Leaders of the 1970s

The man who replaced George Romney had many of the same skills that had made Romney a success. William Milliken was a man who could work well with both Democrats and Republicans. But politics was not Milliken's only concern. He was faced with the problems of the time, which included a recession, or business slowdown, that was affecting the entire nation.

There were serious questions to be answered about education during Milliken's years as governor. Many teachers' strikes had to be settled. There needed to be better ways to finance education. The federal government demanded that schools have more nearly equal numbers of black and white children. That meant many children would have to be bused to different schools.

The money needed to bus children along with the rising costs of education in general, forced the state to borrow money to keep its schools running. But banks in America were afraid to take a

George Romney, who was president of American Motors Corporation, served Michigan in many ways. On several occasions he set up citizens' committees to help solve particular problems in the state.

chance on Michigan. The state finally had to borrow the money it needed from Japanese banks. It also had to find better ways of meeting the costs of education. In 1972 voters approved a state lottery to help raise money. The lottery games, which depend on people's willingness to gamble, brought in money and proved to be a success.

At the end of 1982, Milliken decided to retire from the wearing job of governor. He had served the state for fourteen years, longer than any other Michigan governor. Voters chose Democrat James Blanchard to take his place.

During the 1970s two Michigan leaders played important roles in the national government. One of these was Gerald R. Ford, who was born in Nebraska but grew up in Grand Rapids. Ford graduated from the University of Michigan and the law school at Yale University. In 1948 Ford, a Republican, was elected to the House of Representatives and moved to Washington, D.C. Nearly twenty years later he was chosen speaker of the House.

Ford's position as House speaker ended suddenly owing to some unusual events. In 1973 Vice President Spiro Agnew was forced to resign. The person next in line for the position of Vice President was the speaker of the House. Ford became the first person to become Vice President without being elected to that office.

But Ford's rise to fame did not stop there. In 1974 Richard Nixon was forced to resign from the office of President because of his unlawful acts relating to his presidential campaign. Gerald

William G. Milliken served as Michigan's governor for fourteen years. He was faced with leading the state as troublesome recessions swept the nation.

Ford became the first President of the United States from the state of Michigan. Although people complained that Ford lacked the leadership qualities necessary to be President, he did play an important role as he served in Nixon's place. After the uproar caused by the Vietnam War and the scandals of Agnew and Nixon, the country welcomed a calm period with an honest man at its head. When Ford ran for President in the next election, however, he lost to Jimmy Carter.

The other important Michigan leader in the federal government was Senator Philip Hart. A Democrat especially concerned with civil rights, Hart was greatly respected by leaders from both parties. He earned the title "conscience of the Senate" because of his great concern for the individual worth of all people, regardless of their race, sex, or other differences. A few days before he planned to retire in 1976, Hart died of cancer.

The ups and downs of the auto business

The 1970s and early 1980s were troubled by serious recessions. As always, Michigan's automobile industry was quick to

Gerald R. Ford was sworn into the office of U.S. President after Richard Nixon resigned. Betty Ford watches the event.

suffer, since people without jobs or those worried about losing them do not go out and buy automobiles. But the recession of the mid 1970s was especially bad for the car industry since it was caused by an oil shortage. Oil companies that had been importing large amounts of oil from Arab nations coud no longer do so.

With a new respect for gasoline, the American people bought foreign cars and small American cars that used less fuel. The American car companies could not sell their large, expensive models. Thousands of workers were laid off from their jobs, and other automobile-related industries also sent workers home.

The oil shortage forced the Big Three automakers to change their ways. Except for a few models like American Motors' Rambler and Ford's Pinto, car makers had insisted that Americans wanted large luxury cars. They also insisted that these could not be built with smaller engines that used less fuel. But suddenly there were not enough small cars to go around, and the government was passing laws demanding that cars use less fuel. Remarkably, the auto companies found ways to build attractive cars with smaller engines that used less fuel.

The fuel shortage was not the only factor that forced changes in the auto industry. The huge number of automobile deaths inspired some groups to look at reasons for this problem. Ralph Nader, a leader of one of these groups, placed the blame on the automobile industry itself. As a result, lawmakers forced the industry to put seat belts in cars, use better tires, and make many other changes to keep people safer. Other groups concerned about clean air helped pass laws forcing automakers to add devices that would clean up car exhausts.

One of the companies that suffered most during this period was the Chrysler Corporation. Under the leadership of Lee A. Iacocca, however, many of its problems were worked out with the help of a huge loan from the federal government. Union and non-union workers alike took cuts in pay as the company improved its cars and factory operations. The great success of the undertaking made Iacocca one of Michigan's present-day heroes.

A serious recession in the first half of the 1980s was still another blow to the auto industry and to Michigan in general. This time, however, many workers decided to leave the state to find jobs in other parts of the United States, particularly the South. So many people moved away, in fact, that a popular bumper sticker read, "Will the last person to leave Michigan please turn off the lights."

The auto industry has managed to survive the ups and downs of recent years even though some experts believed it would be impossible to do. Others believe that the industry could have avoided many of its problems, but waited until a crisis before building safer and more fuel-efficient cars. Some people have blamed unions for demanding too much from companies and driving costs too high. Both the companies and the unions, no doubt, often worried more about making money than about the quality of the cars they built.

Even a healthy automobile industry, however, will not supply Michigan's people with enough jobs in the future. Just as the use of new machinery cut down the need for unskilled workers after World War I and World War II, new advances in technology promise to make even further cuts. It is likely that the huge number of workers needed to run Michigan's automobile industry will be part of the state's history.

The problems of the cities

Although Michigan's people had rushed to the cities in the early part of the century, that trend did not continue. Instead, people were moving from the cities to the suburbs. In the 1950s shopping centers outside the city limits began to become popular.

There were a number of reasons for the move to the suburbs. People had more money than ever before and wanted to buy their

Michigan's People · 1980

Since the 1800s people from different parts of the world have been coming to the state to make their home. The 1980 census shows that there are still many people living in the state who have been born in another country. They bring a variety of cultural backgrounds to the state.

Place of birth	Number	Specific homeland
Europe	198,211	United Kingdom, Germany Poland, Italy
North & Central America	94,555	Canada, Mexico, West Indies
Asia	77,476	India, Philippines, Korea, Lebanon
U.S.S.R.	13,142	
South America	5,553	
Africa	5,244	North Africa, Egypt

own houses. They also had cars to help them commute from their homes in the suburbs to their jobs in the cities. In some of the large cities, such as Detroit and Grand Rapids, many wanted to escape the city problems. There were still racial conflicts, poor housing, lack of quality education, and often a lack of jobs. As a result, the crime rate in the cities was rising at a fast pace. In 1971 and 1972 combined, for example, over a thousand murders took place in the city of Detroit, more than had taken place in the whole decade of the fifties. Detroit earned the unhappy title of "Murder City, U.S.A." In the cities of Grand Rapids and Flint, crime also increased.

In many ways people's moving to the suburbs only added to the problems of the cities. Poor people moved into some of the better homes and let them run down. Many popular stores moved to shopping centers. And poor people and empty stores did not provide city governments with the money needed to run the cities. Some suburban areas became part of older cities in order to gain the services of water, fire, and police departments. Other suburban areas, such as Warren in the Detroit area and Portage near Kalamazoo, became cities in their own right.

A number of Michigan's cities have made attempts in recent years to attract businesses and people back to the downtown

Michigan's Population

Year	Population		Year	Population
1800	3,106*		1930	4,842,325
1810	4,762*		1940	5,256,106
1820	8,896*		1950	6,371,766
1830	31,639*		1960	7,823,194
1840	212,267*		1970	8,875,083
1850	397,654*		1980	9,189,000
1860	749,113			
1870	1,184,059			
1880	1,636,937			
1890	2.093,890			
1900	2,420,982			
1910	2,810,173			
1920	3,668,412			

*Does not include the Indians who were not counted in the census.

Martha Wright Griffiths

One of Michigan's political leaders in recent decades is Martha Wright Griffiths. Although neither Martha or her husband Hicks Griffiths was born in Michigan, they graduated from the University of Michigan Law School in 1940, the school's first married couple. After graduation they moved to Texas where Hicks Griffiths had a job. But Martha was not so fortunate. Even with outstanding qualifications, she was unable to get a law position because she was a woman. She and her husband returned to Michigan and in 1946 opened their own law firm with a famous partner, G. Mennen Williams.

Always determined and willing to try again when she faced defeat, Martha Griffiths has achieved many firsts in her career. She was the first woman to serve as judge on the Detroit Recorder's Court, a court which deals with only serious crimes. She was the first woman from Michigan to be elected to the United States Congress. While in Congress, she became the first woman to serve on the important and powerful House Ways and Means Committee.

When she retired from Congress in 1974, Martha took on new kinds of roles. She served on the board of directors of many important corporations and agencies, sometimes becoming their first woman director. She was then asked by James Blanchard to run for lieutenant governor, a position she has held for two terms.

Throughout her career Martha Wright Griffiths has fought for the rights of women, minority groups, and the handicapped. More than achieving "first woman" status, she has made countless contributions to Michigan and the nation.

areas. In Grand Rapids, for example, a rundown riverfront area is now an attractive park. Some old buildings have been restored, and others have been torn down. In their place are attractive new buildings, including offices, a hotel, and a museum. Huge old homes near the downtown area have also been restored and have been put to many different uses.

Even with the improvements in the cities, however, people are still not choosing to live in them. Figures in 1985 showed that every major Michigan city had lost population. Downtown areas, although greatly improved, are mainly centers for business and for visitors. There are signs that city life, although it is not ending, is changing drastically as Michigan moves toward a new century.

Michigan's resources

Michigan today depends nearly as much on its natural resources as it did earlier in its history. Lumbering and mining are still among the state's industries, although neither is as important as in former times. Farmers and a variety of food processing plants continue to rely on the state's rich farmlands. Water resources are used widely for industry and recreation.

One of Michigan's modern industries that is closely tied to its natural resources is the tourist industry. The state's beautiful lakes, rivers, and Great Lakes shoreline attract vacationers from many different states, and even from other countries. As they dine in restaurants, sleep in motels and hotels, and shop in stores, the visitors provide Michigan's people with a number of ways to earn a living.

Citizens and lawmakers have worked hard in recent years to keep Michigan clean and beautiful. Many forests are protected, and others that are cut are replanted. In 1968 Michigan residents voted to spend millions of dollars to find ways to save the state's water resources from pollution. Lawmakers set stricter guidelines so that towns and cities and their industries had to stop pouring waste materials into rivers, lakes, and streams. Even with these steps to control pollution, protecting Michigan's land and water from the chemical wastes of modern industry remains a big job.

Along with the cleanup of lakes and rivers, state officials began an experiment in 1966 to see if a saltwater fish, the salmon, could live in the fresh waters of Lake Michigan and Lake Superior. Within two years the experiment proved successful. Not only did the salmon thrive, they ate small trash fish that died in the summer and rotted on the beaches. The salmon experiment was a

As a U.S. Congressman from Michigan, James Blanchard sponsored the Great Lakes Protection Act of 1982 to help stop the lakes from being polluted by industries.

great boost to the state's tourist industry. It attracted thousands of people who enjoyed fishing and cleaned the beaches for the swimmers and sunbathers.

Other steps have been taken in recent years to help improve Michigan's environment. Many people worked to help cut down air pollution. In the mid 1970s Michigan's factories had to meet new standards so that dirty smoke did not pour from their chimneys. Auto manufacturers had to build cars with cleaner exhausts. Michigan voters also passed a law that placed a deposit on beverage cans and bottles. This helped reduce the litter along roadsides and in other public places as people toted their bottles and cans back to stores. It also was a step in saving resources, since the glasss and cans can be recycled.

At times the protection and the use of natural resources have created conflict in the state. This is especially true in the mining industries. The mining of iron ore, for example, changed in the 1950s when companies began using lower grade ores lying close to the surface. In a process called beneficiation, the iron is separated from the other substances and concentrated in pellets. The pellets are then shipped to steel mills along the Great Lakes.

Small trash fish such as alewives became so numerous in the Great Lakes in the 1960s that trawlers and nets were used to reduce their population. This boat is working off the shores of Holland on Lake Michigan.

Although the process has kept the iron industry alive in the Upper Peninsula, it upsets people who are concerned about the land there. The surface mining scars hundreds of acres of land, while mining deep within the earth does not cause as much damage.

Protecting the environment is also a problem in Michigan's oil and natural gas industry. This industry, which began in the 1920s, has had a new importance in the years of gas shortages and high prices. Some of the deposits lie in the beautiful wilderness area of Pigeon River in the northern part of the Lower Peninsula. Many arguments have taken place between people in the industry and those concerned with preserving the area and its wildlife. Balancing a concern for the environment with the interests of industry remains a tough problem.

Copper mining, which is far less important today than in the past, poses fewer problems for the environment than iron mining or oil drilling. When it became too expensive to mine deep in the earth for the copper, the mining companies began to use new processes. For a number of years they produced copper from the heaps of waste left years before. Today Michigan no longer ranks high among the states in copper production. Its deposits,

The remains of a booming copper industry are still evident in the Upper Peninsula. They are also a reminder of how greatly natural resources have shaped Michigan's history.

however, have not been exhausted. New demands for the metal and improved mining methods could possibly revive the industry in the future.

The treasury of natural resources that helped build Michigan remains just that—a treasury. The state's people have spent and wasted many of these treasures over the years. They have often had to learn the hard way to value and protect their natural wealth. But through the years the message has been clear. Michigan's natural resources are its greatest heritage, and its greatest hope for the future.

Michigan's natural resources have brought tourists to the state for the past century. Mackinac Island has long been a favorite tourist attraction.

Governors of Michigan

Stevens T. Mason	**1835-1839**
William Woodbridge	**1840-1841**
James W. Gordon*	**1841**
John S. Barry	**1842-1845**
Alpheus Felch	**1846-1847**
William L. Greenly*	**1847**
Epaphroditus Ransom	**1848-1849**
John S. Barry	**1850-1851**
Robert McClelland	**1852-1853**
Andrew Parsons*	**1853-1854**
Kinsley S. Bingham	**1855-1858**
Moses Wisner	**1859-1860**
Austin Blair	**1861-1864**
Henry H. Crapo	**1865-1868**
Henry P. Baldwin	**1869-1872**
John J. Bagley	**1873-1876**
Charles M. Croswell	**1877-1880**
David H. Jermone	**1881-1882**
Josiah W. Begole	**1883-1884**
Russell A. Alger	**1885-1886**
Cyrus G. Luce	**1887-1890**
Edwin B. Winans	**1891-1892**
John T. Rich	**1893-1896**

Hazen S. Pingree	**1897-1900**
Aaron T. Bliss	**1901-1904**
Fred M. Warner	**1905-1910**
Chase S. Osborn	**1911-1912**
Woodbridge N. Ferris	**1913-1916**
Albert E. Sleeper	**1917-1920**
Alexander J. Groesbeck	**1921-1926**
Fred W. Green	**1927-1930**
Wilber M. Brucker	**1931-1932**
William A. Comstock	**1933-1934**
Frank D. Fitzgerald	**1935-1936**
Frank Murphy	**1937-1938**
Frank D. Fitzgerald	**1939**
Luren D. Dickinson*	**1939-1940**
Murray D. Van Wagoner	**1941-1942**
Harry F. Kelly	**1943-1946**
Kim Sigler	**1947-1948**
G. Mennen William	**1949-1960**
John B. Swainson	**1961-1962**
George W. Romney	**1963-1968**
William G. Milliken	**1969-1982**
James J. Blanchard	**1983**

*Took over the position as lieutenant governor.

Epilogue

Those who cannot remember the past are condemned to repeat it.

from The Life of Reason, *V. I*
by George Santayana

The 150 years of Michigan's statehood are just a portion of its long and colorful past. Michigan's story has been unfolding for thousands of years. Before it was written it was told in the layers of rocks, the paths of rivers, and the legends of native peoples.

Unlike many other states, Michigan took its own shape and made its own boundaries between the waters of the Great Lakes. Its location made it a crossroads for the Europeans' push into the interior of America. The names of its towns and rivers still bear the mark of the French fur traders and explorers who claimed the Michigan area as their own for more than a century and a half.

But the location that had been a hub for the fur trade in the Upper Great Lakes area became a handicap as activity grew in the thirteen original states. For people moving westward, the Michigan territory was not a crossroads. It was a side trip that few people cared to make. Ohio and Indiana and Illinois were on the main route west, and they offered countless acres of rich farmland. And farmland, of course, was what the settlers wanted.

It was relatively late in our country's history that settlers discovered Michigan and the official 150-year story of the state began. Then they made a dramatic rush for the land, and land offices could not keep up with the paperwork. It was the second rush for Michigan's resources, the first having been for the rich furs of beaver, deer, muskrat, bear, and other animals. And it was not the last.

Michigan's people soon made other discoveries. The state's tall white pines were worth a fortune. The cutting began. Sawmills and other related industries grew up. The lumber business was booming as if there would be no end. But there was. Nearly all of Michigan's forests were cut and there was a price to pay— forest fires, ugly scarred land, and thousands of workers without jobs. And the mining booms in the copper and iron-ore lands of the Upper Peninsula held similar stories . . . a rush to claim the treasury of natural resources. Those booms, too, had their busts.

In the present century Michigan's story has been so tightly linked to its automobile industry that the two are nearly inseparable. The successes of the industry have provided Michigan's people with jobs and good times. Its importance has given Michigan recognition in the nation. But the industry's problems have also been felt by everyone in the state. And at times these problems have been huge ones.

There are a number of valuable lessons that Michigan's people can learn from the past. Industries were built on what was immediately profitable, with little thought to the future. The fur trade quickly used up a resource and in the end left the riches in the hands of a few. Lumbering and copper mining did the same. The rush for wealth in the end held little gain for Michigan's people as a whole.

History has also made it clear that our dependence on a single industry is not healthy for the state. When the lumbering industry began to lose its strength, people throughout Michigan were left without ways to earn a living. When the price of copper fell and mines closed, there were no other jobs for people in the mining area. And finally, the ups and downs of the auto industry have proved again and again that the state needs a variety of businesses.

At the 150-year mark of Michigan's history, steps are being taken to avoid repeating the mistakes of the past. Citizens and lawmakers are working to protect the state's resources. The government is encouraging new types of industry. Workers who flocked to southern states for jobs are beginning to return. The confidence and pride in Michigan that seemed to lessen in recent years is now being restored.

Although the story of Michigan is bound tightly to its location, its resources, and its industries, this story must also be told through the lives of the people. The Indians, the rugged fur traders, the New Englanders, the Polish and Dutch immigrants, the blacks from the South—have all had a part in shaping the state's history. From the little-known settlers who cleared the land and took part in township government to the well-known Lewis Cass and George Romney, countless men and women have helped make Michigan what it is today. And men and women will determine Michigan's future.

Looking back on 150 years, it is clear that Michigan has all that any state could offer. Its heritage is a rich and colorful one, from the birchbark canoes that skimmed along its lakes and rivers to the Tin Lizzies that bounced along its dusty roads. Its beauty, which includes sandy beaches and tumbling waterfalls, encourages many Michigan residents to spend their vacations in their own state. And it brings in countless visitors from other areas. Michigan's people have been survivors who have endured many hardships and have often been willing to begin over again. Building on its resources, its people, and the lessons of its past, Michigan holds every promise for the new century.

Bibliography

The authors have consulted many of the rich sources of Michigan History, but they have especially relied on the work of Willis F. Dunbar, George S. May, and F. Clever Bald.

The complete bibliography includes:

Adams, Julia Hubbard. *Memories of a Copper Country Girlhood.* (pamphlet, no date or publisher).

Bald, F. Clever. *Michigan in Four Centuries.* New York: Harper & Row Publishers, 1954.

Barnes, A. *Vinegar Pie and Other Tales of the Grand Traverse Region.* Detroit: Wayne State University Press, 1952.

Benedict, C. Harry. *Red Metal—The Calumet Hecla Story.* Calumet, Michigan: Roy W. Drier, Publisher, 1952.

Bogue, Margaret Beattie. *Around the Shores of Lake Michigan.* Madison: University of Wisconsin Press, 1985.

Bogue, Margaret Beattie & Palmer, Virginia A. *Around the Shores of Lake Superior: A Guide to Historic Sites.* Madison: University of Wisconsin Press, 1979.

Buley, R. Carlyle. *The Old Northwest Pioneer Period, 1815-1840, V. I & II.* Bloomington: Indiana University Press, 1950.

Carouso, John Anthony. *The Great Lakes Frontier.* Indianapolis: Bobbs Merrill, 1961.

Carse, Robert. *The River Men.* New York: Charles Scribners' Sons, 1969.

Catlin, George B. *The Story of Detroit.* Detroit: The Detroit News, 1923.

Catton, Bruce. *Michigan, A History.* New York: W. W. Norton, 1984.

Cleland, Charles E. *A Brief History of Michigan Indians.* Lansing: Michigan History Division, 1975.

Clifton, James A., Cornell, George L. McClurken, James M. *People of the Three Fires.* Grand Rapids: Grand Rapids Inter-Tribal Council, 1986.

Conot, Robert. *American Odyssey.* New York: Wm. Morrow & Company, 1974.

Dobson, Pamela J., ed. *The Tree That Never Dies.* Grand Rapids: Grand Rapids Public Library, 1978.

Dorson, Richard M. *Bloodstoppers and Bear Walkers.* Cambridge: Harvard University Press, 1952.

Dunbar, Willis F. *All Aboard: A History of Railroads in Michigan.* Grand Rapids: William B. Eerdmans, Publisher, 1969.

Dunbar, Willis F. *Lewis Cass*. Grand Rapids: William B. Eerdmans, Publisher, 1970.

Dunbar, Willis F. & May, George S. *Michigan: A History of the Wolverine State*. Grand Rapids: William B. Eerdmans, Publishing Company, 1980.

Ellis, Helen Harriet. *Michigan in the Civil War: A Guide to the Materials in Detroit Newspapers*. Lansing: Michigan Civil War Centennial, 1965.

Everett, Franklin. *Memorials of the Grand River Valley*. Grand Rapids: Grand Rapids Historical Society, 1984.

Fitting, James E. *The Archaeology of Michigan*. New York: The Natural History Press, 1970.

Fitzgerald, John W. *The Shanty Boy*. Berrien Springs: Hardscrabble Press, 1979.

Fuller, George N. *Historic Michigan. v. 1*. National Historical Association, 1934.

Fuller, George N. *Michigan, A Centennial History of the State and Its People*. Chicago: The Lewis Publishing Company, 1939.

Furnas, J. C. *Great Times*. New York: G. P. Putnam's Sons, 1974.

Gates, William B., Jr. *Michigan Copper and Boston Dollars*. Cambridge: Harvard University Press, 1965.

George, Sister Mary Karl. *Zachariah Chandler*. East Lansing: Michigan State University Press, 1969.

Glazer, Sidney and Quaife, Milo M. *Michigan From Primitive Wilderness to Industrial Commonwealth*. New York: Prentice Hall, Inc., 1948

Harris, Wilmer C. *Public Life of Zachariah Chandler, 1851-1875*. Lansing: Michigan Historical Commission, 1917.

Hemans, Lawton J. *Life and Times of Stevens T. Mason*. Lansing: Michigan Historical Commission, 1920.

Hinsdale, W. B. *The First People of Michigan*. Ann Arbor: George Wahr, Publisher, 1930.

Hulbert, William D. *White Pine Days on the Tahquamenon*. Grand Marais, Michigan: Voyager Press, 1978.

Johnson, Ida Amanda. *The Michigan Fur Trade*. Lansing: Michigan Historical Commission, 1919.

Kern, John. *A Short History of Michigan*. Lansing: Michigan Department of State, 1977.

Kirkland, Caroline. *A New Home or Life in the Clearings*. New York: G. P. Putnam's Sons, 1953.

La Fayette, Kenneth D. *Flaming Brands*. Marquette: Northern Michigan University, 1977.

Lutes, Della. *Country Kitchen*. Boston: Little, Brown & Co., 1937.

Lutes, Della. *Home Grown*. Boston: Little, Brown & Co., 1937.

Lutes, Della. *Country School Marm*. Boston: Little, Brown & Co., 1941.

Martin, John Bartlow. *Call It North Country—The Story of Upper Michigan*. New York: Alfred A. Knopf, 1944.

May, George S. *Michigan and the Civil War Years 1860-1865. A Wartime Chronicle.* Lansing: Michigan Civil War Centennial Commission, 1964.

May, George S. *Pictorial History of Michigan: The Early Years.* Grand Rapids, William B. Eerdmans Publishing Company, 1967

May, George S. *Pictorial History of Michigan: The Later Years.* Grand Rapids, William B. Eerdmans Publishing Company, 1969.

May, George S. and Brink, Herbert J., eds. *A Michigan Reader: 11,000 B.C.—A.D. 1865.* Grand Rapids: William B. Eerdmans Publishing Company, 1974.

Maybee, Rolland H. *Michigan's White Pine Era 1840-1900.* Lansing: Michigan History Division, 1973.

McGeehan, Albert H. *My Cross and Country—The Civil War Letters of John Anthony Wilterdink.* Dallas: Taylor Publishing Co., 1982.

Michel, Sara. *With This Inheritance,* Holland, Michigan: The Early Years. Spring Lake, Michigan: River Road Publications, 1984.

Michigan Historical Society, editors. *Historical and Scientific Sketches of Michigan.* Detroit: Wills & Whitney, Publishers, 1834.

Michigan Pioneer Collections, Volumes 8, 10, 12. Lansing: Wynkoop Hallenbeck Crawford Co., 1908.

Millbrook, Mrs. Raymond H. *Michigan Women in the Civil War.* Lansing: Michigan Civil War Centennial Commission, 1963.

Monette, Clarence J. *The Keeweenaw Waterway.* Lake Linden, Michigan: Welden Curtin, 1980.

Morison, Daniel. *The Doctor's Secret Journal.* Mackinac Island: Mackinac Island State Park Commission, 1960.

Nichols, Alfred. *More Copper Country Tales,* V. II. Calumet, Michigan: Roy W. Drier, 1968.

Nute, Grace Lee. *Lake Superior.* New York: Bobbs-Merrill, 1944.

O'Neill, William L. *Coming Apart.* Chicago: Quadrangle Books, 1971.

Ortig, Victoria. *Sojourner Truth, A Self-Made Woman.* New York: J. B. Lippincott, 1974.

Parkman, Francis. *The Conspiracy of Pontiac.* Boston: Little, Brown & Co., 1901.

Peckham, Howard H. *Pontiac and the Indian Uprisings.* Princeton: Phoenix Books, 1947.

Peirce, Neal R. & Hagstrom, L. *The Book of America.* New York: W. W. Norton & Co., 1983.

Petersen, Eugene T. *Mackinac Island—Its History In Pictures.* Mackinac Island: Mackinac Island State Park Commission, 1973.

Quaife, Milo M. *The Kingdom of St. James.* New Haven: Yale University Press, 1930.

Quaife, Milo M. & Glazer, Sidney. *Michigan.* New York: Prentice Hall, 1948.

Quimby, George Irving. *Indian Life in the Upper Great Lakes.* Chicago: University of Chicago Press, 1960.

Riddell, William R. *Michigan Under British Rule, 1760-1790.* Lansing: Michigan Historical Commission, 1926.

Russell, Nelson Vance. *The British Regime in Michigan and the Old Northwest 1760-1796.* Northfield, Minnesota: Carlton College Publishers, 1939.

The Saga of the Great Lakes. Toronto: Coles Publishing, 1980, reprinted from *History of the Great Lakes,* 1899.

Sagendorph, Kent. Stevens T. Mason, *Misunderstood Patriot.* New York: E. P. Dutton, 1947.

Santer, Richard A. *Michigan: Heart of the Great Lakes.* Iowa: Kendall/Hunt Publishing, 1977.

Schoolcraft, Henry R. *Narrative Journal of Travels Through the Northwest Regions of the United States Extending From Detroit Through the Great Chain of American Lakes to the Sources of the Mississippi River in the Year 1820.* East Lansing: The Michigan State College Press, 1953. (Originally published 1821)

Sheldon, Electra M. *The Early History of Michigan from the First Settlement to 1815.* New York: A. S. Barnes & Co., 1856.

Spencer, Robert F. & Jennings, Jesse D. *The Native Americans.* New York: Harper & Row Publishers, 1977.

Strang, Mark, ed. *The Diary of James J. Strang.* East Lansing: Michigan State University Press, 1961.

Sturtevant, William C., ed. *Handbook of North American Indians.* Washington: Smithsonian Institution, 1978.

Tanner, Helen Hornbeck. *Atlas of Great Lakes Indian History.* Norman: University of Oklahoma Press, 1987.

Utley, Henry Munson & Crutcheon, Byron M. *Michigan As A Province, Territory, and State, The Twenty-Sixth Member of the Federal Union, v. 1.* New York: The Publishing Society of Michigan, 1906.

Waldman, Carl. *Atlas of the North American Indian.* New York: Facts on File Publications, 1985.

Warner, Robert M. & Vander Hill, C. Warren. *A Michigan Reader 1865 to the Present.* Grand Rapids: William B. Eerdmans Publishing Company, 1974.

Wells, Robert W. *Daylight in the Swamps.* New York: Doubleday, 1978.

Widder, Keith R. *Dr. William Beaumont,* The Mackinac Years. Mackinac Island: Mackinac Island State Park Commission, 1975.

Williams, Mentor L., ed. *Schoolcraft's Indian Legends.* Lansing: Michigan State University, 1956.

Wood, Edwin O. *Historic Mackinac.* New York: The Macmillan Company, 1918.

Woodford, Frank B. *Lewis Cass, the Last Jeffersonian.* New Brunswick: Rutgers University Press, 1950.

Woodford, Frank B. & Woodford, Arthur M. *All Our Yesterdays.* Detroit: Wayne State University Press, 1969.

Index